WAGING PEACE

IN OUR

SCHOOLS

WAGING PEACE

IN OUR

SCHOOLS

LINDA LANTIERI AND JANET PATTI

WITH A FOREWORD BY
MARIAN WRIGHT EDELMAN

Beacon Press   Boston

Beacon Press
25 Beacon Street
Boston, Massachusetts 02108-2892

Beacon Press books are published under the auspices of
the Unitarian Universalist Association of Congregations.

· 02   01   00   99   98   97   96   8   7   6   5   4   3   2   1

Text design by Susan Hochbaum
Composition by Wilsted & Taylor

Library of Congress Cataloging-in-Publication Data

Lantieri, Linda.
    Waging peace in our schools / Linda Lantieri and Janet Patti :
with a foreword by Marian Wright Edelman.
        p.   cm.
    Includes bibliographical references.
    ISBN 0-8070-3116-X (cloth)
    1. School violence—United States—Prevention.   2. Classroom
management—United States.   3. Conflict management—United States.
4. Peace—Study and teaching—United States.   I. Patti, Janet.
II. Title.
LB3013.3.L36   1996
371.5—dc20   96-12160

[
To the memory of

Patrick F. Daly,

principal of one of

the first schools

that gave birth

to our dream.

And to all

the young people,

parents, teachers,

and administrators

who are passionately

and courageously

waging peace

in our schools.
]

[CONTENTS]

[FOREWORD]

by

Marian Wright Edelman

President, the Children's Defense Fund

IN 1968, DR. MARTIN LUTHER KING, JR., asked our nation a prescient, urgent, and timely question: Where do we go from here—chaos or community?

Since Dr. King's death, over one million Americans have been killed violently here at home, including tens of thousands of children. Almost seventeen million children have been born out of wedlock, thirteen million to teenage mothers. And at least sixteen million babies have been born into poverty. In America a child is reported abused or neglected every eleven seconds, is born into poverty every thirty-two seconds, is born to a teen mother every sixty-two seconds, is arrested for a violent crime every four minutes, and is killed by guns every ninety-eight minutes.

Behind these shameful numbers are small individual faces and individuals' feelings. We must stop this suffering. Change must come from the highest levels of government but it must also come from our communities, communities that sometimes seem to have forgotten too much of what we have always known is important.

Never before have we exposed children so early and relentlessly to cultural messages glamorizing violence, sex, material possessions, and the use of alcohol and tobacco with so few mediating influences from responsible adults. Never have we experienced such a numbing and reckless reliance on violence to solve problems, feel powerful, or be entertained. Never have so many children been permitted to rely on guns and gangs for protection and guidance rather than on parents, neighbors, religious congregations, and schools.

We must all work together to see that the violence against our children is stopped, that our schools can be turned back into places of nurturing and learning rather than the war zones which some of them have become, and that every child has a safe start in life with the support of caring parents and communities. I hope that we can begin by trying to teach our children that violence is not the way to resolve conflicts. The kind of antiviolence curriculum that Linda Lantieri and others have been working on is crucial. I wish that the Resolving Conflict Creatively Program could be taught in every classroom in America because we are not going to be able to deal with the violence in our communities, our homes, our neighborhoods, and our nation until we learn to deal with the basic ethic of how we resolve disputes and to place an emphasis on peace in the way we relate to one another.

This wonderful book by Linda Lantieri and Janet Patti should be in the hands of parents, teachers, principals, and everyone who cares about the crises confronting our children today.

The Resolving Conflict Creatively Program works. It has achieved amazing success in schools and with many other groups. I've personally seen remarkable responses from their work here at the Children's Defense Fund, at our conferences with child advocates nationwide, and at staff retreats. In addition, CDF has used RCCP at our training workshops for young, college-age leaders who go back to their communities to run Freedom Schools for neighborhood youth.

Teaching peaceful interactions has a ripple effect. A child who had taken RCCP training wept as she told Lantieri and Patti about possibly having saved two lives when, thanks to what she had learned from the program, she was able to mediate a fight between two other students who had knives.

Every life touched today touches unknown hundreds and hundreds of others as the years unfold.

I am honored to have been asked to write the foreword for this most important book. "Blessed are the peacemakers," and most blessed indeed are those who work to bring peace into the lives of children.

[ACKNOWLEDGMENTS]

WE ARE DEEPLY GRATEFUL to all the students, teachers, administrators, and parents who have been at the forefront of our work and are part of the RCCP family, especially all those who graciously agreed to be interviewed for this book.

Our most profound gratitude is to Tom Roderick, who with Linda courageously answered the call to dream together and work untiringly to bring this vision of waging peace to the public schools of New York City.

We stand on the shoulders of many who have been thinking about and developing this vision over a number of years. Among those from whom we have received much inspiration and wisdom are Sheila Alson, Zephryn Conte, Larry Dieringer, Marian Wright Edelman, Mariana Gastón, Daniel Goleman, Emma Gonzalez, Eileen Rockefeller Growald, Larrie Hall, Vince Jewell, William Kreidler, Carol Lieber, Antonia Meltzoff, Robert Muller, Deborah Prothrow-Stith, Priscilla Prutzman, Ted Quant, Jinnie Spiegler, Jim Tobin, Peter Yarrow and Emily Young.

We are also deeply grateful to the RCCP National Center staff, especially Cassandra Bond, Kim Jones, Michael Isaac, Matt Gerber, Mara Gross, and Vivian Otero, whose capabilities, love, and dedication enabled us to juggle home, work, and writing in order to finish this project.

This book would not have come to fruition without the patient and constructive help of two dear friends who know a lot more about writing than we do—Wally Levis and Vivian Otero. Our deepest gratitude also goes to our editors Deanne Urmy, who urged us to write this book, and to Andy Hrycyna, who mentored and nurtured us through its completion.

A special thank-you to Ardeth Cropper, Mara Gross, Bob Holloway, and Paul Teta for guiding Janet's research.

And, finally, we are grateful to our parents, who were the first to educate our own hearts.

[PREFACE]

If we are to reach real peace in this world and if we are to carry on a real war
against war, we shall have to begin with the children.
- Mahatma Gandhi -

THIS IS A BOOK ABOUT a bold new vision for schools—a dramatic departure—that includes educating the *heart* along with the mind. This vision has deep roots in a very specific experience and history. The Resolving Conflict Creatively Program began in 1985 as a joint initiative of Educators for Social Responsibility Metropolitan Area (ESR Metro) and the New York City Board of Education. The program started in three schools in Brooklyn, New York, and by 1988 had expanded to many more within New York City. By 1993, when we opened our national center, RCCP was being replicated in over three hundred schools in five states.

Then as now, we worked with teachers, administrators, young people, and parents to foster emotional and social development by focusing on the skills and practices of conflict resolution and diversity education. Our aim was to create caring, safe school communities in a society that seemed to be giving up on kids, abandoning them to a climate of perpetual violence.

In the late morning of December 17, 1992, we received a phone call at the RCCP New York office. Shortly after 11:00 A.M. on that day, a fourth-grade boy had run out of his classroom in a burst of anger and left the school building. His principal, Patrick Daly—a dear friend, ally, and colleague—had gotten word of what happened and had quickly gone out to find the boy. Pat headed straight for the housing development that surrounded the school. As he was walking through the projects, bullets flared from nowhere, the outcome of a drug deal gone sour. Pat was hit and killed almost instantly.

How could the violence we were helping to stop get this close to us? Pat had been one of the first principals to pilot our program in his school. Interviewed on television just a few months before his death, he had said, "There's a war going on outside this school and it's there and we have to teach our kids to deal with it. We're teaching them that they can get along with each other and there *can* be peace in their lives." As he talked, he had pointed in the direction of the very place where he would be shot.

That day, walking through the doors of Pat's school, a place that had become an oasis of peace for kids and families in the neighborhood, we were struck with the bitter realization that "the Angel of Redhook" would never walk those halls again. The next several months are a blur to many of us who knew and loved Pat. How could this happen? We sank into despair. We weren't winning the war that Pat had talked about. We weren't waging peace fast enough.

Pat was not the only victim. The three boys who were convicted of his murder each got a life sentence. Two of the boys had gone to P.S. 15 as children and had now murdered—however unintentionally—someone they had known, loved, and respected. In the days and weeks following the tragedy, RCCP staff assisted District 15's school-based support team in helping teachers, parents, and students deal with their grief. When Mary Manti, Pat's assistant principal, took over as principal, she announced immediately that as a tribute to Pat Daly she would work to put the philosophy of the Resolving Conflict Creatively Program at the core of the school's mission. We were deeply touched that RCCP was providing hope and meaning for a school and neighborhood that had undergone such pain. The results are plain to see: the culture of the school is now changing as children, parents, and teachers practice nonviolent ways of handling conflict. Pat Daly would be pleased.

After Pat's death it was clear to us that we needed to take a bolder step in bringing our message to the national level. We were running out of time.

One of the many unexpected results of expanding our work is this book. At the Children's Defense Fund's 1994 annual conference, we presented a combination of nitty-gritty "how to's" for school-based programs in violence prevention and conflict resolution, along with individual testimonies from young people, teachers, and principals in the field. Time was running short at the workshop; we could take one last question. "It's not a question. Well, I guess it is," said a woman from the back of the room. "This was so moving today. I feel so much hope hearing the two of you and the voices of these children. Is any of this written anywhere?" We answered flippantly. "Oh, that's the book we have on the back burner."

The workshop ended. Moments later, we met Deanne Urmy, executive editor of Beacon Press, who was in the audience. "I'd like to publish that book you've kept on the back burner," Deanne said. We are grateful for Deanne's faith in us, the kind of faith the Bible calls "the substance of things hoped for, the evidence of things not seen."

The purpose of this book is to take the reader into the heart of our work, focusing on three dimensions of creating safe and caring schools: conflict resolution, valuing diversity, and enhancing social and emotional learning. This book is based on available current research in these fields and on the practical experiences that teachers, parents, administrators, and students have had with this work.

Chapter 1 describes a new vision of education—one that promotes the teaching of emotional literacy, conflict resolution, and diversity education as basic to young people's education—and includes a review of some of the research that informs our work.

Chapter 2 takes the reader into the "peaceable classroom." We provide a sense of what a classroom looks and feels like when the expression of emotions, the peaceful resolution of conflicts, and the appreciation of diversity are interwoven into every aspect of classroom life.

Chapters 3 and 4 provide an introduction to the real core of what we do —the specific concepts and skills we teach young people and adults in the fields of conflict resolution, diversity education, and social and emotional learning.

Chapter 5 focuses on the role of the teacher in creating a safe and caring learning environment. Teachers share with us the various challenges, rewards, and obstacles they face as they embrace this work.

Chapters 6 and 7 talk about how this effort affects young people. Chapter 6 describes the work of mediation in schools and the practical experience we have gained from implementing this component of our work. In Chapter 7, we hear from the young people themselves, from the mediators who have worked intimately with the skills and concepts of RCCP in their schools, homes, and personal lives.

Chapter 8 describes the parent component of our work. As our children's first teachers, parents play an essential role in creating a safe and just world. This chapter outlines what parents can do to create a "peaceable home."

Chapter 9 takes us back in time to the early days of school-based conflict resolution efforts and describes the beginnings of the Resolving Conflict Creatively Program. The second part of the chapter describes the RCCP model in detail.

Chapter 10 provides a picture of the "peaceable school"—what it's like and how to get there. It focuses on creating norms and beliefs that support nonviolent conflict resolution and the valuing of diversity, and explores how school leaders can embrace RCCP as a schoolwide model for change.

Finally, Chapter 11 describes the importance of schools working together with their communities and the steps that can be taken to ensure that these efforts on behalf of children are comprehensive, sustained, and long-term.

This book is in every way a collaboration between the two of us, and every chapter is the product of joint effort. But because so much of the experience behind our conclusions is personal, we did not want to mask that experience with an artificial "we." Therefore each of us tells stories in the first person singular. In chapters 3, 4, 8, 9, and 11, "I" is Linda. In chapters 2, 5, 6, 7, and 10, the "I" is Janet. In this way we hope our individual experience will come through.

From RCCP's beginnings to the present, we have seen all that we are doing as a learning process. Although no one has all the answers on the best ways to wage peace in our schools, in writing this book we thought a great deal about what might be helpful for those of you who are also struggling to find better ways to teach young people and make schools safer for them. We feel grateful and fortunate to be writing this book together as friends of over twenty years, and to share in print our commitment to the work of waging peace in our schools.

We met when Janet was doing her student teaching practicum and Linda (then a full-time faculty member in the Education Department at Hunter College) was her supervisor. Both of our careers began in East Harlem. Both of us were teachers and then administrators in two of the first "schools of choice," the "break-the-mold" public schools in East Harlem that marked the beginning of the school reform movement in New York City in the 1970s. After teaching at Hunter College, Linda went on to serve at the central offices of the New York City Public Schools and there co-founded RCCP.

When Janet moved to California in 1979, she continued in the field of education in a variety of capacities—teacher, bilingual coordinator, school counselor, adjunct university instructor. It was in her role as assistant principal at Roosevelt Middle School, a large comprehensive school in Southern California, that we reconnected professionally. The signs of increasing gang violence were appearing on the school's campus, a reflection of a changing rural and suburban community that was being affected by several gang factions that had trickled down from the Los Angeles area. In order to address these issues, Janet became relentlessly committed to bringing RCCP to the Vista Unified School District. By the time Linda left the New York City school system to become the director of the RCCP National Center, established in 1993 under the auspices of Educators for Social Responsibility, the Vista school district was one of the pilot sites of our national work. Janet is now a senior program associate at RCCP's National Center. We knew early on that we would work together again. This book is our first attempt—and we've used many of our conflict resolution skills in the process!

< I >

A

NEW

VISION

[**1**]

A NEW VISION OF EDUCATION

Indifference finally grows lethal. . . . The act of turning away, however empty-
handed and harmlessly, remains nevertheless an act.
- Cynthia Ozick -
from the Prologue to
Rescuers: Portraits of Moral Courage in the Holocaust

OUR SOCIETY NEEDS a new way of thinking about what it means to be an educated person. We can no longer turn away from the emotional fabric of children's lives or assume that learning can take place isolated from their feelings. We need a vision of education that recognizes that the ability to manage our emotions, resolve conflicts, and interrupt biases are fundamental skills—skills that can and must be taught.

The simple truth is that we as a society are faced with the results of our cumulative indifference—exploding rates of drug abuse, teen pregnancy, and teen suicide, and the highest homicide rate of any country in the world. It is our responsibility to do something about it. Our indifference is lethal. We turn away at our own risk. From the killing fields of our streets to the arguments in our homes to the hopelessness so many of our young people feel—these are arenas in which schools can no longer be bystanders.

Each and every one of us has a role to play—parents, students, teachers, administrators, policy makers, researchers, custodians, counselors, cafeteria workers, bus drivers, and anyone else who comes into contact with the real lives of students. It takes a whole village to raise a child, and it takes a whole village to rescue one, too.

And children can be rescued. We know that now. They can be rescued if instead of turning away we listen—not just hear but *listen*—both to the alarm and to some of the exciting solutions that are emerging.

This is our wake-up call. Pick an urban city, a rural area, a wealthy suburb, an ordinary neighborhood:

> Lake Brantley, an affluent community outside of Orlando, Florida. A fifteen-year-old girl reportedly gashes a classmate in an argument turned violent.[1]

In another school down the block, a sixteen-year-old boy calmly responds to a classmate who is upset because he accidentally bumped into him. He says, "Did you think I did that on purpose? I didn't. I'm sorry. Are you okay?"

> Harper High School, Atlanta. A ninth-grader is killed and a tenth-grader wounded when another student opens fire in the crowded cafeteria. The previous day, the murdered student had had a fist fight with the suspected killer.[2]

Two years later, the same high school has set up a program through which students in conflict can choose a process of mediation to settle their disputes.

> Indianapolis, Indiana. In the first year of operating an electronic frisking device, school officials confiscate two sawed-off shotguns and a .38-caliber revolver.[3]

In a school in Brooklyn, kids are bringing in their toy guns to exchange for books in a "Books for Toy Gun Campaign" started after the accidental death of the brother of a classmate, who was shot by a police officer who mistook a toy gun for a real one.

> Downers Grove, Illinois, an affluent suburb outside of Chicago. A seventeen-year-old student is dressed in a hornet costume as the school mascot. After a football game, a fifteen-year-old student from a rival school reportedly walks over and shoots him once in the head. Tension between the two students had been growing.[4]

In another school, as kids are choosing up sides for stickball, Josh sticks up for another kid who wasn't being chosen because of his racial background and says, "I feel angry when people say things about people because of their race. If you do that again, I'm not going to play."

> Brooklyn, New York. A Thomas Jefferson High School student comes to school with a gun, then shoots and kills one student and critically wounds a teacher.[5]

In the same school system, hundreds of thousands of young people are now being taught conflict resolution skills as a "basic" of their education.

The horror stories go on and on and on, but so do the stories that tell us that there is another way, that many young people in our society today are being rescued, and that our schools have an important role to play.

One fact is clear: the times have changed and we must face the changes. Kids are coming to school more frightened and more angry than ever before. And their fear and anger walk right through the metal detectors set up at school doorways. Families today don't have the luxury of spending as much time together as our own parents spent with us, teaching us the lessons of the heart. Our communities are no longer functional villages, responsive to children's needs. Kids are growing up further and further away from a deep sense of community. Instead of spending meaningful time with friends, parents, and neighbors, America's children are spending more and more time glued to a computer screen or a television set.

For a long time schools have performed a socializing function in our society. They are now among the few places where young people of diverse backgrounds can be found in large numbers on a daily basis. Just by bringing them together, schools give kids a chance to develop their thinking, to practice handling their emotions, to deal with conflicts, and to learn the values of our society—if the schools are organized correctly.

Addressing young people's social and emotional lives is an immediate, pressing, urgent need. The mission of our schools must be expanded to include the critical human skills our children need in order for their lives to be safer, happier, and healthier. The definition of a well-educated person must include an education of the heart.

The goal of this new vision of education is to improve the social and emotional competence of children by teaching these life skills as part of their regular education, not only when they arrive in the principal's office or are labeled as troubled. We believe that this set of skills and understandings is essential for every child, that a child's emotional and social well-being should not be attended to only when emotional outbursts, physical fights, or racial slurs occur; we believe that the teaching of these skills and competencies in our schools is critical for our future survival.

This book offers a look at what this new kind of schooling can and could be like. It will draw on real examples, on recent theory, and on the more than five decades of experience that we possess between the two of us over our careers as educators working with kids and adults.

Our shared background is in one particular school-based program that combines the teaching of social and emotional skills with training in conflict resolution and diversity issues. As noted in this book's preface, the Resolving Conflict Creatively Program (RCCP) began as an initiative of Educators for Social Responsibility (ESR) Metro and the New York City Board of Education. Today RCCP's National Center works with the national nonprofit organization Educators for Social Responsibility in its efforts to make social responsibility an integral part of education by fostering new ways of teaching and learning.

RCCP is one of the largest and most successful programs of its kind in the country. In the 1995–96 school year, RCCP served over 150,000 children in more than 325 schools in eight school districts across the country. The program has been recognized by such national leaders as Children's Defense Fund President Marian Wright Edelman, U.S. Secretary of Education Richard Riley, and U.S. Attorney General Janet Reno. In the national arena, RCCP has been cited as one of the most successful school models by the U.S. Department of Education, the National Institute of Justice, the Harvard School of Public Health, and the U.S. General Accounting Office.

We have found that deep, committed intervention over a period of time begins to change things around. We *can* give young people concrete skills for dealing with conflict and prejudice. We *can* shift around kids' images of a hero and help them realize that the Rambos of this world, far from being heroic, are pathetic because they can think of only one solution to the problem. We *can* help young people realize that the highest form of heroism is the passionate search for nonviolent solutions to complex problems. Young people *can* learn to deal with their anger differently.

We believe in a new educational model, one which includes social and emotional learning from a multicultural perspective. In this model, schools help young people become caring individuals who participate as citizens in a democratic process within a pluralistic community. We have seen adults and young people alike believing and acting on the understanding that a nonviolent pluralistic society is a realistic goal. We have seen adults change, we have seen individual students change, and we have seen whole schools change.

The Research that Informs Our Practice

The new movement for social and emotional learning in schools comes at a time when research is informing and validating this work. In his groundbreaking book *Emotional Intelligence*, Daniel Goleman, social psychologist and mental health writer for the *New York Times*, makes the convincing argument that EQ, or "emotional quotient"—a way of describing people's human skills—may be as important as IQ, intelligence quotient, for success in life. He points out that skills such as empathy, managing difficult emotions, and the ability to motivate oneself may in fact be more important than scores on traditional cognitive tests in determining what happens in adult life.[6]

Unfortunately, these social and emotional competencies are in serious decline among American children throughout all sectors of our society. Psychologist Thomas Achenbach, from the University of Vermont, studied thousands of American children, first in the mid-1970s and then again in the late 1980s. He found that in the course of fifteen years, America's children—from the poorest to the most affluent—displayed a decline across the board in their scores on over forty measures designed to reflect a variety of emotional and social capacities.[7] American children have become more aggressive, more impulsive, more disobedient, more lonely, more sad. This decline in the very nature of the emotional and social life of children may in fact be more alarming than the dip in SAT scores that is also occurring.

That's the bad news. The good news is that people's emotional and social capacities can be strengthened, especially at an early age. Neuroscientists have confirmed that we have a wide window of opportunity to influence and strengthen our emotional and social selves early on in life. Research has uncovered the encouraging news that the centers in the prefrontal lobes of the brain that affect and control emotional impulses are among the last to reach full maturity—in mid- to late adolescence. And from experience we know we can intentionally reshape the emotional lessons learned in childhood, lessons which form the basis of the habits of the heart for the rest of our lives.

As we better understand the connection between the emotional brain and the thinking brain, we realize that we can only be as smart as our emotions let us be, as Daniel Goleman notes. The more we are emotionally distressed, anxious, or angry, the more we are affected by intrusive thoughts. The more of these kinds of thoughts we have, the less capacity we have to devote to working memory, the site of problem-solving and conscious thought. So among the benefits of managing our moods, Goleman tells us, is that doing so can make us smarter.

Recent breakthroughs in brain research and psychological theory have given us the scientific framework to begin to understand this different way of being smart. In 1990, psychologists Peter Salovey of Yale and John Mayer of the University of New Hampshire, building on the work of psychologist Howard Gardner of Harvard, coined the term "emotional intelligence." In his book *Frames of Mind*, Gardner names seven different intelligences and presents the case that schools traditionally teach to only two of them—math and verbal competencies. He identifies two other competencies as forming the basis of the concept of social and emotional literacy—intrapersonal and interpersonal intelligences. Intrapersonal intelligence involves knowing and managing one's own feelings; interpersonal intelligence is the ability to understand others and to get along with them. These intelligences are also often referred to as "personal intelligences."[8]

The theory of multiple intelligences is perhaps most accurately described as a philosophy of education, an attitude toward learning and an approach to teaching children rather than a specific program of fixed techniques or lessons. There is an added benefit. This approach also offers a way to appreciate differences: we each possess different combinations of intelligences. If we recognize this, we have a better chance of managing our emotions and dealing appropriately with our conflicts. Gardner has made a strong link between the cognitive and affective domains, one that is crucial for educators.

The Development of Social and Emotional Competencies

What are the abilities encompassed by the idea of emotional intelligence?

The first component, as described by Goleman in an essay entitled "The Educated Heart,"[9] is that of *self-awareness*—knowing what you are feeling. This ability lies at the base of all other emotional abilities. It's being able to step back from an experience and "be with" what is happening rather than letting the experience take over and getting lost in it. It's the difference between being swept away by emotion and saying, "I hate you," and knowing and saying to yourself, "This is anger," and beginning to think about how you will deal with that anger.

The second ability is how to *handle emotions*. It's the ability to manage the feelings you're aware of. It's thinking about what an appropriate reaction to the feeling would be and not acting impulsively. Managing emotions means being able to break the patterns of the past—the legacy of events and learned responses from childhood—and deal with the events of the present.

The third ability of emotional intelligence is *self-motivation*. This means maintaining hope and optimism in the pursuit of your goals, even when things get frustrating, even in the face of setbacks.

The fourth ability is *empathy*. Empathy, the root of caring, is the ability to imagine and understand other people's feelings without their having to tell you how they feel. People rarely express their feelings in words alone, and empathy includes being able to read facial expressions, gestures, and other nonverbal signals. Empathy is a critical human capacity and is crucial for harmonious relationships. "Empathy," Goleman tells us, "underlies many facets of moral judgment and action." It allows someone to "feel for" the circumstances [of] another, which may or may not result in actions, sometimes even altruistic in nature.[10]

Finally, *social skill*, the fifth ability, refers to the capacity to handle and to respond effectively to someone else's emotions; it includes the social competencies that allow us to relate well to others.

Maurice Elias, associate professor in the Department of Psychology at Rutgers University, and others believe that young people can learn skills in school which will increase and strengthen their social competence and improve both the quality of their own lives and their interactions with others.

The consensus among social psychologists is that socially competent children are those who

>   possess a positive sense of self-worth;
>   feel capable as they interact with others and take on new developmental tasks and challenges;
>   behave ethically and act responsibly toward others;

> appreciate the benefits of a multiracial society and respect the values of others;

> possess skill in interpersonal encounters and communication, get along with others, and develop long-term interpersonal relationships;

> develop sound work habits, motivation, and values;

> engage in health enhancing and health protective behavior;

> are motivated to become productive citizens, serve as contributing members of their peer group, family, school, and community;

> avoid engaging in behavior that leads to negative consequences such as substance abuse, teen pregnancy, AIDS, etc.[11]

In their book *Building Social Problem Skills*, Elias and his coauthor, John Clabby, describe a series of protective factors, a core set of skills which can facilitate social competency and ward off delinquent behaviors, and thus allow a child to grow into a socially competent adult. These skills fall into three areas: *Self-control and self-regulation skills* include skills such as listening carefully and accurately, remembering and following directions, concentrating and following through on tasks, calming oneself down and avoiding being provoked to anger in interactions with others. *Social awareness and group participation skills* include accepting praise or approval, choosing caring friends, knowing when help is needed and being able to ask for it, working as part of a problem-solving team. *Social decision-making skills and problem-solving skills* include recognizing feelings in oneself and in others, being able to describe these feelings, setting realistic interpersonal goals, seeing the effects of one's choices on oneself and on others, selecting solutions that can reach goals, anticipating obstacles, and learning from experience.[12]

Violence Prevention

One particularly urgent task of emotional and social learning is the prevention of violent and other antisocial behavior. The violence in our society has many causes, including obvious social forces such as prejudice, economic inequality, the availability of drugs and guns, and the glamorization of aggression in mainstream American culture. Violence is now considered a serious public health problem. It accounts for about 38 percent of all fatal injuries. The peak age of arrests for serious violent crimes in the United States is eighteen.[13] We also know that homicide is the second cause of death of young men between the ages of fifteen and twenty-four and the first cause of death of African-American males and females in this age bracket.[14]

It seems obvious that schools have an important role to play, and the public is demanding that they play it. Even though recent statistics are showing a nationwide dip in overall crime (except among youth), a 1994 study published by the organization Public Agenda showed that safety remains the public's number one concern in relation to our nation's schools.[15]

The approach we take to tackling violence depends on how we frame the problem. Deborah Prothrow-Stith, author and assistant dean of the Harvard School of Public Health, is a leading spokesperson for the use of the public health model as a lens through which to view violence. Prothrow-Stith explains that we must begin by thinking about the way we approach the prevention of a disease. For example, in addressing the problem of lung cancer we not only treat people who have the disease, we help people quit smoking, and, perhaps most importantly, we teach people about the risks of ever starting to smoke. Prothrow-Stith admits that the analogy between physical health and the issue of violence is not perfect, yet she argues that trying to control violence mainly by punishing its perpetrators is akin to trying to prevent lung cancer deaths only by performing surgery.[16]

The public health approach to violence concentrates on prevention rather than treatment. And schools must accept their role as the main source of this prevention. We need to start addressing these issues proactively rather than reactively. Although schools alone will not be able to create a peaceable society, there is little possibility that we will succeed in reducing violence without educating our young people in the ways of peace.

As youth violence increases, it is essential that we understand the contributing factors. Ronald Slaby, senior scientist at the Education Development Center and lecturer at Harvard University, has found that violent students have a different way of thinking from their nonaggressive peers. Slaby says that kids prone to violence seek fewer facts, have less insight into alternative solutions, and often fail to anticipate the negative consequences of their behaviors.[17]

David Hawkins and Richard Catalano have identified several risk factors in youth which, according to current research, are high predictors of later violent and antisocial behavior.[18] Among these factors are "alienation and a lack of bonding to family, school and community." Research has also uncovered a group of "resilient" children, children who are exposed to the same risks but are able to bounce back and overcome the effects of a high-risk environment. According to the literature on resilience, these children possess, among other qualities, social competence and problem-solving skills.

In other words, we have the power to create conditions that promote resilience in young people; cultivating the emotional and social domain, in the context of one's cultural background, can enhance one's ability for personal adjustment as well as one's resiliency through life. Hawkins and Catalano advocate giving young people "opportunities, skills and recognition"—opportunities to contribute to their family, schools, and community; skills that enable them to participate; and recognition for their capabilities and participation.

William DeJong of the Harvard School of Public Health tells us that upon examining the research on aggression, public health specialists have come to the following conclusions:

> We must improve young people's perspective taking skills.
> We must focus young people on the negative consequences of violence, both for society and for the aggressor as well.
> We must teach young people how to negotiate nonviolent solutions to conflict.
> We must teach young people to be vigilant for signs that a conflict might spin out of control.[19]

Several studies indicate that when young people are taught social skills at an early age they are less likely to commit violent crimes as adults.[20] Another showed how referrals to juvenile court were reduced simply by teaching young people how not to insult, how to praise others, and how to accept feedback from others.[21] Karen Bierman's work at Pennsylvania State University confirms these findings. After ten sessions in which aggressive boys were taught lessons in cooperation, how to ask questions, and how to share, the boys became less aggressive. Bierman says, "Even if a child has a predisposition to aggression, s/he can learn to override it. The more aggressive kids just need more help from their parents, teachers and friends."[22]

This research is encouraging, and it suggests that not only do efforts have to be in place for all children, but targeted interventions—methods for reaching young people at risk for violent behaviors—are also needed. G. D. Gottfredson reports that schools that aim at increasing resiliency in young people can reduce a young person's possibilities of becoming a juvenile offender by 40 percent.[23]

The American Psychological Association's Commission on Violence and Youth reports, "We overwhelmingly conclude, on the basis of the body of psychological research on violence, that violence is not a random, uncontrollable, or inevitable occurrence. . . . Although we acknowledge that the problem of violence involving youth is staggering . . . there is overwhelming evidence that we can intervene effectively in the lives of young people to reduce and prevent their involvement in violence." Their report recommends that schools play a critical part in any comprehensive plan for preventive intervention to reduce youth violence.[24]

Some of the best research available on school-based prevention efforts comes from the work of the W. T. Grant Consortium on the School-Based Promotion of Social Competence. The consortium conducted extensive studies on programs designed to prevent and reduce drug and alcohol use in children and young adults. They looked at the effectiveness of programs aimed at developing social competencies that would decrease risk factors for antisocial behavior, academic failure, alienation and rebelliousness, low commitment to school, favorable attitudes towards drug and alcohol use, associating with drug-using peers, and early first use of drugs. These programs simultaneously sought to increase protective factors such as bonding to school, resisting antisocial influences, and forming positive social relationships.[25]

Research by the consortium has provided us with criteria for establishing effective prevention efforts and for developing appropriate school curricula. This research also tells us that programs designed to have an impact on students' behavior must recognize that change occurs over time, and that learning prosocial skills not only helps young people with their interpersonal relationships but also with their attitudes towards school. They get along better with students and teachers and therefore find school a comforting place to be. This in turn shows itself in higher academic achievement and helps to erase more negative and antisocial behaviors; teachers and schools that have concentrated on social competency programs have reported successes such as fewer behavior problems and a more cooperative school climate.[26]

The research by Hawkins and Catalano indicates that not only do young people need to learn these skills, they also need to see them modeled, and they need to practice them in a setting where they are provided with feedback and with reinforcement for choosing to use these skills and for using them well.[27]

For this to happen, an environment of openness and acceptance that encourages kids to risk this "new way of being" needs to be present, one that fosters cooperation and a belief in teamwork. When these foundation skills are offered to young people, the protective factors that foster resiliency are increased by making bonding possible. Kids can then develop the cognitive and social skills necessary for problem-solving and getting along with others.

Diversity Issues and Prejudice Reduction

In addition to studies in the field of social and emotional development and violence prevention such as those cited above, research in the field of intergroup relations informs our practice as well. One of the pioneer scholars of racial prejudice, Gordon Allport, found that children learn bigotry in two basic ways: by adopting the prejudices of their parents, and by absorbing the lessons of the larger cultural environment when that environment fosters suspicion, fear, and hatred of specific groups of people. Allport tells us that it takes the entire period of childhood and adolescence to master prejudice.[28]

The work of Louise Derman-Sparks provides us with background as to how this happens—how young children begin to form their conceptions about people who are different from themselves.[29] Children are aware of these differences at a very early age. They construct their identities and attitudes as they experience themselves, their own bodies, and their social environments through various cognitive stages. Derman-Sparks notes that a two-year-old child already distinguishes differences in gender and skin color, and a child as young as three has already become aware of society's norms about gender, racial differences, and physical disabilities. Somewhere between the ages of three and five, children begin to describe who they are based on attributes such as skin color, gender, and abilities; by age four or five, they can clearly be heard making biased comments based on racial, gender, and physical differences. Indeed, Adolf Hitler, when he started the Nazi Youth Movement, said that if he had control of a child until his or her sixth birthday, he could plant seeds the child would never overcome.

Our work concentrates heavily on helping young people recognize the effects of prejudice and discrimination, and on creating a school climate that discourages biased acts of any kind and fosters a valuing of diversity.

In examining the research by social psychologists on prejudice, we find that eliminating prejudice itself is not easy. Studies suggest that it is most helpful to identify and have strong sanctions in place against *acts* of bias. In fact, as psychologist Fletcher Blanchard of Smith College has found, when a few very vocal people express dismay at these acts, others are encouraged to do likewise. Blanchard and others point to the fact that when bias acts are ignored they increase, but when people in authority make it clear that such acts will not be tolerated, bystanders are more likely to condemn the acts themselves and to conform to the new social norm.[30]

Another promising approach to combating bias involves putting diverse groups of people together in a cooperative context, working toward a common goal. An early (1979) national study of over 2,000 high school students found that the strongest variable as to whether a student was less prejudiced was his or her involvement in team sports, clubs, or other student activities that brought diverse groups of young people together. A 1989 study of 3,200 students in five middle schools in Florida found that students in racially mixed learning teams were among the least prejudiced. Charles Green, a psychologist at Hope College in Michigan, says that "the idea that if you just get people together they'll start liking each other is naive, but if they are working together for shared goals, it breaks down negative stereotypes they had of each other."[31] Robert Slavin, a national leader in the field of race relations, confirms the learning-team results: "There's nothing as strong as personal, cooperative contact with someone you get to know naturally without saying anything about race."[32] Working together toward a common goal is one way to allow this to happen.

Clearly, these experiences need to be frequent and extensive in order to break down the negative stereotypes people have of each other. We've learned the following from the research cited above and other studies:

> Students will appreciate diversity and will work harder to resolve diversity-related conflicts when they are in an environment that actively values diversity.

> The more pride in and appreciation for their own culture students have, the more they can appreciate other cultures.

> To appreciate other cultures and overcome prejudices, it's not enough for students to learn about those cultures; they need some emotional

connection with other groups and direct positive experiences of being on equal footing with one another.

> For students to overcome prejudices and stereotypes, they need to acquire and understand the vocabulary necessary for talking about prejudice and related issues.

Educational Innovation and Conflict Resolution

Most of the research described in this chapter has been going on in the academic world, with carefully designed interventions targeted at specific societal problems. At the same time, over the past several decades, people working in schools have been translating the lessons from such in-depth research and putting parallel ideas to work in various innovative movements in education.

The affective education movement of the 1960s contributed much to the idea that what was being taught conceptually could be better understood if it was put into a psychological and experiential context. And in the late 1970s and early 1980s, the cooperative learning movement played a critical role in shaping the teaching of prosocial skills, by looking at the role cooperation plays in learning. David W. Johnson and Roger T. Johnson, Robert Slavin, Spencer Kagen, and others looked at the relationship between cooperation and competition. When group goals are established and students are also held individually accountable for their work there have been many successes using a cooperative learning mode.[33] Also key, according to the research in cooperative learning, is the creation of a cooperative climate for learning by the use of an alternative to the competitive reward system of grades. Johnson and Johnson point out that "it makes little sense to teach students to manage conflict constructively if the school is structured so that students have to compete for scarce rewards (like grades of 'A') and defeat each other to get what they want."[34] Cooperative learning strategies are now widely accepted in American classrooms and have paved the way for the cooperative context needed for teaching conflict resolution skills.

Theories and practices from the field of conflict resolution, which has taken root in the business world, have also begun to make their way into the educational arena. The field of conflict resolution emerged about seventy-five years ago as an approach to improving labor-management relations.[35] During the 1920s Mary Parker Follett, an educator and one of the field's pioneers, began showing business managers how to better deal with conflict in the workplace in order to increase productivity. Follett had the insight that many conflicts can be solved in mutually satisfactory ways if the parties can avoid bickering over "positions" and can focus instead on finding creative ways to fulfill their underlying needs. Follett's insight, sometimes called the win-win solution, lies at the core of contemporary approaches to negotiation, popularized in books such as Roger Fisher and William Ury's 1981 bestseller *Getting to Yes: Negotiating Agreement Without Giving In*.[36]

Conflict resolution skills seem to matter in all facets of adult life, from family life to career success. Consider, for example, that more than half of all first marriages in this country end in divorce and second marriages fare even worse, failing 60 percent of the time. In decades of marital research, studies have found that emotional intelligence can make a difference in terms of whether a marriage will last. John Gottman, a psychologist at the University of Washington, studied more than two thousand married couples over a twenty-year period and concluded that the single most important factor in the success or failure of a marriage was how couples work out their differences—their ability to resolve conflicts.[37]

Our ability to handle conflict is also crucial to successful employment, and how we fare in the workplace also seems to be linked to our emotional intelligence. According to a 1994 Census Bureau survey of hiring, training, and management practices in American business, the two qualities employers most value are attitude and communication skills. The survey also shows an alarming failure on the part of most American schools to focus directly on the cultivation of these skills.

Although conflict resolution remains a relatively new focus for most schools, much is already being done, all across the country, by many educators working to create safe schools and effective learning environments that include the cultivation of social and emotional competencies. This good work goes on under many different banners—cooperative learning, affective education, and, more recently, conflict resolution—but the labels matter little. What matters is that in the pockets of successful schools that exist everywhere, even in our most afflicted urban areas, children are known and cared for and respected. And they are learning and succeeding.

Reclaiming Our Schools as Safe Havens

But pockets of successful schools aren't enough. Ultimately, every school in the country needs to adopt a broadly conceived and well-coordinated strategy to cultivate the emotional and social skills necessary to an educated, whole, socially responsible person. This needs to happen for all students and teachers in every school in America. We need to reclaim our schools as safe havens.

We know that this new kind of schooling is possible. Amidst the despair we find great hope. We believe our schools have the potential for supporting the resiliency of children, for counteracting violence, and for providing the cooperative environment in which change can take place. In our long-term vision, we see children entering kindergarten and immediately beginning to learn that differences are accepted, that feelings are okay, and that nonviolent approaches to conflict are the norm. By the time they are in first or second grade, these kids will almost automatically choose conflict resolution skills to mediate disputes among classmates. And later, as they enter high school, they will have the courage and skills to stand up to bigotry and violence and to work for a more peaceful and caring society. When young people can experience this way of being in their schools, chances will be higher that they will fully internalize and employ this approach throughout their adult lives.

This is our vision—bold, grand. Now let's look more closely at how it can become a reality in classrooms across America.

[**2**]

THE PEACEABLE CLASSROOM

Each second we live is a new and unique moment of the universe, a moment
that never was before and will never be again. And what do we teach our
children in school? We teach them that two and two makes four,
and that Paris is the capital of France.
When will we also teach them what they are? We should say to each of them:
Do you know what you are? You are a marvel. You are unique. . . . And when you
grow up can you then harm another who is, like you, a marvel?
You must cherish one another. You must work—we all must work—
to make this world worthy of its children.
- Pablo Casals -
Joys and Sorrows

HOW DO WE MAKE THIS NEW vision of education practical? What kind
of classroom experiences are we talking about?

To begin with, we know what kind of classroom we are *not* talking about.
Too many schools today—partly as a result of the belief that if we take the
time to teach our young people social and emotional skills we will somehow
deprive them of the "academic rigor" they need—foster elitism, competition, isolation, and separation by gender, racial, and ethnic differences. In
such an environment children become unruly, disrespectful, unmotivated,
and hurtful to each other.

Let's look at an example.

Ms. Wagner lines up her fifth-graders outside the classroom door.

"Boys on this side and girls on that side," she reminds them. "Look how nicely the girls are lined up. Boys, you can do much better than this. Samantha, you can lead the girls in first."

Once the children are settled, Ms. Wagner begins.

"Today, children, we will continue learning how to divide fractions."

As Ms. Wagner lectures to her class and writes example after example on the chalkboard, John, a small boy in the second row, bends down and grabs something out of his notebook. A closer look reveals a connect-the-dots puzzle which he slips under his math book and begins to complete whenever Ms. Wagner isn't looking. In the third row, fifth seat, a tall girl with braids passes a note to the girl behind her. The girl reads it, giggles, and then pretends she is listening. The room is very quiet. A boy in the last row, last seat, sticks his tongue out at the student across from him, who throws a paper wad at him. It hits a girl and ends up in the front of the classroom, directly in front of Ms. Wagner.

"Who threw this?" she demands.

No replies.

"Fine," she continues. "We can just wait all day then and miss our recess."

Silence.

"Who did it, Mark?" She glares at Mark, an immediate suspect. "You always think it's me," he blurts out. "I didn't do anything, I swear. It came from back there." He points toward the back of the room.

Still no response.

"Well, then, you've all just lost fifteen minutes of recess and gained another page of math homework," Ms. Wagner informs them.

"So now," she continues, "who can show me how to do problem number fifteen on page forty-seven?" She looks around at the blank faces. Finally, one brave hand goes up and its owner volunteers to go to the board to do the example.

"Good, Henry!" Ms. Wagner exclaims. "I'm glad somebody was listening. What about the rest of you? I'm sure you're all going to pass the test on Friday. What about you, Maria? You haven't had an 'A' paper hanging up on the bulletin board in a long time. Do you think you will this time?" With eyes downcast, Maria replies, "Yes, teacher."

"Well, then, perhaps you can show us how to do number sixteen?"

The silence is broken by a tall, red-haired boy in the back row.

"Hey, give me my pencil back!" he shouts at the boy next to him. "I said, give it to me, you jerk!"

"It's mine," the other boy replies. "I don't have to give it to you. I don't know where yours is."

"What's going on back there?" the teacher interjects.

"Danny took David's pencil," explains a small girl in the third row, "and he says it's his."

With eyebrows lowered, Ms. Wagner commands, "Give him his pencil, Danny." She writes Danny's name on the upper right-hand corner of the board. "That's enough. Give it to him or I'll call your mother tonight. I've had enough of this nonsense."

"But . . . ," he attempts to explain.

"There will be no excuses. Just do as I say."

Danny throws the pencil at David, slumps into his chair, and kicks the chair in front of him with his foot. Silence fills the room. Ms. Wagner goes on.

"It's time for social studies. Please put away your math books and take out your social studies books. Don't forget to do page fifty-five for math homework tonight."

While this fictional scenario may seem somewhat exaggerated, even comical, it is meant to be familiar as well, and it loses its humor when we look at it in light of the failures of emotional and academic learning this kind of classroom manifests.

Let us now turn our attention to a positive vision of the classroom, one that embodies the kind of education we argue for.

Mrs. Frye sits for the moment at her desk, off to the side in the back of the classroom. Tammy, a fourth-grade student, approaches her to discuss a story she's writing. Off in the front right corner of the room, designated "the peace corner" by a student-made multicolored sign, several students are busily working. Two girls are seated on a couch, silently reading books together. Another student has donned a set of headphones and is listening to music while writing in his journal. Others work quietly with their groups at their tables. Suddenly Frank, a short boy at the table near the door, breaks the silence.

"Hey, give me back my pencil, Tom. I know you took it!"

"I don't have your stupid pencil," Tom responds in a shrill voice. This is mine." They continue to yell at each other until Sara, a student mediator, walks over and asks, "Why are you arguing with each other? Do you want a mediation? Would you like me to help?" For a brief moment the boys stop their bickering.

By this time, Mrs. Frye is standing behind the two angry boys. Placing her arm around Sara, she says, "Thank you, Sara." Turning to the boys, she says, "It does seem like there's a problem. I'd like you both to calm down and decide whether you'd like to discuss this with me or whether you'd like a mediation. You know the rules about fighting. I hope you'll think about them before making your decision."

The two boys, still angry, stalk off to different sides of the room. They both know the procedure. They will sit apart for a while and calm themselves down before they attempt to resolve the conflict they are having; they may ask either their teacher or a class mediator for help. Fighting is not acceptable; they know they will be suspended from school if they fight.

During the three or four minutes that this conflict interrupts the class, other students look on, but continue to work at their tables. It's clear that in this classroom this kind of behavior will not be tolerated or supported by either young people or adults.

Consider first the way the two classes we've described are managed. In Ms. Wagner's class, discipline is established by having a teacher set rules which the students follow; when rules are broken, students are punished, with little or no reflection as to what could be done differently to avoid a repetition of the offending behavior. Conflicts are resolved by the teacher, because it is believed that kids lack the skills to resolve their own conflicts. Young people come to expect adults to solve their problems, instead of assuming responsibility for regulating and managing their own emotions and behaviors. When arguments and fights erupt, children may be sent to a cooling-off corner or to the counselor or assistant principal after the problem occurs, but there's no vehicle for defusing the situation before it gets out of hand.

In Mrs. Frye's class, while the rules are very clear, well defined, and understood, students also know that there are many means to address conflicts before they escalate and become physical. In this classroom—and others like it—kids know it's their job to express and control their anger appropriately. Mediation and negotiation are used by staff and students, and discipline is not just a matter of teacher-made edicts; the students have taken part in the rule-making, know what happens if rules are broken, and have skills to resolve conflicts nonviolently. The norms underlying the culture of the peaceable classroom are clear to all of its members. Not only does physically aggressive behavior have strong sanctions against it, but hurtful, painful words and "put-downs" are not tolerated either.

The children become the peacemakers. They encourage their peers to resolve conflicts nonviolently. Student mediators equipped with high-level conflict resolution skills ward off potential fights among friends. They may even prevent violence from occurring.

Mariana, a former classroom teacher who is now coordinator for RCCP in New York City, reported on her early experience with the program:

At the beginning of this school year there was a lot of tension in my class-room. The boys were using put-downs, doing a lot of "dissing" and "rank-ing" and this was intimidating the girls. . . . We did discussions and exercises on dealing with anger and on cooperation and then I helped them process these experiences, talking about [both] the difficult and good parts of their efforts. By January, students began to mix more naturally in cooperative learning groups. Dissing, ranking, and put-downs virtually disappeared. Kids began helping each other by taking time to talk through conflicts that occurred in their school life. The change in the climate of the classroom was palpable and very satisfying for me.

Like Mrs. Frye and her class, Mariana and her students felt an ease of learning in their classroom once they had established a culture of coopera-tion, caring, and respect. Many school reform efforts of today focus on maxi-mizing students' academic learning. While there are many excellent models designed to reach this goal, we must not forget that young people need to be taught how to get along and how to resolve the conflicts in their lives so that they *can* learn effectively.

The Goals of the Peaceable Classroom

William Kreidler—author, conflict resolution expert, and an elementary school teacher for more than twenty years—first coined the term "peaceable classroom" in the early 1970s, inspired by the painting "The Peaceable King-dom," by Edward Hicks, which depicts a beautifully colored world of ani-mals and people living together in harmony. Kreidler was teaching third grade at the time, and a reproduction of this painting that he so loved hung above his desk. He would repeatedly gaze upon it and think, "How can I have a class of students be as peaceful as this painting?"[1]

He considered all the things that caused conflict in the classroom: mis-communication, inability to work together to complete a task, inability to express feelings in constructive ways, exclusion because of differences, and inability to talk things through. Overriding all of these was a general lack of care and respect.

Kreidler began to use cooperative learning strategies in the classroom to teach constructive social skills to his students. In a few weeks he saw an amazing difference in the way children were treating one another. Children began to choose peaceful solutions and to reject fighting and berating one another. Instead of competing, they were helping each other learn and working together in respectful ways to accomplish tasks.

Kreidler was convinced that if he could teach young people how to cooperate, he could also teach them other essential social and emotional skills. Soon Kreidler's third-graders were learning more and they were learning better. His classroom afforded them a safe haven. They weren't fearful and angry anymore. They felt included, respected, listened to, and capable of helping each other learn as well. These experiences sparked Kreidler to develop the model of the peaceable classroom now used in many classrooms across the United States and Canada.

Little did he think that today these skills would be literally lifesaving for many of our young people, who are learning to use words instead of deadly physical violence to express their anger and rage.

Teaching the Themes of the Peaceable Classroom

William Kreidler stresses that the strength of the peaceable classroom is in the synergy that develops from the presence of six principles: cooperation, caring communication, the appreciation of diversity, the appropriate expression of feelings, responsible decision making, and conflict resolution. If these themes have been clearly taught and emphasized, then resolving conflict creatively naturally follows.

Learning new skills is a slow process and the skills of the peaceable classroom are no exception. Whether we are teaching cooperative learning, decision making, or conflict resolution, there are a series of stages that learners go through. At first students may be unaware, unskillful, and even resistant.

They may be uncomfortable using new techniques; they may feel foolish, phony, or insincere because this is not the way they are used to acting. New skills may even seem to contradict ways of being that stem from their cultural backgrounds. We need to honor cultural differences and to provide levels of comfort in accommodating the new skills. We each come with different levels of readiness. For example, in our program it isn't uncommon to hear kids who are practicing the "I-message" (a basic technique taught in conflict resolution) say, "This stuff seems silly. How will I say this to someone who's angry at me and doesn't know anything about I-messages?"[2] Teachers have to provide plenty of practice, and allow for creative adaptations and lots of feedback to the students on how they are doing. Practice in a variety of contexts will help students integrate this new learning into their active repertoires.

Cooperation

Cooperation is a prerequisite for many other school tasks, and teachers often assign collaborative projects in the hope that young people will work together, only to become frustrated when the projects fail because kids argue, interrupt one another, and don't work as teams. It's important to remember that kids aren't born cooperative and certainly haven't been encouraged to be so in this society.

In our curriculum, children are taught that cooperation is about working together toward a common goal, and that it has many advantages over competition because it allows people to help one another. For some children this is a familiar theme, reinforced by a tight-knit collective culture at home, but others are taught at home that competition is essential to achieve success.

In a cooperative classroom, young people learn that they can come together and use people's different strengths to collectively solve problems. If there's a job to be done, working cooperatively often gets that job done better. Young people begin to view cooperation as fun and to see that it gets easier with practice. They learn that there are times when working coopera-tively benefits them greatly and that there are times when they must work alone.

At first, working in cooperative groups may be difficult for very young children. Developmentally they are still very much into the "me" and "mine" way of thinking about their world—sharing is usually not number one on their list of skills. But with guidance and the support of a well-designed curriculum, they can be very successful in extending themselves and learning valuable lessons about cooperation. In one project used in our program, for example, young children build imaginary monsters together, using a set of improvised materials. They discuss what their monster will look like and decide who will create the different parts of the monster. Then they join their efforts and present the final product to the class.

Older children can work in collaborative ways throughout their day. They can be given the responsibility to decide together what best works for the team, whether it's about what game they will play in physical education class, for example, or what part of a science project each of them will com-plete. Language arts activities can be enhanced when kids write stories to-gether; each person in the group supplies a new sentence to the paragraph, creating group ownership and wonderful, creative narratives. In math, they might make group estimates of the number of beans in a jar; discussing their estimates with their teammates, they inevitably find that collaboration makes their estimates much more accurate.

We have found that it is also important that kids have time to reflect on the workings of cooperation. In small groups, children can listen to their teammates talk about what it feels like to work cooperatively. In this confi-dential sharing time, it becomes safe to express feelings like "I feel disap-pointed when you don't complete your part of the assignment because I work so hard at completing my work so the group will do well," or simply to affirm each other by saying, "I think we all really worked well today and I feel good about working in this group." This evaluative process allows young people to set goals that will help each member of the group take responsibility for completing group assignments. They see how much they depend on each other.

In our experience, it is essential that students explicitly evaluate how well they did in using specific social skills they are working on, skills such as listening to one another, encouraging, praising. This is often the piece of the process that gets lost in the time crunch to "get everything in," but teachers report that when they take the time to analyze these behavioral skills with their students, academic tasks are accomplished even more swiftly and with fewer interruptions.

Once students know how to work cooperatively, cooperation becomes second nature, even the preferred way of accomplishing tasks. Maureen, a teacher at the Roosevelt Middle School in Southern California, shared the following experience with us.

The idea was born in the classroom during a brainstorming session on "What will be our theme this year?" It received unanimous acceptance: a "peace quilt" celebrating our awareness of how conflict resolution can make a difference. My students, eighth-graders, [had been] given the task of deciding on a theme for our annual quilt, a collaborative, hands-on product of our Pioneers Unit in our U.S. History class.

The kids wanted to design a quilt to show what they were learning from those lessons in class, and to send the message that together we can work out our problems without resorting to violence. Each square uniquely reflects how each student sees conflict, or conflict resolution, affecting his or her life. The kids [each tried] to find a symbol or saying that captured the essence of concern or hope: gang jackets, peace signs, hands clasped, a beautiful globe, a love poem, weapons with the "no" circle superimposed on them, a pebble rippling in a pond, and many more creative images. . . . The students were very proud of its effect upon the rest of the campus and the community. The peace quilt will remind all of those who see it of what [the] peacemakers of the future really care about.

The impressive, multicolored quilt stands seven feet long and five feet tall. Loved by all members of the school, the quilt took on an even greater significance as a symbol of important schoolwide core values, and it now marks the entrance to the building.

Caring Communication

Two people can be in the same place at the same time and hear the same words spoken and each translate those words into a different meaning. In a classroom, the possibilities for miscommunication are multiplied many times over.

Real discussion and dialogue, central in any classroom, depend on honest, open communication. In our program, we teach young people that communication works best if the speaker is clear about what is being said and if the listener actively listens and asks clarifying questions. We stress that observing with all of our senses helps facilitate good communication, that poor communication causes unnecessary conflicts, and that everyone has different points of view and brings the richness of their own individual and cultural experiences to the group.

We've found that as teachers teach communication skills to children they need to be aware that in some cultures and families communication patterns are hierarchical; out of respect for authority, some children may not freely express their opinions or engage in free-flowing conversations. Teachers' sensitivity to such differences in background can help children explore ways of communicating that don't come easily. Sometimes, after asking a question that a student doesn't respond to, a teacher simply needs to say, "Take some more time to think about it. I'll come back to you later," or, "Do you feel comfortable in answering that question now? Please let me know if you don't."

There are many activities that help foster young people's communication skills. In a primary classroom, we often start with simple ones such as asking children to draw figures based on descriptions given. "Draw a circle in the middle of your paper. Above the circle make a dot." The kids are encouraged to ask clarifying questions to be sure that they have enough information. Then the children check their papers and compare their drawings with the one the teacher was describing. Often the results are very interesting, and kids are invited to brainstorm other questions they could have asked in order to get a more accurate reproduction.

To explore the concept of point of view, we ask kids to talk about how characters in books could have said things differently or asked questions that would have avoided their misunderstandings. Or we might discuss, for example, a new version of "Little Red Riding Hood," called "The Maligned Wolf," in which the poor wolf tells us his point of view about what really happened:

When the girl arrived, I invited her into the bedroom where I was in the bed, dressed like her grandmother. The girl came in and the first thing she did was to say something nasty about my ears. I've been insulted before so I made the best of it by suggesting that my big ears would help me to hear her better. Then she made another nasty remark, this time about my bulging eyes. I ignored her insult and told her my big eyes help me see better. But her next insult really got to me. She said something about my big teeth. At that point I lost it. I knew I should have been able to handle the situation, but I just couldn't control my anger any longer. I jumped up from the bed and growled at her and said, "My teeth will help me eat you better."[3]

Kids begin to see that there are "many sides to a story" and that often people have very different thoughts about similar events. (Imagine feeling sorry for the wolf. But he sure is convincing!) They begin to act out roles that demonstrate differences in point of view. We ask middle school and high school students to do "role plays" in which they see how communication potholes—such as giving unsolicited advice, passing judgment, or avoiding the issue—break down communication. We encourage them to open up communication by paraphrasing and reflecting feelings, by agreeing to disagree, and by using I-messages.

Kids often say hurtful, unkind words to one another. They poke fun at one another by playing upon their weaknesses and differences. In the vocabulary of peaceable classrooms, we refer to these hurtful words as "put-downs."

We do an activity with both children and adults in which we hold up a large red paper heart representing a young person's self-esteem and tell a story like the following:

David gets up in the morning to get himself ready for school. As he heads out of his room to get breakfast, he is stopped by his sister, who says, "Yuk, David, that shirt is horrible. It has stains on it and it's nerdy. You look terrible." David quickly changes his shirt and heads to the kitchen where he greets his mom. "Morning, Mom. What's for breakfast?" "Breakfast?" Mom responds, somewhat disgruntled. "Do you realize what time it is? I can't make it now. You've got to get up early, David, if you expect me to give you a warm meal." David grabs a banana and runs out the door to catch the school bus. Just as he gets to the corner, the bus passes him by. A boy calls out the window, "Tough luck, David! Have a great walk to school."[4]

The story continues. Each time David hears a defeating, negative, derogatory remark, we tear off a piece of the heart and throw it on the floor. People sit speechless, eyes on the heart, as they feel David's pain, bit by bit. When we ask the question, "How many of you have been hurt by put-downs at some point in your life?" every hand goes up. When we ask the group to think of ways that negative statements can be put constructively, not only do they begin to avoid using put-downs, but they begin to see the usefulness of "put-ups," statements that accept feelings and validate and affirm.

Sometimes as young people are learning to practice this new way of communicating, we suggest that they create a signal, agreed upon by the class, which they can use when they notice that a put-down has been issued. In a classroom in Anchorage, Alaska (where many deaf children are included in regular classrooms), one of the students suggested signing the word "love" as the signal.

Learning to stop using put-downs takes practice. A teacher might say, "Can you say that in another way?" Teachers have to be careful not to use put-downs themselves in making a young person aware that he or she has used one.

Young people learn that not only do words hurt, but they can escalate conflict. Words that blame and judge are referred to as "You-messages." We point out that they attack and cause the receiver to be defensive and that they are often responded to with equally painful expressions. We encourage adults and young people to carefully evaluate the language they use with one another. If we prepare our children at an early age to communicate effectively, they'll have more of a chance of reducing conflict in their lives. They'll also be able to model these ways of talking and listening for others.

Expressing Feelings

Another key theme of the peaceable classroom is helping young people to express their feelings and to know that it's healthy and desirable to do so. Dan Goleman reminds us that according to the research, people who know and manage their own feelings well and who can read and deal effectively with other people's feelings are at an advantage in any domain in life.[5] How we handle our emotions affects our intimate relationships and our professional interactions. Educators need to take note of these facts.

To begin with, teachers can help their students expand their understanding of the range of emotions. Often children lack the words to describe the feelings they are having. Teachers can help children build vocabulary to match their feelings, prompting them to translate "I'm feeling bad" into something more precise: "I'm feeling disappointed,' or "frustrated," or "concerned."

In our experience, children need to be taught constructive ways to deal with anger in particular. Young people need to know that anger is a normal, healthy feeling that they can respond to by suppressing and ignoring it, or by being aggressive, or by asserting the way they feel and channeling their anger into constructive action. They need to be helped to examine what makes them angry and to learn ways to handle that anger.

We teach young people that suppression—keeping in angry feelings that later boil and maybe erupt—is a *weak* way of dealing with anger. If anger goes unexpressed it may become internalized and result in physical or psychological illness. Adolescents especially, in seeking an escape from anger, may be prone to taking drugs and alcohol. Everyone deals with anger differently. Phoebe, a ten-year-old, once told us, "When I get angry, I just keep it inside and when somebody talks to me I just yell, like it makes me mad and then I just blame it on somebody else."

Without outlets to release anger positively, children often resort to physical responses. With a mean look on his face, seven-year-old Bobby, remembering a fight with his brother, said, "One time he pushed me off the bed and I landed on the pillow. I pushed him down and body-slammed him."

Aggression has become a commonplace way for people, young and old alike, to release their anger. Children who have witnessed or experienced violence often see the world as a mean one and protect themselves by responding in mean, aggressive ways themselves. In some ways, they see being mean as safer than being a victim. Young people who see the adults in their lives act aggressively towards each another, for instance, will respond aggressively themselves in conflict situations. Children whose parents are abusive to each other often harbor a lot of unresolved anger towards one or both parents. We recall five-year-old Jarrod, who was sent to the assistant principal's office one day for biting another student. Jarrod's reason was "He made me mad." Further discussion with Jarrod and his parents revealed that he had overheard his father beating up his mother the previous week.

An eight-year-old named Steven put it well: "People get so violent because something happens to them and they don't like it very much and they feel like they want to take it out on someone. Sometimes they do that but they don't realize that they're hurting someone. They just like to take it out on someone."

Through various activities, students in the peaceable classroom learn that when they respond to anger assertively and say what they feel in a way that other people can hear, they are acting *strongly*, because they have put themselves in a position where they can best change what it is that's angering them. One game we've used to help children practice being strong involves kids pretending to be "strong message machines." They line up facing one another with an aisle between them and imagine that they have switches on their chests. When they are "switched on" they give out a "strong message," practicing what they would say if someone calls them a mean name, takes something of theirs and won't return it, trips them and laughs when they fall.

We teach young people that what we do with our anger is what makes the difference between a violent situation and a nonviolent one, between a destructive use of anger and a constructive one. And we teach specific techniques for coping with anger. Jamie, in his kindergarten class, learns how to "drain" his angry feelings.[6] He tenses all his muscles and breathes in and out for five seconds and then, starting with his head, begins to relax downward. Once Jamie knows this technique, he can use it when something or someone angers him, imagining that the anger is draining out of him "through the tips of his toes"; once it has drained out he can leave the "puddle of anger" behind, then try to understand it.

"Ballooning" is another cooling off technique we teach small children; they fill their lungs with air and raise their arms as if they were balloons.[7] Another way to release anger is to have "grump and growl" sessions where kids can complain about all the things that are angering them, no questions asked.[8] Puppets can help small children act out feelings; even self-made paper puppets can help them talk about the way they feel at different times throughout the year.

Kids can also be taught effective ways to use their anger constructively. Learning how to deliver I-messages helps young people express these feelings in an assertive and positive way. Throughout the curriculum, at all age levels, children and young adults practice using I-messages, saying how they feel without putting the other person down. One of our kindergarten teachers had just finished teaching her students about I-messages; as she brought the lesson to a close, she wasn't really sure if they had gotten the concept or whether it was a little beyond kindergartners. A few minutes later, when the class was really noisy, she said, "I get upset when you take so long to settle down because I want to make sure to have time for our next project." No sooner had she completed her statement than Benjamin raised his hand and said, "Good work with that I-message, Mrs. T."

In many classrooms, "morning dialogues"—quiet times when young people write in their personal journals—provide another kind of chance to express their feelings. Sometimes they exchange with a friend and discuss happy or sad, angry or confused feelings. Topics for the morning dialogues are generated by teachers and students together, and each day begins with a new one: What are my feelings about homework? My best friend? . . .

A great method for having children express how they are feeling is the "feelings boxes" devised by Sandy, a kindergarten teacher from New Orleans. Sandy writes students' names on a tongue depressor or popsicle stick with brightly colored markers. Each day as children come into the room, they find their sticks and place them in the feelings box that describes how they feel that morning: "Happy," "Sad," "Angry," "Scared," "Other." Sometimes children will discuss these feelings in their morning circle time. Others might discuss them with their friends, or with the teacher. For some children it may be culturally inappropriate to express their feelings anywhere but at home or with a family member. Throughout the day children sometimes get up, find their stick, and place it in a different box; they are aware that feelings change. Children know that it is okay to express emotions in Sandy's classroom, and they know that someone will always listen.

As people who work with conflict resolution, we're honestly surprised by how easily even very young children can grasp these concepts. We simply have to provide them with the skills and the opportunities to express themselves.

The peaceable classroom is an environment where children feel safe and confident that they are appreciated for who they are: each person is unique, every student feels special, and everybody works together to assure that diversity is honored at all times. Various activities, like those described below, provide a vehicle for expressing and exploring feelings about being different from one another.

Small children team up with partners to explore their similarities and their differences. They ask each other many questions about themselves, including what their favorite games, foods, and hobbies are. They note the things that they have in common and the things that make them different from one another. They learn about how their families are different and ways they might be the same. They make banners that tell about their families, and shields that tell about themselves. They are asked to think about what life would be like if we were all the same. When their curriculum includes activities like these, young people begin to see that differences make life more interesting—to truly appreciate diversity.

In one exercise/game we use, pairs of kids are asked to select a potato from a pile in the center of the room. They spend some time "getting to know" their potato by looking at it closely and talking about it with their partners. After a brief time, they return their potatoes to the center pile. The challenge is that each team must then be able to select their own special potato from a circle of many apparently similar ones. In almost all cases, the children are able to find their own potatoes. A follow-up activity might be to have the children sit face to face and notice the similarities and differences they themselves have. Together with the class, they list these. When we take the time to notice differences, we are also able to know something or someone much better.

Older children and adolescents are introduced to the word "culture." They come to understand that different groups have values, beliefs, and customs that are an important part of their culture. Often parents of different backgrounds are invited to the class to talk about their lives and about the things they value. The more young people learn about each other's cultures, the more they will learn to respect their differences and release their prejudices. But it isn't enough to simply celebrate multicultural activities in isolation from the regular curriculum; traditions, customs, histories need to be honored continuously. And when a classroom is not reflective of a wide range of diversity, the teacher is even more obligated to find ways to expose students to differences, in order to dispel the myths about people who are different from themselves and to create a feeling that diversity is in fact desirable.

Teachers also need to be sensitive to those Anglo-European children who sometimes feel that they have no culture. Louise Derman-Sparks, noted educator and author in the field of diversity and social justice, reminds us that culture is a part of what we live each day—how we interact with our families, our foods, values, stories, spiritual beliefs, and language. Derman-Sparks notes, "White children come from ethnic groups with specific customs or mixtures of customs, just like the more 'visible' ethnic groups, even if some white families do not consciously carry out their ethnic culture."[9]

In the peaceable classroom, teachers explicitly address the harm caused by prejudice and discrimination, teaching young people how to intervene and interrupt prejudice toward themselves or toward others. In fact, the curriculum and class environment are designed to raise students' awareness of their own biases as well as their awareness of larger social injustices. Firm policies are established to let young people know that bias will not be tolerated. As mentioned earlier, cooperative learning groups in which children work together to complete a specific task, each party having an equally important role in the project, help to break down the divisive lines that can separate young people.

We help young people to identify and explore their own stereotypes and to see that these are based on misinformation. Teachers provide students with opportunities to ask questions about diversity, as well as with knowledge and factual information about physical differences and cultural or historical events and traditions.

I (Janet) still remember beginning this work with an eighth-grade class at Roosevelt Middle School that had been experiencing a lot of conflict related to issues of diversity. Anger and hurt were prevalent and many of these young people were frequent "visitors" to my office as a result of physical and verbal disputes.

I began the session by asking the thirty-five students to form a large circle with their desks. I explained that the purpose of my visit was to address these issues, and that I would be visiting for the next few weeks to conduct RCCP sessions with them. I began with an activity designed to help them get to know more about one another. I told the students that we were each going to state our full name and then tell the group something about it. I asked them to include whatever history they knew about their names, especially their ethnic backgrounds and personal connections to their names. I went first.

Then, while everyone else remained silent, one at a time, students' voices rang clearly: "My name is Manuel de la Luz. I was born in Sinaloa, Mexico. I got my name Manuel from my grandfather. My father wanted me named after his father who had died when he was very young. My last name, de la Luz, means 'of the light' in Spanish. I came to this country when I was five years old and didn't speak any English." "My name is Lillian Suzuki. My mother is white and my father is Japanese. My grandparents were born in Japan. I was born here. I don't speak Japanese, but I am trying to learn it." "I'm Raymond Wood. My mother is from the Philippines and my father is African-American. I was born in Louisiana and moved here when I was ten."

The brief personal accounts, rich with the essence of these young people, continued. At the close of the class, when I asked them how they felt about the lesson, I struggled to hold back the tears of joy as I heard them share their feelings. "I learned so much about people in this class today, even some of my close friends." "I feel different inside about so many of you now," one girl said to the class, "now that I know more about who you are. Why don't we take time to learn about each other?" "Maybe we'll be able to get along better now that we're beginning to know each other more," said another student.

Their statements revealed that we had begun to chisel away the barriers with one simple activity. I realized that I had embarked on a new journey with these young people. I knew that, in time, they would see not only their peers, but also the world, through very different eyes.

In our program, we encourage students to look at how prejudice and discrimination have an impact on their lives and those of the people around them. Small children start by thinking about gender stereotypes and how they influence their own play and behaviors. They then can think about other forms of prejudice. They play different roles in scenarios designed to show how people are excluded and how this feels to them. Students in upper elementary grades make "discrimination webs." They see that prejudice is the judgment, the negative thought, and that discrimination is the act. Older students look at how society creates social biases, how discrimination becomes institutionalized, how some groups have more privileges than others.

Once young people have a good understanding of the impact that biases have upon themselves and others, the peaceable classroom teaches them the skills of interrupting prejudice, ways they can intervene to stop biased behavior. Using puppets, young students role-play what they might do if they were to see teasing in the class or on the playground. Children brainstorm lists of qualities that a person would need to fight injustice. They ask for a quality that would help them prevent or resist prejudice and discrimination as their classmates hold out their hands and in unison offer them that quality as a gift. They practice ways in which they could stop people from talking in a discriminatory way. They think of the questions they would ask and how they would respond to others' comments. Then they actually practice this intervention in small groups.

Responsible Decision Making

We can begin to help kids learn how to make effective and responsible decisions about themselves and the world by providing opportunities for them to contribute to decision making at the classroom and school levels. Working together to make decisions helps build a strong sense of community. So, in the peaceable classroom, students feel that they have a say in making rules, deciding on certain activities, planning class trips, mediating disputes, and other aspects of school life.

Learning how to approach making decisions in the face of problems is an essential prerequisite to resolving conflicts, so in our program we begin with small children. They read or listen to stories and when the story reaches the point of conflict, the class analyzes ways to resolve it. When students have a conflict they normally bring to the teacher, the teacher might ask them to go to the peace corner to think it through; there the older students could write down several ways of handling the conflict. Small children use "problem puppets" to act out their conflicts. This allows them enough distance so that they don't feel threatened. William Kreidler says that he makes a big deal out of the problem puppets. "They live in a specially marked shoe box. The kids have names for the puppets and they have a big P across their chest."[10]

Decision making can seem overwhelming at times, so we teach young children certain steps to follow:

[1]   *Tell what the problem is.*
[2]   *Find as many different solutions as possible.*
[3]   *Decide which solutions are "good."*
[4]   *Choose one solution and act.*

With elementary-age children we brainstorm a list of actual conflicts or pose an invented problem such as whether or not they should go on a class field trip if during the last field trip several students wandered away. Children are taught to describe the problem, rather than accusing or taking sides with someone. They talk about different people's point of view. How did the teacher feel when the kids strayed away? The parents? The students? Then they brainstorm solutions and list them on chart paper. If all goes well, they come up with the best solution, one that everyone in the class feels good about.

William Kreidler suggests a great strategy he calls "blockbusting" for thinking of different solutions. He tells kids to:

[1]   *Picture the situation and what it would look like if it were solved.*

[2]   *Wait for a while, at least half an hour, before doing anything else.*

[3]   *Change perspective; think about how someone else might see this conflict if they were in it. How would a bird in a tree view it? How would a Martian view it?*

[4]   *Think silly about it. Come up with solutions that are far out or funny. Laughter often helps to change perspective.*[11]

Sometimes decisions have to be made instantly; there isn't a whole lot of time to think things through. So Kreidler also teaches kids how to make quick decisions. Either in role-play demonstrations or using a "hassle line" (a double line where kids face each other and role-play with the partner who faces them), he times them, giving them about thirty to sixty seconds to come up with a solution to a given situation. They repeat this practice and eventually they're making better decisions in shorter amounts of time.

With older students, we expand upon this process in more sophisticated ways. In our middle school curriculum, students explore the negative and positive consequences of different ways of handling conflict: aggression, collaboration, compromise, giving in, avoiding, delaying, appealing to authority.[12] They improvise short skits to identify and evaluate ways of handling a conflict. Sometimes teachers videotape the students so they can play back the skit and "reframe" the situation. Older students, like younger ones, learn about win-win solutions—how to think through conflict situations so that both parties get their needs met and feel good about the solution.

High school students can learn very sophisticated concepts about how to work in groups so that conversation is open, thoughtful, and respectful. Carol Leiber, an experienced conflict resolution trainer, has produced an excellent high school curriculum in conflict resolution—one which we have drawn upon—called *Making Choices about Conflict.*[13] In one activity suggested by this curriculum, students brainstorm about the kinds of decisions they make daily and they think about decisions made for them by their families, the school, the government. Then they talk about the *constraints* and *limitations* that accompany every decision. For example, in thinking about where they might go for college, constraints might be money, distance from home, grade-point average or a relationship with a boyfriend or girlfriend; in deciding what to do this weekend, the opinion of a best friend or groups of friends might matter, a parent might put some limitations or constraints on the weekend plans, transportation might need to be considered, and so on. With a partner, the students discuss recent decisions they themselves have made or are about to make.

They also consider and evaluate how decisions are made when groups of people are involved. They learn to distinguish four decision-making styles: autocratic—I decide or you decide; participatory—getting input from others; democratic—voting on it; consensus—everybody agrees. They are encouraged to visit and observe groups making decisions—families, clubs or other extracurricular organizations, school board meetings, civil court, traffic court, and so on—and to share their experiences with their classmates.

When discussing decisions, students are asked to address questions like the following:

> Does the decision respect the rights and needs of people affected by the decision?

> Are people who are supposed to implement the decision involved in making it?

> Do you have what you need (people and resources) to make the decision work?

> Does it seem fair to everyone involved?

> Is it moral? Legal? Smart?

"Conflict toolboxes" include cards which say: *share, take turns, say "I'm sorry," listen, paraphrase, reflect, ignore it and walk away, ask questions, ask for help, make a request, compromise, check it out, offer help, say how you feel and what you need, talk it out and problem-solve, take responsibility and fix it, agree to disagree.* In reviewing conflict situations, students can go into their "tool boxes" for alternatives before they decide what words or actions would work best in a given situation.

One of the best means of involving young people in decision-making processes is through regularly scheduled class meetings in which young people problem-solve about class issues. In his book *The Quality School Teacher*, William Glasser describes the class meeting as an essential vehicle to help young people recognize their needs and why they act the way they do.[14]

In class meetings kids have a chance to use all the skills they have previously learned to say what they feel in non-attacking ways, to listen actively, and to be open to different points of view. Teachers and students together establish certain ground rules for the group, including not using put-downs and listening to each other without interrupting. Regular scheduling for meetings is important because students look forward to them. When I was teaching fifth grade I often heard young people say to one another, "Save it for our class meeting." At the kids' suggestion we established a "problem-solving box" in which they placed concerns they would like to discuss. When meeting time came around, we would see how many problems there were, prioritize them, and accomplish all that we could. If we felt more time was needed we would sometimes schedule another session. Many times children resolved issues amongst themselves modeled upon what we had done in our meetings. They would then inform me that they had taken care of the problem and it didn't need to come back to the group.

Central to this practice is that young people learn that they can resolve problems themselves. The teacher facilitates the meeting so that ideas come from the students; it is not the role of the teacher to solve any of the problems that are brought to the group.

Once, when Linda was conducting a class meeting in her fifth-grade class, her students brought up the fact that they had gotten in trouble for misbehaving with one of their resource teachers earlier in the week. They had just returned from an assembly, missing their accustomed break, and the material the teacher was covering had already been done once before. The kids were upset with their own behavior, but they wanted the resource teacher to know how they felt and why they had acted that way.

At first they wanted Linda to tell the teacher how they felt. Then they decided that they should tell her themselves, but they didn't know how. Linda, acting as facilitator, asked, "If you were going to tell her, what would you say? Let's imagine we send a person to talk to her, and let's have one person play that part and another play the part of Ms. X." The students then role-played a possible scenario, in which one brave student told "Ms. X" how the class felt. "We've been talking about the problem that we have in your class, and we decided that we don't behave because . . . well, we're bored. We've already learned the stuff you're teaching us." The child playing the part of the resource teacher responded, "Well, what do you think would be more interesting?" At this point, the students were able to talk about what they thought would work better (a five-minute break was high on the list of needs).

While the students never actually confronted the teacher themselves, they agreed to ask her to listen to a tape of the session (Linda always taped her class meetings in case they needed to refer to information shared at another time). When the students went to her class that week, she told them she had listened to the tape, would be willing to give them their five-minute break, and wanted to discuss with them other units of study.

There are many ways to run class meetings and many types of class meetings that offer opportunities to discuss problems ranging from messy classrooms to kids' reactions to course content to interpersonal conflicts. A well-run class meeting is an effective tool for creating responsible decision making and instilling a sense of ownership among young people for what goes on in their schools.

Conflict Resolution

The final theme, conflict resolution, is a central goal and element of the vision that stands behind the peaceable classroom. As early as kindergarten children can learn about I-messages, win-win solutions, and active listening, and to use their words instead of responding in a mean, physical way when problems arise. By third grade, we introduce students to the concept of win-win negotiation and mediation.

In Chapter 3, we will discuss the particular conflict resolution skills that we teach children and adults in our program—expanding on the theory and practice of this essential component of educating the heart and waging peace in our schools.

In Summary

The peaceable classroom is a caring community responsive to the needs of young people. It teaches young people skills in cooperation, communication, expression of feelings, bias awareness, and decision making and conflict resolution, with the result—one among many that we'll focus on throughout this book—that young people become empowered to manage their own emotions and handle their own conflicts as they arise. In this kind of classroom environment young people achieve their very best, supported by each other and the adults who teach them. The teacher of the peaceable classroom models the same beliefs and values that they teach young people throughout their day. The interaction between student and teacher and between student and student reflects genuine care and respect.

At a time in education when many feel that they can't possibly give even one little bit more or teach one more "new" thing, teachers are embracing this program. Perhaps Mildred, one of our New Orleans teachers, said it best:

This has always been a rough area, but now it's a different kind of roughness. The children will say "I'll kill you" to children, and I never heard that before. It's all this concentration on guns and killings. . . . It's harder to deal with kids in the classroom. Much harder. And I've got older kids in my room. Some of these children now thirteen and fourteen years old are going on to become drug dealers. RCCP is important to me because they [the kids] don't know how to really deal with their conflicts. Even to the point of someone just looking at them. Even if you look and don't say anything, they want to fight. It's a constant battle. I have to teach conflict resolution every day.

We all have to become involved in teaching the children that there is another way.

< II >

THE
CORE
CURRICULUM

HOW TO WAGE PEACE:
THE SKILLS OF
CONFLICT RESOLUTION

WE WANT TO MOVE now to the real core of what we do—the concepts and skills of conflict resolution and diversity education. We will be shifting gears in the next two chapters to talk about the content of what we teach rather than the mechanics of how we teach it.

Not only are children today living in an increasingly violent society, they are also growing up in more diverse communities. Therefore, we at RCCP believe, we have a responsibility to teach children how to manage conflict nonviolently and to understand and value the pluralistic society they are living in. The following two chapters are meant as a mini-course in the ideas that are at the heart of our work.

Training Ourselves First

A woman came to Gandhi, asking him to give her ideas of ways to get her little boy to stop eating sugar because it was doing him harm. Gandhi gave a cryptic reply, "Please come back next week." The woman left puzzled but returned a week later, dutifully following Gandhi's instructions.

"Please don't eat sugar," Gandhi told the young fellow when he saw him, "It's not good for you." Then he joked with the boy a while, gave him a hug and sent him on his way. But the mother, unable to contain her curiosity,

lingered behind to ask, "Why didn't you say this last week when we came? Why did you make us come back?"

Gandhi smiled. "Last week," he said, "I too was eating sugar."

Since the field of conflict resolution is a recent innovation in education, most adults we come in contact with need to be immersed in the concepts and skills of conflict resolution before they can even think about teaching this body of knowledge in the classroom.

Moreover, we recognize that this work differs from teaching a new math or social studies curriculum. With this work, the medium—who we are and who we become—is the message. And so our work with adults is often a fine balance between introspection and skill building. St. Francis of Assisi put it this way: "While you are proclaiming peace with your lips, be careful to have it even more fully in your heart."

Conflict resolution requires inner work of subtlety and depth, a journey within. Like Gandhi in the story, we must struggle, change, and work on ourselves before we can offer authentic help to others. We present the following material on conflict resolution in that spirit.

Defining Conflict

In many of our RCCP classrooms, we do an activity called a conflict web. We write the word "conflict" on the board and draw a circle around it. We then ask students what comes to mind when they hear the word, and create a web by connecting their responses to the circled word. Even when we do this activity with adults, chances are high that most of the other words mentioned have negative connotations. One third-grade boy said, "Conflict is anything bad that could happen to you." Another student came up with the word "evil."

One of the first myths to dispel is that conflict is always bad. Conflict is actually a natural, normal part of life. The day we die we'll still have a list of conflicts yet to be resolved. Conflict is not bad in and of itself, yet for many of us, especially young people, it has come to equal violence. This is an equation we have to break.

Conflict is part of living and growing. Like a stone-tumbler tumbling a raw stone, conflict has the potential of polishing us or breaking us. There is a lot of emotion connected to conflictual situations. Past experience has taught many of us that they can escalate, hurting us physically and emotionally; feelings sometimes come up that remind us of hurtful moments in our lives and in the lives of those we love. And so conflict can sometimes break us. But it can also be an opportunity for growth and change. It can polish us, make us better than we were before. Consider the Chinese way of writing the word "crisis": two characters make up the ideograph—one means danger and the other means opportunity. Conflict is a fact of life, sometimes destructive and bad, at other times constructive and good.

Too often we think that we have no control over the conflict in our lives, we feel helpless. But when we have the skills to assert ourselves in nonviolent ways, we begin to feel empowered, able to draw upon our past experiences to approach the situation differently. If we have been trained in conflict resolution skills, we can open up communication and confront conflict nonviolently. Resolving conflict creatively can be taught—it relies on a set of practical tools. Alberto, a senior at Schomburg Satellite Academy in the South Bronx, has incorporated these skills into his everyday life:

No one goes out in the morning looking for a fight, but things happen in split seconds. Conflict resolution teaches you how to use your mind more. How to step back from the situation and quickly analyze it before things get nasty. Your posture and eye contact should symbolize strength—that you can handle the situation. And that you want to handle it peacefully.

In schools where conflicts are resolved peaceably by adults and student mediators, young people grow up seeing this way as the norm. The culture of the school reflects this active process; fights diminish, arguments become discussions, and kids feel emotionally and physically safe.

Exploring our own histories allows us to understand why it is that we respond to conflict in the way that we do. In our work, adults and young people reflect upon the messages they received from the people who raised them:

"If he hits you, hit him back."
"If you have nothing good to say, then don't say anything at all."
"I'm your mother, that's why."

Sometimes thinking about early days brings back laughter, sometimes sorrow and tears. Either way, we realize that these early messages are now echoed in our communications with colleagues, students, and loved ones.

Recently, Cassandra, a middle school teacher in New Jersey, was asked by her administrator to take on the organization of the school's drug awareness week. Because she didn't want to disappoint her principal, she accepted the responsibility even though she was overloaded with other projects. She was angry with herself for taking on the extra work, but instead of talking with her principal and expressing how she felt, she begrudgingly completed the project. She also got sick in the process. When someone in authority tells her to do something, Cassandra tends to respond as she did when she was told to do something as a child: grin and bear it.

Conflict styles are set when we are very young. We either live out those early messages or rebel against them. Training in conflict resolution equips us with the tools to start to change old patterns. As an ancient Chinese proverb tells us, "if we do not change direction, we are likely to end up where we are headed."

Roger Fisher and William Ury, authors of the bestseller *Getting to Yes*, were among the first to identify and analyze conflict styles. They outlined three distinct styles of negotiation: soft, hard, and principled.[1] Although most people employ a combination of all three, some of us "get stuck" in one style or another, using that style all the time, even when it's not appropriate.

For instance, a person who is locked into the "soft" negotiation style is usually intent on concentrating more on the quality of the relationship than on the problem; a soft negotiator puts a high stake on how others perceive his or her needs and is willing to let go of those needs for the sake of a relationship. This, of course, is not without cost. As Langston Hughes asks in the well-known poem, "What happens to a dream deferred? Does it dry up like a raisin in the sun? . . . Or does it explode?" When people are locked into this style, their unmet needs build up and they eventually lash out at themselves or at someone else. They may also somatize their emotions and impair their health. Our dear friend and colleague Lindamichellebaron gets right to the point in the following poem:

Even weeds have needs, you know,
Don't make me creep through cracks,
or race for space to grow.

Even weeds have needs, although,
I've been known to survive on dried up rain
and left over sun.

Even weeds have needs, you know,
And this weed needs a great big garden,
with a gardener who's not afraid
to let me grow.[2]

At the other end of the spectrum is the "hard" negotiator, who aims to win no matter what the stakes. Hard negotiators often gravitate to career choices that affirm them in playing out such a style. A hard negotiator approaches conflict as a contest, one in which he or she wins and the other person loses; self-esteem is connected to seeing conflict as a contest to be won at any cost. Hard negotiators are often so intent on proving their point by whatever means necessary that their relationships with other people suffer. One student from Phoenix Academy in New York City described his style this way: "I was the type that would yell, get overly emotional, and use physical violence in order to get my point across." Hard negotiators may win, but often they have no one to celebrate with them at the finish line.

Soft and hard negotiation styles are not solely the product of individual personality. Cultural and gender differences also influence negotiation techniques. In a tightly knit culture, for instance, the focus is usually on collective needs first, individual needs second—similar to a soft negotiation style. Loosely woven societies tend to focus on individual needs and sanction other styles, mainly hard negotiation.

The third approach—principled negotiation—is distinctly different, and it is upon this approach that conflict resolution as a discipline is based. In principled negotiation we "separate the people from the problem": we are hard on the problem but respectful of the people in the process. When he was in jail in South Africa, Gandhi "separated the person from the problem" by making sandals for the man responsible for imprisoning him,[3] and during the struggle for India's independence, he sent Princess Elizabeth (later Queen of England) a beautiful teacloth that he himself had woven.

The principled negotiator doesn't have a bottom line. Participants become problem-solvers. The goal is to reach a wise outcome efficiently and amicably. Principled negotiation supports both getting one's needs met and treating the other person with respect. This approach offers a strong possibility of a win-win solution.

The model used by the Alternatives to Violence Project (see figure 1) offers an outline of possible responses to conflict and another way at looking at response styles.[4]

As shown, we can attempt to avoid conflict, diffuse it, or confront it. When we confront conflict, we have a choice of doing it violently or nonviolently. At times, we are unable to see creative alternatives because we are

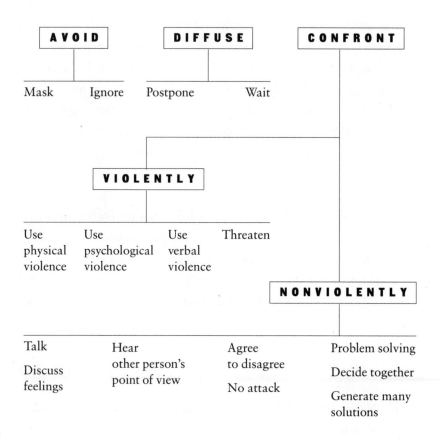

Figure 1

locked into a particular style. The secret is to free ourselves enough to take charge of our responses.

For instance, avoidance may be an appropriate response to certain conflict situations. Imagine that while walking down a dark, empty city street someone approaches you with apparently harmful intentions; you might decide to enter the next building in order to avoid your pursuer. However, soft negotiators tend to overuse avoidance. In fact, soft negotiators don't choose avoidance, avoidance chooses them. One of our RCCP teachers decided to get a transfer to another school because she was upset with the way her colleagues were treating her, but when asked several weeks later how her new placement was working out, she described a situation much like the previous one. Because soft negotiators try to avoid conflict, they often fail to develop concrete skills to handle problems effectively. Instead they repeat old patterns.

Hard negotiators tend to approach conflict by threatening, intimidating, and even by using physical abuse at times. Hard negotiators put up lots of roadblocks in their communication with others. This causes emotional distance and decreases the ability to actually solve problems. Psychologist Thomas Gordon identifies these roadblocks to communication as "the Dirty Dozen":

[1]   Criticizing: "Don't blame anyone else for this. You got yourself into this mess."

[2]   Name-calling: "What an idiot!" "Just like a woman." "You men are all alike, totally insensitive."

[3]   Diagnosing: "I know exactly why you're doing this—to make me angry."

[4]   Praising evaluatively: "You're such a good boy. I know you'll do your homework."

[5]   Ordering: "Clean up your room right now." "Why? Because I said so."

[6] *Threatening: "Stop arguing with your brother or I'll cut off both your allowances."*

[7] *Moralizing: "You shouldn't leave your husband—think what will happen to the children."*

[8] *Excessive/Inappropriate Questioning: "Are you sure that you did it?"*

[9] *Advising: "If I were you, I'd never talk to her again."*

[10] *Diverting: "You think that's bad? Let me tell you what happened to me."*

[11] *Logical Argument: "Let's face it. If you'd been on time we wouldn't be eating cold food."*

[12] *Reassuring: "Don't worry, tomorrow you'll be laughing about this whole mess."[5]*

These are all examples of interpersonal responses that tend to close down communication. Whether they occur in one interpersonal act or in more systemic forms, we know that each such response breeds another like it.

William Kreidler uses the image of an escalator to describe every behavior in a conflict situation as either stepping up or stepping down.[6] Every step up the "conflict escalator" has feelings that accompany it. As the conflict intensifies, so do the feelings. And no one gets on the escalator empty-handed. We always have the baggage we bring to the conflict. This baggage can be filled with lots of things. First, there's our past experience with the people and issues involved. Then, there are all the feelings about the specific conflict itself, as well as the "mood of the day" and issues of diversity and cultural perspective. All of these may move us either up or down the conflict escalator and affect the outcome.

The higher we go on the escalator, the closer we come to violence, and the harder it is to come down. And yet it is possible to descend the escalator at any time. This is what the skills and awarenesses of nonviolent confrontation are about. In fact, in any situation, even a potentially violent one, if our next act can be one which is positive and assertive, then we have the possibility of descending the conflict escalator.

One strategy William Kreidler offers to help us approach a conflict in this way is called CAPS, an acronym based on the following steps:

> Cool Off: Take some deep breaths, acknowledge your feelngs.

> Agree to Work It Out: Show a willingness to solve the problem by not escalating it further and letting the other disputant know you are ready to discuss the issues involved.

> Point of View on the Problem: Using "I" statements, give your points of view.

> Solve the problem: Brainstorm solutions, decide how to implement a win-win solution.[7]

Several years ago, before I (Linda) could have verbalized them easily, it seems that I had somehow already internalized these steps. Faced with a life-and-death situation, I intuitively did the things we teach.

It was about 6:00 P.M. on a warm May evening. I was walking along 99th Street between 1st and 2nd avenues in New York City's East Harlem. I had walked these familiar blocks many times during my years as a teacher and an administrator at Community School District 4. The street was desolate, lined with the remnants of deserted buildings. The thought did occur to me that it might not be safe to be walking this way right now, but my intuition didn't kick in soon enough. Before I knew it I was surrounded by three young men, about thirteen or fourteen years old. One of the boys reached into his pocket and took out a knife with a shiny four-inch blade. As all three pressed closer to me, the young man with the knife said, "Give me your purse. Now."

Inwardly panicked, I took some deep breaths and found myself saying, "I'm feeling a little uncomfortable. You know, guys, you're a little into my space. I'm wondering if you could step back a little bit?" I waited cautiously. I glanced down and was shocked to see three sets of sneakers take three steps back. "Thank you," I said. "Now I want to hear what you just said to me, but to tell you the truth I'm a little nervous about that knife. I'm wondering if you could put it away?"

I waited for what felt like an eternity and then watched the knife slip into a pocket. The boys and I were working it out.

I quickly reached into my purse and took out a twenty-dollar bill, realizing that this was no time to ignore such a request. I was glad I had it. But how to stay neutral—not take sides?—was what went racing through my mind. I caught the eye of the young man with the knife in his pocket and asked, "Who should I give it to?" "Me" was his response. I looked over at the other two guys and asked if they were in agreement. One of them said, "We could cash it at the corner at the bodega." My God, I thought, we're actually problem-solving together.

"Great," I said, as I handed the first boy my twenty. I focused on all three and said, "Now here's what's going to happen. I'm going to stay right here while you walk away." They looked quite puzzled. The script had changed. Without a word, they started to slowly walk away, glancing back at me as I managed to keep my two feet firmly planted, although my knees began to quiver.

Then I saw the power of nonviolence in action. They began to run away from me. My response had so disarmed them that *they* felt in danger. This moment is etched in my memory. I call upon it whenever I need to remember the power we possess when we use the skills of nonviolence. Even in a potentially dangerous situation, the opportunity to go down the conflict escalator always exists.

I remember another example of this power in action, one with even wider implications. There was a time a few years ago in New York City when wearing a sheepskin coat could be deadly. There were several incidents of kids being held up by other kids and getting shot when they refused to give up their coats. Around this time, Raymond, a mediator in a local high school, got off the subway at a stop in East Harlem and found himself surrounded by three guys who demanded he give up his jacket. Instead of resisting, Raymond looked at the three boys and said, "This is incredible—I was just getting ready to do that." As he unzipped his coat, he asked his assailants who he should give it to. One of the young men took the coat and all three began to run.

If it had ended there, it would have been only a partial vindication of conflict resolution, since although Raymond had used his skills to de-escalate a potentially violent situation, he'd still lost his coat. But when Raymond got back to his school, a teacher had the insight to expand the lesson in emotional learning; he called a group of kids together so that Raymond could share his story and express his rage. Within moments, one of the other kids asked, "How much was that coat?" Raymond responded, "It was $119." "Well," said another student, "there are ninety-two seniors in this school—that's a little over a dollar each." In about three days' time they collected enough money to replace the coat. Raymond learned an important lesson. He was rewarded by his peers for using his conflict resolution skills in a potentially deadly situation to control anger and express it in a more appropriate place.

We liken these skills in nonviolent conflict resolution to training in cardiopulmonary resuscitation: when we know CPR, there are very few times when we'd hesitate to help in time of need. I have a childhood memory of my Uncle Angelo, who saved someone's life one day with his CPR training. One minute he was on his way to his niece's wedding, dressed up in fine clothes; the next minute he was down on his knees on the grimy city pavement, working feverishly to save a stranger's life. When we have skills in nonviolent conflict resolution, we too are always on duty. Sometimes calling upon these skills can mean the difference between living and dying. When I need another level of conviction in the power of creative nonviolence, I think of another true story.

Sara, an eighty-three-year-old woman who lived alone in a log cabin in rural Virginia, turned on her radio one day and was frightened to hear that three inmates had just escaped from the maximum security prison less than a mile from her home. Each of the convicts was described in utmost detail, in hopes of alerting the community. Just as the announcer had finished the description of the third convict, the doorbell rang. Sara opened the door and there stood the three inmates. Her first words to them were, "You guys look like you need breakfast and I can make a good one." Moments later they were eating her grits, bacon, and eggs as she chatted with them, never sure of what their next move would be. After they had finished eating, they unexpectedly hugged her, thanked her, and quietly left. Several hours later they were apprehended. To this day they probably wonder what power took hold of them that would cause them to stop and have breakfast in the middle of an escape.

From India's struggle for independence to our own civil rights movement of the 1960s to Sara's breakfast table, our society yearns for this power to come forth again. Gandhi's belief was that humankind can get beyond violence only through creative nonviolence: "Hatred can be overcome only by love. Counter-hatred only increases the surface as well as the depth of hatred." Holocaust survivor Viktor Frankl put it this way: "Everything can be taken from us but one thing, which is the last of the human freedoms—to choose one's attitude in any given set of circumstances, to choose one's own way."

Win-Win Negotiation

There are many, more ordinary, conflict situations where win-win solutions—those that meet the underlying interests and needs of all parties involved—can be achieved. Too often we assume that one side must win and the other must lose, or that both must give up something and thus neither will get what they need or want.

This happens because conflict is seen as a contest. In a contest, one person wins and the other person loses. Some conflicts do end that way—in what is called a win-lose resolution. And of course it's possible that neither person will get what he or she wants, in which case the result is called a lose-lose resolution. But it is also possible that both parties can get what they want or need in the situation, resulting in a win-win resolution to the conflict. This is the type of resolution we emphasize in our work.

A parable frequently told to illustrate this approach involves two sisters who both want the only orange in the kitchen. "I need the orange," says one. "You can't have it," argues the other. "I saw it first."

If one sister gets the orange and the other doesn't, we have a win-lose resolution. In a lose-lose outcome, during a fight over the orange both sisters get hurt. (An apparent compromise—dividing the orange in half—also turns out to be a lose-lose situation in this case because neither of the two parties gets enough of what she needs.)

In our story, however, the sisters stop arguing long enough to explore the situation, and they find they can work out a win-win solution: both can get what they need from a single orange, since (as they discover) one sister wants to eat the orange, while the other needs the peel to flavor the icing on a cake.[8]

In a conflict situation it's important to make the distinction between needs and positions. A position is a statement of what a person wants. It represents just one way in which the person's needs can be met. Needs or interests are short-term, but frequently represent concerns underlying a position. When we are able to separate positions and demands from actual needs, then we can achieve win-win solutions. In the case of the orange, the sisters were able to separate the demand "I've got to have the orange" from their real needs, allowing both of them to get what they needed.

The win-win approach to negotiation helps identify and separate needs and positions, making the distinction between what we say we want and our reasons for wanting it.

It's important to note that good communication is essential in moving from positions to considering underlying interests; it provides room for brainstorming possible solutions and eliminating those that are unacceptable to either party. And our values come into play here as well. Deeply held beliefs—religious, ideological, or cultural—must also be understood and taken into account. These values are so firmly rooted that they seldom change in a negotiation.

In win-win negotiation, we choose the solution that will meet the interests of everyone. It's not necessarily our first choice, but it's one we can all live with. It makes us feel like all parties are winners.

In win-win negotiation, a cooperative climate is created, and this allows for a reframing of the situation: both parties ask the question, What kind of agreement would allow both of us to get important needs met? Furthermore, in our program we teach that a win-win negotiation always ends with the parties deciding on how the solution they have chosen will be carried out—what first steps need to be taken, who will do what, and when they will do it.

In summary, the win-win negotiation process as we teach it in schools involves the following steps:

[1]   *Identify positions and interests. When you negotiate, "positions" are what you say you want, "interests" are the reasons you want it.*

[2]   *Present and listen. Say what your positions and interests are. Listen to what the person you're negotiating with says about his or her positions and interests. Try not to call people names. Try to be specific. Use active listening to move from positions to interests.*

[3]   *Brainstorm possible solutions. Think of all the possible ways to solve the problem. Try to think of many. Write them down. Don't say if the ideas are good or bad (that will happen next).*

[4]   *Eliminate solutions that are unacceptable. Read over all the ideas. Draw a line through any idea that either of you doesn't like.*

[5]   *Choose a solution that will meet the interests of everybody involved. Read the ideas that are left on your list. Choose the idea or ideas that will meet everyone's interests. You want to help everyone feel like a winner.*

[6] *Make a plan to take action. Once you choose a solution, decide how you will make sure it happens. Decide what the first steps will be. Decide who will do what and when they will do it.*[9]

In our experience, people generally feel they've gained from going through these steps; however, many cultural and gender differences come into play as we learn to negotiate well. For example, some of us tend to minimize—even withhold—negative feedback, while others are equally able to give and receive both negative and positive feedback. Some of us can talk about conflict anywhere, others need a quiet, casual, private space. For some of us, timing is very important; for others, sooner is better. Some of us require a lot of thinking before we speak, while others think out loud and express gut feelings early on in a conversation. This means that although two parties might be totally committed to a negotiation, many other factors need also to be taken into consideration. As we try for win-win solutions, we can keep in mind some words of wisdom from Henry David Thoreau: "Thaw with her gentle persuasion is more powerful than Thor with his hammer. The one melts, the other breaks."

While the win-win approach can be helpful in many situations, resolution of a conflict is not always possible. Sometimes the best strategy in a conflict-laden situation may be one that simply prevents the outbreak of physical violence or the rupture of a relationship. In any case, the primary goal is to be creative and resourceful in the face of conflict.

Active Listening

The practice of creative response to conflict entails more than a collection of isolated skills, but acquiring specific skills helps us develop a systematic way of thinking about how to handle conflict.

Communication is an essential part of conflict resolution. In fact, the process is described in shorthand terms as "talking things through." You cannot resolve a problem you don't understand, and you can't understand the problem until you have complete, accurate information. People involved in a conflict situation need to be able to talk about concerns and feelings, to speak about what they would like to change, and to discuss what they feel they need. Clear communication is a necessary tool for getting to the bottom of conflicts and finding satisfactory solutions; unclear communication may itself be the cause of conflict.

We can think about the process in terms of senders and receivers. Senders observe something using their senses of sight, hearing, touch, smell, and taste. They process this information by comparing and contrasting it with previous experiences and information, and evaluating it according to their beliefs and needs; they can then encode a message and transmit it through speech and body language. Receivers take in messages and decode them, sorting out and interpreting them according to their own experiences, beliefs, and needs. Thus, messages received also pass through perceptual filters. A Haitian proverb says it this way: "We see from where we stand."

In order to improve communication it's helpful to have receiving as well as sending skills at our disposal. In fact, the technique of *active listening*, also known as empathic listening, is one of the most important skills needed to de-escalate conflict. (Yet in a typical conflict situation, listening is often the last thing we do.)

Active listening is really listening with the heart. In and of itself it is a gift—a priceless gift that can be given freely to help heal and reconcile differences. It helps us defuse anger and hostility and gain information.

Active listening requires us to put our lives—our thoughts, feelings, values—on hold. Not an easy feat when we all have unprocessed feelings, unfinished projects, unresolved concerns, and deeply held values that must be set aside in order to redirect our attention to the other person. Active listening requires that we clear a mental and emotional space and allow the speaker to fill that space. At this point the listener is able to go beyond accepting differences to offer the speaker full freedom to be who he or she is.

The active listener is able to walk a mile in the speaker's shoes. In that walking, we offer the gift of empathy as we make ourselves available and present. To do that—to walk in someone else's shoes—we've got to be barefoot first. We don't want to turn our desire to listen into speaking ourselves, interrupting the speaker to tell our own stories; we don't want to advise or judge or go on mental side-trips to plan what we're going to say next. To really listen with one's heart, mind, and soul is to be able to fully engage ourselves not in what *we* are thinking or feeling but rather in what it is like for the *other* person.

For Faydra, a teacher in New Orleans, listening has gained a new dimension: "I try to be more sensitive with my kids. When I really stop and listen, I see why some of them hurt. And even when I'm frustrated, I step back and look at it from a different perspective. This has helped me to give them the benefit of the doubt. . . . And I see behavior changing in them and in me."

Active listening is useful in a variety of situations. Active listening can help two parties get a sense of how each views a situation as well as the feelings surrounding it. Active listening can shed light on a conflict by clarifying issues and concerns. It is also helpful in regulating emotion, especially when strong feelings are being expressed.

There are several active listening techniques we can use to help the other person to talk. Added to our repertoire, they provide us with a range and depth in our ability to actively listen. Some of these techniques are

> paraphrasing,

> clarifying,

> reflection,

> encouragement,

> summary, and

> validation.

Most of us are familiar with the simplest form of active listening: repeating back the information expressed, or *paraphrasing*. This practice may seem artificial at times, especially when we don't have other techniques at hand. I recall an incident an RCCP teacher related to us after we had first introduced her to the idea of active listening. When her husband picked her up after the initial training session, she proceeded to repeat back word for word everything he was saying. After a while, in exasperation, the husband declared, "Aren't you listening? That's what I just said!" Clearly, the teacher needed to expand her "tool chest" of techniques.

Another way to actively listen is *clarification*. Clarification, a way of acquiring information, generally presents itself in the form of questions:

> What did you mean when you said that?

> When did this begin?

> How long have you been feeling this?

Clarification can be particularly helpful in getting details and building a more complete version of the issue presented. Many years ago, when I was teaching fifth gade, clarification once helped me get through a teacher's nightmare—a child's disclosure of sexual abuse.

Ten-year-old Tanya came to me one day at the end of class and said that she wanted to talk to me about something personal. She sat down next to me, stared out the window, and began to tell me that her uncle had made her feel very uncomfortable the previous night. I didn't know what to do with my own anger at what this vulnerable young person was revealing to me, so I began asking clarifying questions, which helped both Tanya and me get through the difficult moment: When did it happen? How long has this been going on? Who was in the house? What did he do? I realized that active listening was not only helping me to be there for Tanya, it was also allowing me to think on my feet about what I should say and do next. I was glad that asking these difficult questions helped Tanya relate her story. In hearing her answers, I was able to be more fully present as well.

I feel obliged, however, to offer a cautionary note about using clarification. Adults especially love using this technique in talking to young people, but questioning can feel too confrontational when answers are expected instantaneously. The key to using clarification is to accompany it with other active listening techniques.

There are times when one's culture and forms of expression dictate much subtler forms of active listening. Our Lakota friend David Whitehorse, professor at California State University at San Marcos, tells us that, traditionally, one should never expect an immediate answer from a Lakota person: "When a Lakota is asked a question, the reflective nature of the native thought process is to seek wisdom before responding. This may require asking guidance from the powers associated with the four directions, from above, and from below. The Lakota pattern (and other similar native patterns) is to think and feel one's way through the question and its broader sociocultural implications. Only when one senses and understands these relationships does one provide an answer." This, David Whitehorse adds, "is in contrast with the Euro-American trial-and-error method, where the answer is often provided [by] 'raw data' without understanding the larger context for the question and perhaps the question itself."

Reflection is similar to paraphrasing, but in this active listening technique we focus on the underlying feelings the speaker is experiencing. With reflection, we try to echo back the feelings behind the statements. We might simply venture, "You seem pretty upset about this," for instance, when the speaker clearly wants to identify his or her feelings and needs help to move from a statement of fact to the emotions beneath it. When we "reflect" carefully, the listener often expresses a sigh of relief that we have listened beyond the words to hear what was coming from the heart. It's helpful to ask if you are accurately reflecting the feeling: "You seem very sad about it. Is that true?"

It is best to use reflection sparingly, however. The difficulty with its overuse with young people especially is that adults tend to identify feelings *for* children, without giving them a chance to do it for themselves. It is equally important to help young people name their feelings and develop their own repertoire of feeling words. We all need a degree of trust and rapport before we are ready to allow our feelings to be identified. We've all been in the situation where we say to someone, "You seem really angry," and he or she unequivocally denies it; the speaker wasn't ready for the listener's evaluation of his or her feelings.

Active listeners can also listen by encouraging and validating. In *encouraging*, we simply say any phrase that lets the person know we are ready and willing to listen: "Go on, tell me more." A simple but effective phrase for delving into a deeper level of a problem is "Anything else?" In a conflict situation, our first way of describing the issue usually exposes its surface; asking "Anything else?" can reveal what is really happening underneath.

Validation is a form of active listening that proves effective in a variety of situations. With this technique, we let the person know that we appreciate and respect their sharing. We acknowledge the value of talking and show our appreciation for being part of the sharing as well. For those whose cultures favor minimizing or even withholding difficult feelings, validation is essential, especially when sharing a painful memory or an angry feeling. We can acknowledge their effort by saying, "I know this is difficult for you and I'm glad we're talking about it." Validation is helpful in situations where disclosure is not customary for the speaker, but the person nevertheless has a desire to break through his or her own cultural or individual reticence. In our diversity work, when we ask people to share stories about times they have witnessed or experienced prejudice, we often use validation to support them through the painful moment and help them continue.

I remember one of those moments, when I was conducting a training in the Iñupiat village of Barrow, Alaska. The participant was talking about his experience of prejudice in front of the group. Visibly overwhelmed with grief, Bill made frequent pauses until he finally dropped the microphone and became silent. It was clear to me that part of him wanted to let the hurt out and another part felt very uncomfortable doing that in front of two hundred people. Bill would have probably felt more comfortable doing this sharing in an intimate space, perhaps sitting around a fire at home. He said the words

"I can't go on" and the room stood still. No one moved or spoke for what seemed like a long time. Then one of the Native Alaskan women, a village elder, stood up and said, "You've got to go on with this story. It must be told. It's our story." One by one, others stood up to validate his experience in this way. Bill picked up the microphone and through his tears managed to finish his story. In so doing, just as he himself had been validated by the group, he also validated many other Iñupiat people in the room.

Finally, another way to actively listen is to *summarize*—to voice the main ideas or themes the speaker expresses in order to review them as well as to acknowledge that we have heard everything that was said. It is helpful to summarize when we have little time available to let the person know we are listening. A child may come home from school and start to unwind by telling a string of stories about his or her day, and a parent might say, "So you've had a really full day today, and spent lots of time with your friends." Summarizing is also useful in situations when we are in the role of third-party intermediary and two disputants are almost to the point of being able to talk to each other directly. Summarizing helps the dialogue continue and assures reiteration of the main thoughts and feelings.

As we teach active listening to people from a variety of cultural perspectives, we discover that, depending on our backgrounds, some of us have had a great deal of practice in listening whereas others have had less opportunity to develop good listening habits. I grew up in a family where a minimum of two people were always speaking at the same time. I'm not certain how much active listening actually went on; in the rare moments when there were a few seconds of silence at the dinner table, we assumed that the persons speaking had simply forgotten what they were about to say. This differs greatly from the experience of people whose cultures honor the value of silence and consequently give the speaker the opportunity to reach a deeper level of response. A Hebrew sage once said, "The beginning of wisdom is silence." The next stage is listening.

Eye contact is another case in point. Establishing eye contact means different things in different cultures. For some of us, eye contact is a sign of disrespect; for others it is connected to feelings of intimacy and reserved for showing deep affection. For some, eye contact is important as a means of picking up deeper cues to what the other person is thinking and feeling. However, although our cultural and personal norms about eye contact differ, most of us would agree that active listening suffers when we glance around the room when another person is speaking. This is why, in teaching people to actively listen, we ask them to *focus* on the speaker. There are many ways in which our body language lets someone know when we are giving them our undivided attention, including gestures and postures as well as eye contact behavior.

Thus, again, in practicing any of these skills, it is important to realize that we may need a bridge from our cultural pattern to someone else's in order to improve communication.

We also have to keep questioning our assumptions at all times. Most of us would agree that body language plays a key role in active listening, that our body language needs to be open and receptive. But how close or how far away from someone must we be to show receptivity? Once again, this varies from culture to culture, and there are individualities within each cultural group as well. When we as listeners get too close or too far away, we may cause anxiety on the part of the speaker. Since we are attempting to be in another person's shoes when we actively listen, we must sometimes cross over to what feels comfortable for them, not us. In doing RCCP training in Barrow, I began to slow the rhythm of my speech to match the rhythm I was experiencing around me. My co-trainer began to think I was losing my train of thought. Instead, I was shifting to a pace that enhanced silence and, in this case, also encouraged more dialogue.

Active listening is one of the most powerful skills we teach. Learning to do it well gives us a variety of options for communicating and resolving conflict. The following are examples of instances when active listening can be a valuable tool:

> To improve the quality of a conversation, especially when the discussion is a sensitive one

> When someone needs help in expressing his or her feelings, and welcomes someone's help in problem solving

> When a strong emotion—whether painful or joyful—is present and the person needs acknowledgment

> When you disagree strongly with someone and feel that you are about to begin arguing and criticizing

> To check accuracy before you act on something you've heard

Active listening is not just behavior. When we decide to listen empathically, we choose to engage our own feelings. It is not enough to learn all the techniques and put them to practice. We must *become* those techniques. It is the intent to have our hearts fully present, to engage ourselves in the other person's feelings, that makes actively listening an act of compassion. The technique then becomes a gift we can offer others, a powerful, effective way to transform a difficult situation.

Using I-Messages

Just as conflict is a natural part of life, so are anger and a host of other feelings. Our emotions can signal that something isn't quite right in a relationship, alert us to the presence of a problem that needs to be addressed. All emotions have the potential of enhancing personal awareness, deepening relationships, and aiding us in resolving conflict.

The feeling we normally associate with conflict is anger. Anger often drives us to aggression, either verbal or physical. Even so, we can develop interpersonal and communication skills to express our anger and other strong feelings in beneficial, nonaggressive ways.

We first need to develop the ability to identify our anger. Sometimes our bodies give us cues: rapid breathing, racing pulse, rising voice pitch. It is also important to become aware of the kinds of behaviors and situations that trigger our anger. Finally, we need to think about which behaviors can lower the intensity of the angry feelings. We may need to remember to breathe deeply, count backwards, think about the consequences of our anger should it get out of control.

Once we have this level of introspection in place, it is useful to have concrete techniques to help express what we need and want in ways that keep communication open and receptive. I-statements, or I-messages, are one way to do that. When strong feelings surface in a conflict, we frequently use "You-messages" instead. You-messages accuse, blame, judge, and belittle: "You're always doing that." "You're so irresponsible!" You-messages tend to generalize, make demands, or bring up past grievances, thereby shutting down communication. You-messages are aggressive. I-messages, on the other hand, are assertive. Social scientist Virginia Satir estimates that less than 5 percent of the population can be expected to communicate assertively.[10] We either can't say what we want to say or we say it with a conscious or unconscious motive to hurt the other. Using I-messages allows us to state our needs and feelings and send a clear message to the receiver. This doesn't guarantee a positive response, but it does keep our own integrity intact.

An I-message generally has three parts to it, sometimes four: *I feel* (state the emotion) *when you* (state the other person's specific behavior) *because* (state the effect the behavior has on you), *and I would like* (state what you would like to have happen—something doable).

The I-message formula has appeared in numerous training programs, books, and articles over the last thirty years. Most of us in the field don't even know to whom we should give credit for the concept because it has become so widely used, but a few years ago, Janet and I enjoyed meeting

Thomas Gordon, whose effectiveness training courses for parents, teachers, and leaders are taught throughout the world. Tom shared with us how he first coined the term:

I had taught the first three or four classes of my Parent Effectiveness Training [P.E.T.] course in Pasadena, California, in 1962. One night after class, I shared with my wife that the course taught parents the value of empathic listening [active listening] when their children encountered problems in their lives, but that parents also needed to know what to do when children's behavior caused them *problems. How can we help parents get their children to listen to them and change their behavior?*

Before I knew it, I took a napkin and wrote the word "you," the pronoun I typically used as a professional counselor trying to help my clients to "own" their problems, as in "You are really feeling angry" or "You don't know what to do." Then I drew a vertical line down the napkin and on the right side I wrote, "I have a problem." That's when it really dawned on me that when a child has a problem, parents should use a You-message, as in "You're upset," but when a child's behavior causes the parent a problem, the message should logically begin with an "I," as in "I can't hear on the phone when the TV is on so loud." So I-messages were invented that cold night on a white napkin, and were soon added to the P.E.T. course.

I-messages are one of the most difficult techniques to add to our repertoire. We all lack experience in talking this way and require a lot of practice before it becomes natural.

Let's take the formula one step at a time. Our first task is to say how we feel about the effect the other person's behavior is having on us: "I feel . . ." Those of us who tend to withhold negative emotions or feel that confrontation should be discouraged are faced with a challenge right from the start. Moreover, it takes a lot of awareness to determine what we are feeling: we may be expressing anger when really we are frightened. Asking ourselves what the "first feeling" was when we experienced a specific behavior helps.

If we don't have a wide range of words for feelings in our vocabulary, then it may be difficult to communicate the emotion clearly: when we say we're angry, do we mean mildly irritated or completely furious? In some cases, we use words that are heavily charged: "I feel taken advantage of," "I feel abused or ignored." It is best to use words that are less judgmental.

The disclosure of feelings carries different "baggage" for each of us. Some people grow up in homes where they receive messages that only some feelings are okay ("If you have nothing good to say, then don't say it at all"), or that emotion itself is dangerous ("You're making my blood pressure go up"). If we cannot own our feelings, we tend to blame others for our reactions. Eleanor Roosevelt reminds us, however, that "no one can make you feel inferior without your consent." When I send an I-message, I take responsibility for my actions.

An I-message is ideally an act of love and concern, an act of communication, not manipulation. I've heard many adults and young people say, "My mother (father) never told me she (he) loved me or was proud of me." No wonder many of us have difficulty in practicing gut-level communication. Repressed emotion may be an important variable connected to illness. As Thomas Delbanco, director of the Division of General Medicine and Primary Care at Beth Israel Hospital in Boston, says, "When someone's belly hurts, I ask very quickly what's going on in the mind as well as in the abdomen. When someone is depressed, I think also about what might be going on in the body that's leading to the depression. Mind and body are inextricably woven together."[11]

The next part of the formula, "when you . . . ," can also be tricky. It is important to express this part in clear, specific terms. The tendency is to add judgment to the description and to be vague. An example would be, "I feel angry when you ignore the school rules," as compared to the more precise statement "I feel angry when you arrive late to school three times a week." Another tendency we have is to go beyond reporting specific behavior to make inferences about another person's personality or motives: "I was upset when you left the party early because you were bored" or "I was upset when you left the party just because your friends weren't there." One way to think about whether you have actually described the other person's behavior objectively is to ask yourself, Is this behavior observable? Do I really know why she left the party? A common mistake is to use words which are global and absolute—"always," "never," "every time." Instead of telling someone that they are often late we tend to say "You're never on time." Another roadblock to delivering a clear, descriptive statement about someone else's behavior is to say something about their character or worth. For instance, when you feel a person is endorsing a stereotype and you respond by calling him or her a racist or a sexist.

The final part of delivering an I-message requires that we let the other person know the effect their behavior has had on us. Again, describing this only in tangible and observable ways is helpful. Rather than saying, for instance, "I feel nervous when you call me at work and talk a long time because you think that I'm not listening," one might simply say, "I feel nervous when you call me at work and talk for a long time, because then I can't get my work done on time."

A fourth element is becoming widespread in the use of I-messages—telling the person what you would like to see happen, as in "I feel frustrated when you don't let me know until Thursday that I have to work on a Saturday because I can't plan my weekend, *and I would appreciate knowing at least one week in advance.*" When I asked Tom Gordon what he thought about adding this fourth component to the standard for I-messages, he said, "I like to leave it up to the higher side of the person to come forth without asking. It almost seems like a demand." So you'll see I-messages presented in two ways, with or without this final ingredient.

As is true for all conflict resolution skills, culture and family communication patterns influence one's comfort level in using I-messages, and societal context dictates how safe or appropriate it is to be either assertive or nonassertive in a given situation. In families and communities that are hierarchical, where engaging in free-flowing discussions and expressing opinions is discouraged, delivering a straightforward I-message would be considered disrespectful. The level of expression around the emotions is influenced by both gender and cultural norms, and differences in culturally appropriate ways to express feelings should not be confused with either a lack of emotion or too much emotion.

An important consideration in teaching young people about I-messages is to become aware of the context in which a young person operates—his or her ethnicity, race, culture, and gender. Children of color, who live with racial oppression every day, have many opportunities to deliver I-messages, but they have to deliver them in a society that still supports their oppression. A young boy named Troy described it this way: "Do you know how it feels to have people cross the street to get away from you? To have a security guard follow you around the store? To have women clutch their purses to their chests when they see you? Well, that's how it is to be black." Who in our society will support Troy's message if he has the courage to deliver it?

Gender plays an important part in delivering I-messages as well. Assertiveness and aggression are culturally condoned for boys in our society, while girls are encouraged to be submissive. All this must be taken into consideration.

Robert Bolton, author of *People Skills*, makes an important point: "Virtually all creatures defend their space using a variety of tactics which fall into one of two basic categories—fight or flight. Only humans have a third option—verbal assertion."[12] I feel it is useful to teach young people and adults how to use I-messages, but until we all share power equally in this society, these messages will be riskier for some of us to deliver than for others.

Mediation

There are times when we are neither perpetrators nor victims in a conflict, but rather bystanders. Bystanders can become active participants in solving conflict when they have the skills to intervene. An intervention by an adult in a conflict involving young people often means that the adult will exercise power or authority, controlling both the situation and the outcome. But a different method of intervention exists—one through which a neutral third party helps create an environment where the disputants themselves can find a mutually acceptable solution. This is the method of mediation.

Mediation is similar to arbitration, but differs in that an arbitrator listens to both parties and solves the problem by offering a solution, while in mediation the power for solving the problem lies with the disputants themselves— the mediator simply uses his or her skills to facilitate problem-solving between them.

Mediation has been used in a variety of settings to help settle conflicts. One of its first uses in the United States was as an alternative to court proceedings. At first, community disputes involving minor complaints were settled in a less official way through mediation; today the skill of mediation is helpful in divorce and child custody cases, and in disputes between employers and employees, and between labor and management. Recently it has become a valued practice in schools.

A person trained in mediation can be a neutral, third-party intermediary in informal settings such as public places, family gatherings, and classrooms. The skill of mediation can also be used formally, as in community mediation efforts between a landlord and a tenant. The mediation process can also be formalized in schools where peer mediation programs are in place.

Mediation is the conflict resolution skill of effective communication and problem-solving. It is based on openness and honesty, attempting to equalize power between two parties. Mediation is a cooperative future-oriented process based on nonthreatening, nonpunitive solutions. Mediators seek win-win solutions and are willing to deal with underlying issues and emotions. They maintain neutrality and confidentiality, using the skill of active listening to create trust and separate the disputants from the problem.

Mediators make decisions for neither party. Self-awareness on the part of the mediator is important, as he or she must maintain neutrality and treat both parties without bias. Mediators are skilled at using neutral language, remembering that suggestions and judgments are not objective; they are

THE CORE CURRICULUM

trained to catch themselves before saying things like "One of you is lying" or "The best thing you could do here is to avoid each other." Skillful mediators use open-ended questioning to help the disputants clarify and problem-solve. They tend to not ask questions that lead to one-word or yes-no responses, asking "What happened?" rather than "Did you push into him?" or "Are you sorry for doing that?" A skillful mediator delves into the interests and needs of both parties and helps separate those interests and needs from their positions. Each person's perspective is given attention.

The main task of a mediator is to help both parties approach the conflict in a new way, to shift their perceptions as they better understand, communicate, and trust one another in the hope that this understanding and trust will eventually lead them to a solution they can both agree upon. The steps of mediation follow a similar process regardless of the length or formality of the intervention. The process usually comprises the following components:

[1]   Setting the Stage: The mediator introduces him or herself as a third-party intermediary. The disputants agree to try to solve the problem with the mediator's help. Ground rules are also shared and agreed upon: the disputants will avoid violence, physical or verbal; speak directly to the mediator; let each other finish speaking without interruption; and maintain confidentiality.

[2]   Getting the Stories Out: The disputants discuss what happened and how they felt, while the mediator reflects and restates what they have said. The mediator summarizes the whole story, including key facts and feelings, before the mediation proceeds.

[3]   Brainstorming Solutions: The mediator moves back and forth between the two disputants, helping them both focus in on the question, What can you do here and now to help solve the problem? Active listening on the part of the mediator continues as he or she restates ideas and potential solutions.

[4]   Resolution: At this final stage, the mediator helps the disputants reach a solution that works for both, repeating the solution in all

its parts. The disputants are asked individually whether they are in agreement with the solution. They are also asked what they might do differently if a similar situation comes up again. The mediator continues to restate their comments and finally congratulates them on a successful mediation.

Seeking the help of a third party to mediate feels more natural to some of us than to others. Using mediation or having designated mediators feels especially familiar for people from backgrounds where open confrontation is discouraged and seeking the counsel of a person in a position of authority is the norm. For others, a third-party intervention may seem cowardly. Some may feel that it is easier to just think aloud, express gut feelings openly, and try to resolve a conflict as soon as it emerges; mediation, which entails scheduling time to meet about the conflict, may be perceived as artificial. Some of us feel very comfortable using traditional, tried and true procedures; we welcome solid, consistent intervention by an authority figure. For some of us, sharing our inner feelings is reserved for family members and school mediation is not an option unless the school environment feels familial.

Mediation is acknowledged in many cultures, even honored as a process. In Buddhist monasteries, practices have been in place for the last two thousand years to settle disputes with the help of a third party—in this case the entire community. Thich Nhat Hanh, Zen master and author, describes the technique:

In a convocation of the whole Sangha community, everyone sits together with the willingness to help. The two conflicting monks are present and sit face to face knowing that everyone expects them to make peace. People refrain from listening to stories outside the assembly. Everything must be said in public, in the community. Both monks try to remember the whole history of the conflict, every detail, as the whole assembly just sits patiently and listens. Everyone expects the two monks to try their best for reconciliation. The outcome is not important. The fact that each monk is trying his best to show his willingness for reconciliation is most important. The next step is "covering mud with straw." One respected monk is appointed to represent each side of the conflict. These two monks address the assembly saying something about each monk that will cause the other monk to understand better and de-escalate his anger or resistance—covering their mud with straw. The next stage is voluntary confession. Each monk reveals his own shortcomings without waiting for others to say them. Finally there is decision by consensus in accepting the verdict. It is agreed in advance that the two monks will accept whatever verdict is pronounced by the whole assembly. After exploring every detail of the conflict, a committee presents a verdict. It is announced three times. If the community remains silent that means "okay." This is the end of the session and the monks abide by the decision.[13]

Buddhist monks and nuns have been practicing this form of mediation for thousands of years in India, China, Japan, Vietnam, Korea, and many other countries.

Africa also gives us examples of dispute resolution being completely interwoven into the community. Nicole, an RCCP teacher, told us of one method of mediation which was a natural part of the regional culture among the Dogan people in Mali. In every village she visited in the area, she came across a low platform that triggered her curiosity. When she asked about their use, she was told that these were places to reconcile conflicts. When two people in a village had a dispute, the tribal elders would bring them to the platform and they would sit beneath it until the conflict was resolved. The platforms are built low so that disputants are not able to stand up and engage in physical fighting. The elders serve as mediators and apparently perform their task nonverbally. To Nicole, the spaces under the platforms resembled quiet, private mediation rooms—sacred places that hold a history of peaceful solutions in their very structure.

Native American conflict resolution practices have found their way into mediation circles everywhere. Indeed, they are probably at the root of many commonly used mediation processes in this country. The native people of Hawaii, for instance, have an ancient family problem-solving process called *ho'oponopono* (to set right), in which a *kupuna* (elder) or another respected person who is not involved in the issues at hand serves as *haku* (facilitator). The *haku* becomes a vital element in facilitation and in setting the tone of *aloha* or love and affection which is at the center of the *ho'oponopono*. There are five conditions that must be understood and agreed upon by each participant before the *ho'oponopono* can begin:

> Each individual in the *'ohana* (family) must share a common commitment to be a part of the problem-solving process.

> All words and deeds that are part of *ho'oponopono* will be shared in an atmosphere of *'oia i'o* (the essence of truth).

> The *o'hana* must share a common sense of *aloha* for one another or be committed to reinstating that spirit.

> Everything that is said in a *ho'oponopono* is done in confidence and will not be repeated when the session is complete.

> The *haku* must be commonly agreed on as a fair and impartial channel through which the *ho'oponopono* is done.[14]

The *ho'oponopono* is a complicated process consisting of several phases. Because it has so much to offer as a model, we feel it's worth describing in some detail. The initial phase, *kukulu kumuhana*, consists of clearly identifying the family's general problem and outlining the procedures for the whole process for the benefit of all participants. This phase also involves the pooling of emotional and spiritual forces through prayer. The *mahiki*, or discussion phase, is the time when the family talks about what has happened. Each person talks with the *haku*, one by one, about the incident, taking into account each person's feelings and reactions to the specific issue. In the *ma-hiki*, only one issue relating to the general problem is dealt with at a time. Everyone is given a chance to speak, and the discussion of the problem is led by the leader, who functions as an intermediary, keeping individuals from directly confronting one another. The problem is unraveled layer by layer to enable family members to see how a network of negative entanglements called *hihia* has bound members together in a distressing relationship and caused the problem. Family members see how the initial act of wrongdoing, the *hala*, caused a chain reaction of compounded hurts and angers that led to larger misunderstandings.

When the discussion is complete, the resolution or forgiveness phase, called *mihi*, takes place. This is a time of confession, repentance, and forgiving. It is expected that forgiveness be *'oia'i'o* (true, sincere), and that it be given whenever asked. If restitution is necessary, the family arranges it and agrees upon the terms.

In the closing or final phase of the *ho'oponopono*, the leader summarizes what has taken place. He or she also reaffirms the family's strength and enduring bonds. As a final step, the family has a closing ritual or *pani*. Traditionally, *pani* involved food offerings to the *'aumakua*, or family guardian spirits, followed by feasting. Today, the *pani* frequently consists of the sharing of a snack or a meal together.

This ancient process has much to teach us today, and we are grateful to Native Hawaiian educator Manu Aluli Meyer for documenting this tradition.

Finally, of course, mediation has also been welcomed as a tool in schools throughout America. In many of our schools, educators are working in many different ways to create a culture which finds room for mediation as a way of resolving conflict. As we shall see in chapters 6 and 7, children from many backgrounds are benefiting from this effort.

Gandhi wrote, "My optimism rests on my belief in the infinite possibilities of the individual to develop nonviolence. The more you develop it in your own being, the more infectious it becomes till it overwhelms your surroundings and by and by might oversweep the world." Our goal is to encourage those trained in conflict resolution to make these skills a way of life, to make a decision to be nonviolent. By decision I mean an act that doesn't have to be revisited everytime one has a choice. When both my parents gave up smoking within the same week, they struggled with this change until about a month later, when they each made the *decision* to never smoke again. From then on they no longer had to think about how they would act when cigarettes were available.

This is what we want the skills of win-win problem-solving, active listening, and I-messages to do—empower us to make the decision to be nonviolent. Thich Nhat Hanh put it succinctly in the title of his book, *Being Peace*. It is the difference between simply practicing conflict resolution techniques and choosing to *live* nonviolence. We know we've internalized these skills when Gandhi's words ring true to us: "Nonviolence is not a garment to be put on and off at will. Its seat is in the heart, and it must be an inseparable part of our very being."

How to Make Peace

The following pointers to remember in resolving a conflict nonviolently were formulated by Tom Roderick, executive director of Educators for Social Responsibility Metro.[15] We at RCCP have found them invaluable.

> *Slow down the action.* Many fights and arguments get out of control very fast. Before reacting, think. Remember the conflict escalator.

> *Listen well.* Don't interrupt. Hear the other person out. It helps to paraphrase or state in your own words what you hear the other person saying.

> *Give the other person the benefit of the doubt.* In a conflict between two people, each person has feelings, each person has a point of view. You

may not agree with the other person, but try to understand where s/he is coming from. Ask open-ended questions to get information about how the other person sees things. Try to listen with an open mind. If you see that you have done something wrong, don't hesitate to apologize.

> *Acknowledge the other person's feelings.* When people believe they've been listened to, they generally become less angry and more open to listening to what the other person has to say. Statements like "I can see you're angry" or "You really feel strongly about this" tend to diffuse anger and open up communication.

> *Be strong without being mean.* Express your needs and your point of view forcefully, without putting the other person down. Use I-messages to communicate how you are feeling rather than you-messages that put the blame on the other person. Name-calling, blaming, bossing, and threatening tend to block communication and escalate conflict.

> *Try to see a conflict as a problem to be solved, rather than a contest to be won.* Attack the problem, not the other person. Try to get away from frighting over who's right and who's wrong. Ask instead: What do I need? What does the other person feel they need? Is there a way we can both get what we want?

> *Set your sights on a win-win solution.* In a win-win solution, both parties get what they need and come away happy. This requires good listening on both sides and creative thinking. If a win-win solution is not possible, you may have to settle for a compromise, where each person gets something and each gives up something. A compromise is a lot better than violence.

> *If you don't seem to be getting anywhere in solving a conflict, ask for help.* Of course, you'll need agreement from the other person that help

is needed and you'll have to agree on who the third party should be. But a third party can be helpful. Try to find someone who is a good listener. Tell the third party their role is to help the people in conflict talk with each other, not to take sides.

> *Remember that conflict, handled well, can lead to personal growth and better relationships.* Try to see the conflict as an opportunity. Working through the conflict with a friend can lead to greater closeness. Hearing other points of view can introduce us to new ideas and increase our understanding of ourselves and other people.

> *The true heroes of today's world are not the Rambos.* They are those men and women who have the courage and intelligence to deal with conflict in creative, nonviolent ways.

[**4**]

VALUING DIVERSITY:
CREATING INCLUSIVE SCHOOLS
AND COMMUNITIES

It began to seem that one would have to hold in the mind forever two ideas which
seemed to be in opposition. The first idea was acceptance, the acceptance, totally
without rancor, of life as it is, and people as they are: in the light of this idea, it
goes without saying that injustice is a commonplace. But this did not mean that
one could be complacent, for the second idea was of equal power: that one must
never, in one's own life, accept these injustices as commonplace but must fight
them with all one's strength. This fight begins, however, in the heart and it now
had been laid to my charge to keep my own heart free of hatred and despair.

- James Baldwin -
Notes of a Native Son

Why Include Diversity Education in Conflict Resolution Programs?

IN THE PAST, PEOPLE in the fields of conflict resolution and emotional
literacy have rarely attempted to integrate prejudice reduction and issues of
equality and justice as part of their emphasis. But in our work we have found
that one of the most pressing problems in schools and among youth in general is cultural and racial bias. From the start, our work in conflict resolution
has been intertwined with diversity and anti-bias education. Our K–12 curriculum focuses as much on helping kids develop skills to confront prejudice
as it does on teaching skills in conflict resolution, and we have found that
conflict resolution skills are extremely useful for enabling students of different races and cultures to work through bias issues.

For too many of us growing up in our society, our differences have been an excuse for prejudice, stereotyping, and discrimination. Clearly, we have a great deal of difficulty with differences at all levels—global, local, and individual—and we are too often unable to recognize the remarkable diversity of the human family as a source of wonder and a cause for celebration.

Many of us were taught at an early age who to watch out for, who to fear, who to scorn. My mother tells me (Linda) about growing up as a German American in New York's Greenwich Village in the 1930s. She was taught that the only way to get to a certain part of lower Manhattan was the long way around Little Italy rather than through it: "Those people are dangerous." Imagine my grandparents' shock when she married my Italian-American father some twenty years later. It wasn't until my birth (I was the firstborn) that the ethnic tensions within my family began to lessen.

These early messages surround us as children, before we can critically assess them. We aren't responsible for the scenario we grew up with or for the misinformation we received about people different from us, whether these differences are visible, like race and gender, or less obvious, as with sexual orientation or some disabilities. It is necessary to understand that most often the negative stereotypes we have are not our creation but the result of the conditions of discrimination and oppression that exist around us. Nevertheless, it is our responsibility to unlearn these messages. We must be a part of breaking the cycle of oppression. Think of it this way: you didn't start the fire but you'd better be on the bucket brigade.

If we think about how diverse our world is in human cultures, our need for greater awareness is obvious. In 1990 the World Development Forum gave us a glimpse of what a village of 100 people representative of the earth's population would look like:

57 Asians
21 Europeans
14 North and South Americans
8 Africans

70 of the 100 would be people of color, 30 would be white

30 of the 100 would be Christian, 70 would be adherents of other faiths

50 percent of the world's wealth would be in the hands of only six people, and all six would be citizens of the United States

70 would be unable to read

50 would suffer from malnutrition

80 would live in substandard housing

only one person would have a university education[1]

In light of this microcosmic model and current demographic trends, we begin to get a picture of what the United States will look like in the year 2000. A report from the Hudson Institute, a policy research organization in Indianapolis, tells us that white males are already the minority in the U.S. workplace and that throughout the rest of the century 85 percent of the net growth in the country's labor force will be people of color, women, and immigrants. Already one American in four defines him- or herself as Latino or nonwhite.[2] *Time* magazine reports that in the year 2020, the number of U.S. residents who are Latino or nonwhite will have more than doubled to nearly 115 million. The white population will not increase.[3]

Our schools will continue to reflect this diversity. The U.S. Department of Education reports that by the year 2000, 15 percent of the country's schoolchildren will have limited English-language abilities and that children of color will constitute at least one third of the students in American public schools.[4]

The shift is taking place so quickly that most of us are still struggling with it. In her book *The Future of White Men and Other Diversity Dilemmas*, Joan Lester illustrates the pressing need for change:

Everybody seems to be getting a seat at the table these days. People who once carried the trays are sitting down, people who sat at the foot of the table are now honored guests, and people who took notes at the meetings are now running those meetings. And now the rules are changing right in the middle of our lives. We are all learning—those of us newly seated at the table and those who are having to move over to make a little more room.[5]

Even so, as Lester points out, "twenty-five percent of the U.S. population are white heterosexual males—who currently hold more than 90 percent of the political, economic and cultural directorship seats."[6] In spite of vast demographic change our society is still divided between dominant groups who have more privilege and access to power and oppressed groups with less privilege and power.

We who work in our schools must prepare young people to live in an America which is in fact already very heterogeneous. Issues of diversity need to be faced openly and honestly, otherwise we may leave our children with an even more exclusive, inequitable, and unjust society. We are already seeing the results of neglecting these issues in our schools and our communities. Virtually every organization that monitors bias-related violence and harassment, from the U.S. Department of Justice to the Anti-Defamation League of B'nai B'rith, reports a significant rise in hate crimes over the past few years.

To turn this trend around is not easy. It is a task for committed, caring individuals. In some cases we will have to take responsibility for dealing with the pain caused by the insidious reality of bigotry. One of our students at Phoenix Academy in New York City describes it this way:

Violence has been a problem in our city for a long time, and in recent years it has spread to our schools. Some schools have even installed metal detectors hoping to stop violence. But weapons aren't the only problem. No metal detector on earth can stop people from bringing fear, prejudice, and conflict to school, and no metal detector can prevent students from bringing that fear, prejudice, and conflict back to the street at 3 P.M.

In our work with RCCP, we recognize that facing these difficult issues concerning diversity and bias requires an examination of our own attitudes and beliefs first. Only then can we begin to improve interpersonal relations

THE CORE CURRICULUM

and create institutional change. The good news is that because prejudice is learned—from parents, friends, and society—it can also be unlearned. The challenge, though, is great. Too many people feel excluded, and that they must earn their right to belong. This anonymous poem, entitled "The Cold Within," reflects what we face as a society:

Six humans trapped by happenstance
and bleak and bitter cold;
each possessed a stick of wood,
or so the story's told.

Their dying fire in need of logs,
the first man held his back,
for of the faces round the fire,
he noticed one was black.

The next man looking 'cross the way
saw one not in his church,
and couldn't bring himself to give
the fire his stick of birch.

The third one sat in tattered clothes,
she gave her coat a hitch.
Why should her log be put to use
to warm the idle rich?

The rich man just sat back and thought
of the wealth he had in store,
and how to keep what he had earned
from the lazy, shiftless poor.

The black woman's face bespoke revenge
as the fire passed from her sight.

All she saw in her stick of wood
was a chance to spite the white.

The last person of this forlorn group
did naught accept nor gain.
Giving only to those who gave
was how he played the game.

Their logs held tight in death's still hand
was proof of human sin.
They didn't die from the cold without,
they died from the cold within.

We have to come to the realization that we need to keep the fire burning because it is *our* fire. We approach our work in diversity knowing that we are all longing to grow and discover new awarenesses, that we want to be open to change rather than assume guilt or expect to be perfect.

Assessing Cultural Competence

Depending on our various experiences, backgrounds, and understandings, each of us comes to this work in diversity with varying degrees of "cultural competence." Tools for Diversity, a training group in Portland, Oregon, offers a perspective on this. They present a learning curve along which we understand our own group and culture and learn about other groups and their cultures. It consists of four levels of cultural competence: unconscious incompetence, conscious incompetence, conscious competence, and, finally, unconscious competence.[7] Adaptations of this model have been useful in understanding where we are in the continuum and where others might be.

Unconscious incompetence refers to a lack of awareness of how issues of diversity have an impact on our lives. At this stage, although we may recognize differences among people, we downplay their importance. We might say,

"I don't know how many kids of color are in my classroom. Kids are kids. I'm colorblind." One of our RCCP students from Anchorage, Alaska, had entered a middle school where people were struggling with issues of diversity. After seeing a play at her new school, she was prompted to write the following letter to the editor of the local newspaper:

To the Editor:
A few weeks ago Clark Junior High's sign language group put on a signing skit where they sang and signed to a song called "Why Can't We All Just Be Colorblind?"

They did a nice job. However, I sat there listening to the lyrics of the song and the more I listened, the more I began to say to myself, this song is stupid, just plain stupid. The song was asking why we couldn't just be colorblind so the different races and ethnic groups could get along better, because we could not see their skin color.

I totally disagree. The song sets a bad example to everyone. Racism begins with what is passed down from parent to child and from the TV/radio to the eyes and ears of its viewers. If we want to end racism, we must begin there and not with some crazy wish to be colorblind. We must learn to live with the different colors, cultures, languages and ethnic backgrounds ourselves.

To be colorblind would just take away who we really are and our inner selves.

To be colorblind is an awful wish and should not have been permitted at our multicultural assembly. Color-blindness is not the answer to racism. We must learn to live with and appreciate the different races and ethnic groups of the world—that is the answer to racism.

> *Nichole Young, eighth grade*
> *Clark Junior High, Anchorage Alaska*[8]

Even in our efforts to improve intergroup relations, we are still learning in the process.

In the next stage, *conscious incompetence* (according to our model), we begin to see ourselves as cultural beings and to realize that we have a lot to learn about multicultural issues. Things don't seem so simple anymore. We begin to take in the reality that we don't all share the same values, beliefs, or behaviors. In this stage, we move from an ethnocentric view of the world—"only my culture, my perspectives, and my values are appropriate"—to a multicultural perspective. We start to have a respect for cultural differences and for points of view other than our own.

The next stage, that of *conscious competence*, actively engages us in a give-and-take dialogue around issues of diversity. We are comfortable giving and receiving information and coaching to better understand and appreciate differences; we can easily ask others about themselves and their experiences, and feel comfortable responding to inquiries about ourselves. We engage in dialogues about our backgrounds, values, and beliefs in this stage. (Living in New York City allows me to do "ethnic sharing" during most taxi rides; I get a chance to hear the "authentic voice," the experience of someone from a country I may know very little about, simply by asking, "Where are you from?") At this level of cultural competence, we'd feel pretty comfortable asking someone of another faith, for example, about the significance of their holidays, or explaining our own traditions to them.

The final level of cultural competence in this model is *unconscious competence*. At this stage, we are meeting each other on the same plane, engaging in an equal, democratic interaction. We are more and more comfortable with conflicts that arise during intergroup interactions. We feel at home adjusting the way we perceive and experience our world to consider other points of view. At this stage, we are not likely to go into an intergroup interaction with the naive thought that "all people are alike," but we are able to build bridges naturally and easily from one cultural pattern to another as we interact with people from different backgrounds. At this stage, we truly value inclusion and feel our lives are richer when people with a variety of perspectives enter our classrooms, schools, and neighborhoods. We believe we *need* other viewpoints to enjoy all of life's possibilities.

There is an image we use in our curriculum in teaching about differing points of view, the well-known story of four blindfolded people who encounter an elephant: "This is a large tree trunk," said one, touching the elephant's leg. "No, it's more like a hose, with a wide entrance," said the one holding the trunk. "It is definitely a wall, flat and wide," said the person feeling the sides of the animal. "No, it's a rope," said the one grasping its tail. To get the whole picture, we need everyone's point of view. For people at the unconscious competence level the world includes the richness of diversity.

Valuing Diversity and Preventing Prejudice

Just as metal detectors can be mistakenly relied upon as the approach to decreasing violence in our schools, what we've come to call the tourist approach is often being used in hopes of countering bias in schools. With this kind of program, young people are immersed in learning about a particular culture for a brief period. The next week they move to another culture. The research reveals, however, that to overcome prejudices and appreciate other cultures, it is not enough to be exposed to a classroom unit about them. And although it helps to see more members of various groups on TV and in our history books, we have a real chance of dissolving our stereotypes only through direct contact with each other. We need a strong emotional connection—usually a direct, positive experience where we are on an equal footing with one another.

It is not always easy to create true multicultural experiences for adults and young people. The changing demographics of our society have not touched every community. Diversity is not visible in all parts of our country. Segregation is still evident. In many school districts, we have "pockets" of various ethnicities separate and unequal within the same district. Even when adults working in schools are experiencing quite a bit of diversity in their classrooms, they may still go home to communities where everyone looks like them.

We all have an internal list of those we still don't understand, let alone appreciate. We all have biases, even prejudices, toward specific groups. In our workshops we ask people to gather in pairs and think about their hopes and fears in relating to people of a group different from their own. Fears usually include being judged, miscommunication, and patronizing or hurting others unintentionally; hopes are usually the possibility of dialogue, learning something new, developing friendships, and understanding different points of view. After doing this activity hundreds of times, I'm always amazed how similar the lists are. At any moment that we're dealing with people different from ourselves, the likelihood is that they carry a similar list of hopes and fears in *their* back pocket. Elise Boulding, peace activist and educator, suggests that we "try to think of those we used to call enemies as strangers [instead] and see what that does for our capacity to establish relationships."

When people say they don't feel prejudiced toward any particular group, I suggest that they give themselves a litmus test. I ask them to think of the last twenty people they spoke with personally as well as the last ten people who walked through the front door of their home. How much did these folks look like them, think like them, act like them? How many shared their values?

At RCCP, we believe that schools have an important role to play in inciting young people and adults to question stereotypes and prejudice.

Beginning with Ourselves

We must begin with ourselves in unlearning the myths we have about others. All of us, depending on our culture, background, values, and experience are in a different place in terms of cultural competence. As we examine our own backgrounds, we begin to uncover emotions, biases, and opinions we didn't realize we had.

Some of us have never had to think a lot about differences. We grew up with a sense that our background and behavior represented the logical and correct way to experience the world. We have little awareness that what we think of as universal is often exclusionary, or that our idea of the norm is quite limited. In our workshops we ask people to share where their grandparents were born. A surprisingly common response is "I've never thought much about my cultural background."

Sometimes people resist our work in diversity because of deep-seated feelings about prejudices or personal injustices they themselves have experienced. I remember Renee, a seventeen-year-old African American, telling a class, "I've been through so much where prejudice is concerned. Don't even talk about it. Don't even think about it. Just leave me alone." Creating a safe and trusting atmosphere is essential because talking openly and honestly about these issues usually illicits strong feelings. It is common for groups with more power and privilege to feel guilt, shame, and anger, and for oppressed groups to feel shock, rage, and rejection. As the Haitian proverb says, "Rocks in water don't know the misery of rocks in the sun."

In this work we also go beyond individual beliefs and interpersonal relationships. We begin to explore the notion that our society is set up in a way that our institutions—our schools, government agencies, courts, businesses, religious organizations, and the media—perpetuate the systematic mistreatment of groups of people who do not belong to the dominant social group. Most of us have experienced individual acts of prejudice or bias against us. Some of us, however, have experienced long and systematic historical discrimination. And so the experience of prejudice is vastly different for different people and for some has serious impact and consequences. We try in our work to help people understand that there are levels of prejudice. Prejudice is a pre-judgment based on stereotypes and assumptions. Discrimination is acting on these prejudices. And yet another level exists—a system of advantage based on race, sex, class, and other differences.

Violence in our society is not only interpersonal. It exists on a continuum from the personal to widespread forms of institutionalized oppression. One can visit one school in NYC on Monday where there's a ratio of one computer for every three kids, then go to a school in another school district on Wednesday and find that there students are able to work on a computer only once a month. That's also a form of violence. Gandhi said, "An unjust law is in itself an act of violence."

Our work with individuals therefore also involves working for long-term institutional change. It is essential to examine issues of power and oppression. South African Bishop Desmond Tutu tells us, "If you are neutral in situations of injustice, you have chosen the side of the oppressor. If an elephant has his foot on the tail of a mouse and you say you are neutral, the mouse will not appreciate your neutrality."

Oppression is based on a power relationship. Privilege is given, often in subtle ways, to a certain group or groups, and society supports the system of advantage. This doesn't mean that excluded groups such as women, people of color, or gays and lesbians are intrinsically powerless. Differences don't *cause* the power imbalance, they are used to justify it. But these groups are targeted for more violence, and discrimination becomes institutionalized and socially sanctioned. Those in groups with less privilege learn lies about themselves. Those with privilege also learn lies about targeted groups and about their own superiority. This physical, emotional, mental, verbal, economic, and political form of mistreatment is *oppression* and if it goes on long enough, members of the targeted group begin to believe the lies. This is the condition known as *internalized oppression*, a pervasive one in which people are induced to attack each other instead of the oppressor, to give up on each other, to separate themselves, to compete and blame within their own communities.

Whether we realize it or not, the negative messages of oppression are always at work in our minds. Every group that is a target internalizes this misinformation and begins to believe it. Internalized oppression is an involuntary, often unconscious reaction to the experience of oppression. It is certainly not our fault, and yet it is our responsibility to learn the truth. When we appreciate our own culture and differences, we can build bridges within our own group. We can then build bridges to reach groups of people who are different from ourselves.

It is important to recognize that both oppression and internalized oppression exist in our society. Leo Tolstoy's words illustrate the part some of us may be playing: "I sit on a man's back, choking him and making him carry me, and yet assure myself and others that I am very sorry for him and wish to ease his lot by any means possible, except by getting off his back."

Many of us from dominant groups have accepted that discrimination is present in our society, but we haven't fully taken in the fact that we have certain privileges simply by belonging to a dominant group. Peggy McIntosh of Wellesley College's Center for Research on Women describes her experience of "white privilege" in this way:

I will give here a list of special circumstances and conditions I experience which I did not earn but which I have been made to feel are mine by birth, by citizenship, and by virtue of being a conscientious, law-abiding, "normal" person of good will. I have chosen those conditions which I think in my case attach somewhat more to skin-color privilege than to class, religion, ethnic status or geographical location, though all these other factors are intricately intertwined [list slightly abbreviated].

[1]   *If I should need to move, I can be pretty sure of renting or purchasing housing in an area which I can afford and in which I would want to live.*

[2]   *I can be pretty sure that my neighbors in such a location will be neutral or pleasant to me.*

[3]   *I can go shopping alone most of the time, pretty well assured that I will not be followed or harassed.*

[4]   *I can turn on the television or open to the front page of the paper and see people of my race widely represented.*

[5]   *When I am told about our national heritage or about "civilization," I am shown that people of my color made it what it is.*

[6]   *I can be sure that my children will be given curricular materials that testify to the existence of their race.*

[7]   *Whether I use checks, credit cards, or cash, I can count on my skin color not to work against the appearance of financial responsibility.*

[8]   *I do not have to educate my children to be aware of systematic racism for their own daily physical protection.*[9]

These privileges are actually *rights*, or would be if we all belonged equally in our society. It isn't that European Americans don't deserve every one of the privileges listed—it's simply that *everyone* does. And so our job is to allow ourselves to risk the personal transformation it takes to acknowledge all the manifestations of oppression and to gain the courage to say that we will not accept any of them.

Before we can build bridges to people of other groups, our first task is to build alliances with people within our own. I was reminded of this in a powerful way several years ago, when I was asked to intervene in the aftermath of a serious racially motivated incident in New York City.

In 1989, in the Brooklyn neighborhood known as Bensonhurst, an African-American teenager named Yusef Hawkins was beaten and murdered by a group of Italian-American youth. The incident, which made national headlines for weeks, occurred right in front of an elementary school that had recently become part of RCCP. It happened because Yusef was in the "wrong neighborhood." He was answering an ad for a used car in a Brooklyn paper. The honors student didn't realize that when he got off the N train at the Avenue U stop he would find himself in the middle of a very insular and isolated Italian-American enclave. Most of its residents have lived there for two or three generations, and many of them—grandparents, parents, daughters, and sons—still live close to their extended families. A group of teenagers saw Yusef Hawkins at the train stop. Their fear and hatred escalated. They began to beat him with baseball bats and eventually killed him.

I was coordinating RCCP for the New York City Board of Education at the time. Being the highest-ranking Italian-American in the chancellor's cabinet, I was immediately sent to the neighborhood. I convinced an RCCP teacher, Beatrice Byrd, who was then Brooklyn president of the NAACP, to accompany me. We spent many evenings in Bensonhurst, trying to open up dialogue between two groups of people who shared only a well-defined border—between the African Americans who lived in a housing development on one side of town and the Italian Americans who lived in tenements and two-family homes on the other. To make things more complicated, every Saturday following the incident, several black churches bused in hundreds of parishioners for nonviolent protest marches through the streets. Fear and embarrassment ran high within the Italian-American community. During the weekday evening meetings, we attempted to keep the dialogue open as each march was announced.

The meetings usually went right through dinnertime. So we were all pretty hungry at the end, and I kept a ritual of gathering a group of African-American folks to go out and get a bite to eat before going home. Once the nightly meetings were over, I couldn't bear to go anywhere near my Italian-American brothers and sisters. I was afraid I would hear them repeating the same discriminatory remarks I had heard some of my aunts and uncles make when I was growing up. Keeping my rage inside was difficult enough during the public meetings.

I wished I'd remembered Gandhi's example sooner. When violence broke out between Muslims and Hindus on the eve of the partition of India, Gandhi went to the province of Bengal, where the fighting had begun, and spent as much time with those who had committed the violence as with those who were hurt by it. Her served both equally.[10]

We were about three weeks into the Bensonhurst incident when I experienced a new awareness of how important it was to fully embrace those of my own ethnicity in spite of what they were doing and saying. A courageous African-American pastor helped me break through my own shadow.

It was a Tuesday night during our usual evening meeting. The pastor from Brooklyn was sharing an experience that had happened to him on the previous Saturday. He had been chosen to lead the protest march through Bensonhurst that day. Three or four congregations had bused several hundred people in. As folks got off the bus, they prayerfully and peacefully lined up behind him. The marchers had moved about two blocks when several on-lookers began to throw tomatoes and pieces of watermelon at them. Since the minister was right up front, it wasn't long before his crisp, tailored gray suit and white shirt was smattered with red juice. While he was telling the story, I began to think I could not go on listening, it disturbed me so much. All my stereotypes about my own heritage were building up inside.

I forced myself to keep listening. He continued,

When I was hit with the tomatoes, I made the mistake of glancing down at my shirt. Deep humiliation engulfed me and the pain and despair of centuries began to overcome me. I didn't know how I was going to take another step. I looked back and saw the hundreds of faithful followers being humiliated as well. Feeling I was losing courage quickly, I did the only thing I knew to do. I looked up to the heavens for spiritual sustenance. And when I looked up, I saw an angel disguised as an elderly Italian-American woman. She was probably about eighty years old and precariously hanging out her fourth floor tenement window, giving me the peace sign!

At the sight of this woman, the minister's spirit reignited. He pointed upward. The whole group of marchers were now looking upward and walking forward. The old woman had the courage to hold up her hand for several more minutes before she became tired. The pastor finished the march that day and so did the three hundred people behind him.

The pastor is among those who know that there is a rescuer in every group of oppressors. That night when he finished his story and it was time to go to eat, I cautiously crossed over to the other side of the room and went out to dinner with the Italian-American group for the first time since I had been going to Bensonhurst. At the restaurant, we had chianti and pasta and wished for harmony to return to their shattered community.

I'm convinced that we have as much work to do in breaking the cycle of oppression within our own ethnic groups as we have in building bridges to link us with those who are different. I often need to remind myself that not every-one in any one group acts, feels, thinks, and behaves the same when it comes to issues of prejudice. When I need reassurance of this, I remember the precious old woman who transformed a protest march—and my thinking—with one kind move of her arm.

Those of us from dominant groups have an important role to play in the struggle against oppression. To take on this task, it is helpful to learn more about people in our group who have resisted the oppressor role. We all need new heroes and models to convince ourselves that dismantling the "isms" in our society is possible. Not only do our textbooks give minimal mention to slavery in America or the Holocaust in Europe, they also tend to exclude resistance movements of any kind. As an American of part German and part Italian background, I grew up defining myself as an Italian American because of the guilt I felt in being of German ancestry in view of the atrocities committed in Germany during World War II. If I had also learned in school about the town in France, Le Chambon, where three thousand gentiles hid an equal number of Jews, giving up their own beds and risking their lives, then somehow I might have felt differently. Since the release of the film "Schindler's List," I have immersed myself in literature about other rescuers. I am redefining the role I can play in helping to be "part of the solution." People in targeted groups also need to get strength and courage from one another. The challenge is for all of us to empower ourselves to let go of internalized prejudices. As Samuel Betances, a leader in multicultural education, tells us, "We have to help young people reject rejection instead of rejecting themselves."

The Skills of Interrupting Bias and Prejudice

The Reverend Martin Neimoeller gave us this oft-quoted parable in the voice of one who merely stood by:

In Germany they came first for the communists and I didn't speak up because I wasn't a communist. Then they came for the Jews and I didn't speak up because I wasn't a Jew. Then they came for the trade unionists and I didn't speak up because I didn't belong to a union. Then they came for me and there was nobody left to speak up.[11]

In fact, even on an every-day level most of us have a hard time interrupting bias and prejudice. We may try not to participate in discriminatory jokes, slurs, or remarks, but we lack the commitment or the skill to approach such a situation assertively.

We usually have three choices in attempting to interrupt prejudice. We can argue or attack back by saying something like "That was a very racist remark you made," or "I don't believe you just said that, and you're a classroom teacher, too!" Or, out of embarrassment and uncertainty, we may attempt to ignore or gloss over a prejudiced remark. The person making it then has no idea what we are thinking or feeling. We aren't collaborating with prejudice or discrimination, but we aren't really taking a stand either. We respond this way because we are at a loss for what to do.

Finally, and most effectively, we can try to interrupt the remark or action *and* keep the lines of communication open and the relationship intact. As Martin Luther King, Jr., said, "The ultimate measure of a person is not where they stand at times of comfort or convenience, but where they stand at times of challenge and controversy."

Conflict resolution skills are very useful in this context. We can engage a person in a dialogue using active listening, paraphrasing what was said and acknowledging feelings. We can also use I-messages, expressing ourselves with statements that begin with "I feel" rather than "You are." I have ample opportunity to put these skills to work, (once again) especially during taxi rides in New York. I'm often confronted with a driver who makes comments about the driving ability of certain groups of people we'll call so-and-so's. It usually goes like this: "Did you see what that so-and-so just did? They shouldn't be allowed on the road. They must get their driver's license at Woolworth's!" I am now thrust into a situation of choosing a course of action. I could make no response to the driver's statements and hope the conversation shifts to another topic. Not a likely scenario. Given the high stress of the job, venting like this helps. I could decide to confront the situation aggressively and say something like, "You just made an unfair comment about so-and-so's. I don't have to hear this, I'm paying good money for this ride." Most likely I would now be facing a less pleasant trip.

I could try a third approach. "You think that person made that move just because they're from such-and-such a place?" "Yes," the driver says. "Haven't you noticed it's always so-and-so's driving like that?" I might ask, "How long have you been driving a taxi? What's it like? Have you always felt that way about so-and-so's?" With more give and take and a lot of active listening, I might eventually decide to say, "I feel uncomfortable when I hear something about *all* people from one group. There are probably so-and-so's who are good drivers and others who aren't so good. So let's change the subject. How's your day been so far?"

When these situations of prejudice and discrimination arise, I see it as my job to have the courage to engage and "complicate" a person's thinking, to have them consider another perspective. Whenever I do find the courage to face discrimination and bias directly, I never know how many times this person has been confronted about this issue. I don't know if my remark will cause anger, contemplation, or transformation. It is not necessary for me to know; I'm really doing this in large part for my own liberation.

Sometimes it is a little easier to interrupt prejudice when we ourselves have less pain around what is being said because we haven't experienced that particular kind of discrimination. If I were from the group the biased comment was directed at, I might need to approach the situation quite differently. I might not feel safe baring my soul and telling the other person that I am from that group and that I feel hurt by the remark. However, depending on the personal work I've done with my own issues around this difference, saying something might also be empowering, especially if my emotional pain has been processed in safer situations previous to this encounter.

This is why the role of allies is so important. Those of us in dominant groups have the experience of being conditioned to take the oppressor's role.

Yet we can also assume that a targeted person would want us as an ally, that we have every right to be concerned with these issues, and that is in our own best interest to combat prejudice. Thus we may begin to engage the bigoted person on our friend's behalf and become an ally not by obligation but by choice.

William Faulkner put it this way, "Some things you must always be unable to bear. Injustice and outrage and dishonor and shame. No matter how young or how old you have gotten. Not for kudos and not for cash, your picture in the paper nor money in the bank, neither. Just refuse to bear them."

The encouraging thing about becoming an active partner in breaking the cycle of oppression is that if enough of us are out there and engaged in the work, then our positive actions and words will accumulate. Our act of interrupting prejudice may be the one that, after a string of other comments, makes someone see things another way. Jacob Riis, a Holocaust survivor, uses the image of the stonecutter: "When nothing seems to help, I go look at a stonecutter hammering away at a rock perhaps a hundred times without as much as a crack showing in it. Yet at the hundredth and first blow, it will split in two and I know it was not that blow that did it but all that had gone before."

Whether our act of interrupting prejudice is the first or the last before a change occurs in a person, our job is to keep hammering the stone until it breaks.

Diversity and the Conflict Escalator

There are several ways in which issues of diversity can affect the escalation of a conflict.

Even where initially they aren't relevant to the dispute, these issues can be dragged in as ammunition, usually in the form of name-calling. The racial slur or derogatory label then adds another layer to the conflict. It is important to help those involved to separate their feelings from the name-calling. Suppose you overhear Johnny calling Robert a "faggot." You may need to confront the situation directly, explaining that you are aware that Johnny called Robert a name. You may ask whether or not Johnny was angry at Robert, reflecting back his feelings, and assuring him that you want to help settle the dispute but first you need to address the name-calling. Remind him that I-messages might be much more appropriate, that name calling is not an acceptable way of dealing with anger. You may go back to helping with the conflict at hand. It may also be useful to shed light on the history behind the derogatory words used, so that the young people involved have a sense of how serious it is to use such language. One teacher, Lenore Gordon, says, "When I hear a child use the word 'faggot,' I explain that the word means a stick used for kindling a fire. I also explain that gay people used to be burned in medieval times simply for being gay, and that they had to wear a bundle of sticks on their shirts to indicate they were about to be burned. After the discussion that ensues from this revelation, I make it clear that the word is not to be used in my classroom again, and it rarely is."[12]

Slurs usually have a negative history to them. We at RCCP encourage people to make these derogatory words completely unacceptable in our schools and classrooms, even when they are used by members of the targeted group against themselves or others from that group.

Issues of diversity and conflict intersect in another way when cross-cultural misunderstanding and miscommunication occur. The parties involved may not understand each other because they aren't familiar with the nuances of each other's cultures. They then respond, based on erroneous assumptions and on misinterpretations, to the behavior of the other. Sandra, who is an African American, has just become friends with Sung Quat, a Cambodian classmate. As Sandra gets off the bus one morning, she sees Sung Quat across the schoolyard. She shouts and waves to her, but, to her surprise, Sun Quat folds her arms and turns her back. Sandra is hurt, thinking she has been rejected by her new friend. What she doesn't realize is that, in line with her Cambodian culture, Sung Quat feels humiliated by her friend because everyone in the schoolyard turned to look at her.

Conflict and diversity also intersect, of course, when one or both parties act on prejudice against the other—sometimes consciously, sometimes unconsciously. One of my former college students told me of a high school guidance counselor who felt he was being well-meaning in steering her away from college. Maria was told by this counselor that she just wasn't college material. She almost believed him, but she also had a relentless determination to be a teacher and to give back to the neighborhood she had grown up in. Maria has taught for the last ten years in East Harlem. Fortunately, she was able to reject the biased messages she received. But she remembers the conflict she had with her counselor quite vividly.

Healing Together

We can create a future for our children and ourselves in which no individual is automatically advantaged or disadvantaged because of any arbitrary standard, but this will take commitment, know-how, and skill. Dealing with issues of diversity early on and continuing throughout life is important. It is possible to build rather than tear down our social mosaic. We can create safe, equitable, inclusive schools, classrooms, and communities where differences are valued and where the norm is to nonviolently interrupt bias, prejudice, and discrimination.

Opening up these issues without commitment, responsiveness, and follow-through can be counterproductive. There is a deep level of risk and discomfort in breaking the cycle of oppression. Yet we will be richer for it. The quality of all of our lives will be enhanced.

Janet remembers an occasion in which the rewards of teaching the RCCP curriculum became evident during a weekend retreat with thirty-seven eighth-grade mediators. She and her colleagues wanted to provide the kids an opportunity to really get to know one another—to bond—as some of these students never spoke to one another except when they were brought together to mediate a conflict.

That weekend, students and teachers together looked closely at the concept of oppression and talked about groups of privilege and groups of non-privilege. They discussed the "isms"—ageism, sexism, adultism, racism, etc.—and how they play themselves out in our communities, our schools, and our own lives, and the young people began to see how society has actually catered to certain groups.

People of color began opening up and telling their stories. The hurt and pain they had been through because of discrimination became a reality to all students. Many of the white kids were hearing this kind of personal testimony for the first time. Everyone sat in silence, listening wide-eyed and in disbelief at the painful experiences of some of the students. At one point, Matthew, a tall, red-haired, seventh-grader, stood up and said to Stan, an African-American mediator who had shared his story of discrimination, "I feel terrible that people who look like me have done this to you. Slavery wasn't enough, but now you're still dealing with this every day. I feel responsible for this. I feel terrible." Stan stood up, walked over to Matthew, embraced him, and said, "Matthew, it isn't your fault. You're not responsible for what's happened in my past. But I need you to take a stand and help others realize what it's like for me and other people of color who are still dealing with this stuff every day." At that point, several kids spontaneously stood up and walked over to hug one another. Before you knew it, everyone was walking around crying and hugging each other. There wasn't a dry eye in the room.

A great healing took place that day. Thirty-seven mediators and several teachers experienced the power of compassion and the healing that takes place when we are able to confront our prejudices, listen to each other's stories, and take responsibility to stop the injustices. The bond that was established between these young people was strong, genuine, and long-lasting.

Everyone is hurt personally by oppression, because it gets in the way of genuine, trusting relationships with others. An Australian Aborigine woman once said, "If you have come to help me, you are wasting your time. But if you have come because your liberation is bound up with mine, then let us work together." All forms of oppression are linked by the common bond of the abuse of power over others. Breaking this cycle requires thinking in a new way. It also includes a meshing of the mind and the heart, a deep commitment, and the courage to take a stand. This work will take our whole lives. The Talmud reassures us: "It is not for you to complete the task but neither are you free to abstain from it."

Guidelines for Challenging Racism and Other Forms of Oppression

This list is based on guidelines written by Patti DeRosa, of the organization Cross-Cultural Consultation.[13]

[1]   *Challenge discriminatory attitudes and behavior!* Ignoring the issues will not make them go away and silence can send the message that you are in agreement with such attitudes and behaviors. Make it clear that you will not tolerate racial, ethnic, religious, or sexual jokes or slurs, or any actions that demean any person or group. Your intervention may not always take place at the exact time or place of the incident, but the issue should be addressed promptly.

[2]   *Expect tension and conflict and learn to manage it.* Sensitive and deep-seated issues are unlikely to change without some struggle and in many situations conflict is unavoidable. Face your fears and discomforts and remember that tension and conflict can be positive forces that foster growth.

[3]   *Be aware of your own attitudes, stereotypes, and expectations*, and be open to discovering the limitations they place on your perspective. None of us remain untouched by the discriminatory messages in our society. If you aren't sure how to handle a situation, say so and seek the information or help that you need. Practice not getting defensive when discriminatory attitudes or behaviors are pointed out to you.

[4]   *Actively listen to and learn from others' experiences.* Don't minimize, trivialize, or deny people's concerns; make an effort to see situations through their eyes.

[5] *Use language and behavior that is non-biased and inclusive* of all people regardless of race, ethnicity, sex, disabilities, sexual orientation, class, age, or religion.

[6] *Provide accurate information* to challenge stereotypes and biases. Take responsibility for educating yourself about your own and other people's cultures. Do not expect people from different backgrounds to automatically educate you about their culture, or history, or to explain racism or sexism to you. People are more willing to share when you take an active role and the learning is mutual.

[7] *Acknowledge diversity and avoid stereotypical thinking.* Don't ignore or pretend not to see differences. Acknowledging differences is not the problem, but stereotypes and negative judgments about differences are always hurtful because they generalize, limit, and deny people's full humanity.

[8] *Be aware of your own hesitancy to intervene* in these kinds of situations. Confront your own fears about interrupting discrimination, set your priorities, and take action.

[9] *Project a feeling of understanding, love, and support* when confronting individuals about discriminatory behavior. Be nonjudgmental but know the bottom line: issues of human dignity, justice, and safety are nonnegotiable.

[10] *Establish standards of responsibility and behavior* and hold yourself and others accountable. Demonstrate your personal and organizational commitment in practices, policies, and procedures, both formal and informal. Maintain high expectations for all people.

[11] *Be a role model* and be willing to take the risks that leadership demands.

[12] *Work collectively with others. Organize and support efforts* that combat prejudice and oppression in all its forms. Social change is a long-term struggle.

< III >

NEW
ROLES
AND
NEW
TASKS

[**5**]

I've come to the frightening conclusion that I am the decisive element
in the classroom. It is my personal approach that creates the climate. It is
my daily mood that makes the weather. As a teacher, I possess a tremendous
power to make a child's life miserable or joyous. I can be a tool of torture
or an instrument of inspiration. I can humiliate or honor, hurt or heal.
In all situations, it is my response that decides whether a crisis will be escalated
or de-escalated and a child humanized or de-humanized.

- Haim Ginott -
Teacher and Child

When I first started teaching almost twenty years ago, the problems of
young people were vastly different. Children seemed to have more hope for
the future. Too many of our children have lost hope because so many
people around them have lost hope. I feel like it's one of my responsibilities
to give them that sense of hope they lack.

- Mildred -
Fifth-grade teacher,
New Orleans, Louisiana

THIS IS A CHAPTER FOR and about teachers. It describes teachers committed to the principles of the peaceable classroom—how we work and why
we do what we do.

Because teachers must serve as true models for the qualities and skills
they are helping young people develop in the peaceable classroom, changes

in self and in teaching style have to occur. With these changes come many special challenges, challenges that extend beyond the already great demands that the teaching profession brings with it. There are five in particular that teachers must continually address: adapting to the role of facilitator, the shift of power in peaceable classrooms, the need for personal transformation, the practical issue of instructional time, and the resistance to change.

The Teacher as Facilitator

In contrast to what we think of as more traditional models of teaching such as lecturing or delivering information, the peaceable classroom approach (like other educational reform efforts past and present) emphasizes the teacher as facilitator. We assist kids in coming to their own insights and resolutions. We help young people explore their highest potential: to think critically and produce solutions to a wide variety of problems, solutions that they themselves are satisfied with. This comes naturally with the work we do in emotional learning, but it extends to other parts of the curriculum as well.

While a lecture is certainly appropriate at times, it isn't the only means of disseminating knowledge. Matt, an eighth-grade mediator from California said of his teacher, "I don't know how to describe Mrs. A since she began teaching those RCCP lessons. She's different. . . . She asks us what we think all the time and really wants to hear what we have to say. She isn't like a teacher anymore."

The peaceable classroom teacher consistently provides opportunities for students to learn in the way they learn best, so we teach to a variety of learning styles. We create learning experiences in which young people become actively involved, including traditional pencil-and-paper work, but also including methods that ensure retention in different ways, from combining the work with art, music, drama, and dance to asking students to teach each other. Teachers as facilitators revel in fostering young peoples' creativity and individuality. Affective strategies like the use of role-playing and brainstorming throughout the day ensure that young people are really "connecting" to what they are learning. And when conflict arises, teachers continue in their facilitator role by presenting negotiation or mediation as a vehicle of resolution rather than by arbitrating decisions.

This role of teacher as facilitator is new for some teachers, but once they begin to take it on, they are pleased with the results. They encourage students to work together to complete their work as much as possible. As eighth-grade teacher and RCCP trainer Jane says, "One of the skills young people need to know is how to work well with others, to work well in a group. You can be as bright as can be, but today people even build cars in a team."[1]

Shifting Power

In order to be a facilitator, a teacher has to be able to "let go" of much of the control that has traditionally been a part of the classroom teacher's role. This brings with it a shift in power, a sharing of power. But this is a shift that need not entail a loss in respect, student productivity, or cooperative behaviors.

While discipline guidelines are defined and clearly enforced, young people are now encouraged to participate in more decisions around conflict, and to resolve conflicts independently of teachers. Basma, special education teacher from New Orleans, shared these feelings about the work:

RCCP makes the kids have a happy circle of good thoughts, good feelings and an outcome of good actions. It helps them see that I'm not always the big, bad wolf. Solutions to problems are shared among the children and it brings them closer together. It takes some of the work off of the teacher and puts some of the work and responsibility on the children. It makes them feel responsible.

In many classrooms young people even participate in the making of rules. This move from a more authoritarian teaching style to a more democratic approach feels strange at first for some teachers. Mariana came from a very traditional Cuban background:

When I first started teaching, I was a lecturer, an "enlightener." Conversations were controlled. I trusted the fact that my students could learn but I had a traditional perspective. Gradually, however, I began to look at them as sources of information. My evolution was to take myself out more, giving up power.

Mildred explains the contrast between learning to be a facilitator and traditional teacher education:

It takes special effort because you've gotten used to teaching a certain way for a long time and this is another way of teaching, you know, it really is; unless you've been doing it that way all the time. We usually teach basically the way we are taught. I grew up learning, "You be quiet because I'm telling you to be quiet." And that's how it was. And most of my teaching has also modeled that. My class would be the most quiet class because that's what I expected. I'm beginning to tolerate a little more noise. If you want kids to work cooperatively, you have to have some noise. If you're telling kids to speak their mind, you can't expect them to be quiet all day! The transition has been hard for me.

For some teachers the changes are less drastic. Ilene, a sixth-grade teacher from New York City, told us that learning these skills helped her reduce conflict in her classroom: "The language we use made it easier to deal with problems. It gave me a procedure, words to say. I always felt I was diplomatic, but this gave me some real guidelines."

Elaine, an eighth-grade teacher from Vista, California, explains, "I used to think I was a great teacher. But I think I was much more of a disciplinarian. If students can't get along with the person sitting next to them, they're probably not going to learn very much about the subject being taught."[2]

Power struggles escalate when students and teachers hold oppositional goals, and as teachers we sometimes get pulled into power struggles because we have lots of competing concerns to deal with at the same time. We want to de-escalate a confrontation; we want the inappropriate behavior to stop; we want children to know when they have been disrespectful; we want to show that we are in control; we want children to do the task; we want to identify the problem for the student; we want to continue the lesson without losing a lot of time.[3] The key is to decide on which concerns to address "in the moment" of a power struggle and which to address later, perhaps individually with the student. RCCP teachers learn to avoid and defuse confrontations. In the long run, teachers don't win anything from power struggles. Almost always, digging out of them is frustrating, painful, and humiliating and generally gets no point across.

William Kreidler reminds us to reflect before intervening in a conflict: to consider the urgency of the conflict, how much learning is likely to come out of dealing with it, and whether it is better to deal with it publicly or privately. It's important to remember to let a young person save face. Power struggles will only intensify if there's no way for students to back out of a situation while still feeling that their integrity has been maintained. Sometimes a sense of humor can be most helpful in defusing a conflict, especially with older students, allowing them to back out in an acceptable, easy way.

One result of shifting some power to young people is a building of community. Values and attitudes that are acceptable to both teachers and students are established together. There is an agreement about consequences, rights, and responsibilities. Logical consequences are emphasized rather than punitive ones. There are many opportunities for students to make choices and to feel powerful in positive ways. Procedures are established for how students and teachers will work together. Young people know that what they have to say matters and there are lots of opportunities for them to work with partners and groups to learn, reflect, assess, give feedback, and solve problems.

Personal Transformation

One of the biggest challenges in moving toward a classroom capable of transforming kids is that as teachers we have to transform ourselves before we can expect to see changes in young people. In order to model the behavior of the peaceable classroom we must first come to terms with our own approaches to conflict, our own biases. For instance, in order to help young people confront their prejudices, we have to confront our own. Only then can we help young people understand such deep concepts as what racism is and how our society has oppressed people of color and others because of their differences.

In RCCP our introductory training gets at the heart of these issues. Teachers come together for several days and are given the time to be self-reflective. We think about our own feelings about conflict and examine our conflict styles. We talk with one another about our ethnic backgrounds and about what is wonderful and what is difficult about these histories. Often teachers find that the skills they learn in training are useful to them both professionally and personally.

But change is not an easy process, and change in self is perhaps the most difficult of all. Ilene spoke about what the process of inner change was like for her and how difficult it is for many teachers:

I just think that teachers have been teaching for many years and we have a particular philosophy about teaching—it's hard to give it up. It's like being in a marriage where you believe that it should be working or it used to be working—and things changed and it's not working and you still refuse to change. That's the same in a school—you have teachers who don't flow well with change, or don't even realize that there's a need for change. Something doesn't feel right, but they can't express it and they don't know what to do with it. So they'd rather stay just where they are.

Not too long ago, a principal was trying to recruit a new group of her teachers into RCCP introductory training and realized that it might be a good idea if one of the veterans of the program shared a little bit about the impact the training had had on her school life and her life as a whole. During the faculty meeting, the principal said, "Mrs. Baker, maybe you could give us a little idea of what benefits you received from being a part of the RCCP last year?" Much to the staff's and the principal's surprise, Mrs. Baker responded, "Oh, it's very simple—it saved my marriage. The kids benefited a lot too." (Needless to say, new teacher recruits were forthcoming!)

More and more we are finding that growth at a personal level has been one of the deepest and most unexpected benefits of RCCP. Teachers tell us that there's a transformation that takes place for them when they embrace this work. As they look within themselves, they realize that the way they've dealt with conflict in the past is not productive. They see alternative ways to manage their own responses. With practice of the skills they learn, and a deeper wisdom derived from self-reflection, they come to have more positive interactions with the people they care so much about, in both their private and work worlds. As a result, their commitment to the work deepens, and as this commitment grows they start to model the behaviors they want to see in their students.

A 1990 study of RCCP teachers in the New York City public schools showed that

> 83.9 percent said that their listening skills had improved;
> 89.3 percent said that their understanding of individual children's needs and concerns improved;
> 87.7 percent said that their own use of specific conflict resolution techniques had increased in the classroom;

92.9 percent said that their attitudes about conflict and conflict resolution were more positive;

78.6 percent said that their sensitivity to children whose backgrounds were different from their own increased;

89.3 percent said that they were more willing to let young people take responsibility for solving their own conflicts.[4]

Cindy put it this way, "There's a different way I look at how I deal with kids who get into fights, how I encourage kids to interact with each other, how I interact with students. I watch kids and don't allow disagreements to escalate into fights; I defuse them earlier on."

Faydra, a second-grade teacher from New Orleans, shared that peaceable classroom skills have helped her in dealing with her own frustration level. She's able to step back and look at situations from another perspective; to listen when it feels difficult to do so. Faydra told us of a time when a change in the way she responded proved to be crucial in the life of one of her students:

A week ago, there was a fight in the neighborhood and a mother of one of our students was hospitalized. I didn't know this had happened. I just knew the student's behavior had changed from what was normal for him—calm, basically obedient, a happy little kid. Monday came and he was terrible. He was hitting, biting, fighting. I was upset with him and I said, "Come here!" But rather than fuss at him, I hugged him. I said "You need some lovin' today. Let me give you a hug and sweeten you up." Thirty minutes later, I found out what had happened. And I think that without RCCP, I probably wouldn't have given him the benefit of the doubt. It would have been, "Go to the office. Get out of here. You're disrupting everything." This would have just added to his problems.

In supporting teachers, we need to be sensitive as they begin to recognize what they already feel strong and good about and what they want to change.

As teachers attempt to teach children the new skills, they are often still practicing them themselves. Linda and I have been genuinely moved by the level of honesty on the part of teachers who have shared this growth process with us.

Tom, an eighth-grade teacher, struggled regularly with teaching his students about not using put-downs even though his dry, witty sense of humor led him to use put-downs repeatedly. One day one brave student said to him, "You teach us not to put each other down, but you're always putting us down." Tom realized that he had to work hard to change an old pattern if he expected his students to respect one another. Joel, a sixth-grade teacher from New York, shared his difficulty with modeling these new behaviors and accepting criticism from his students:

I remember doing an active listening lesson and one of my students asked, "What about for teachers? . . . Well, you, Mr. Brooks, I came to your desk last week and you said, 'Yes, yes,' but you didn't even look at me." And that's what I was doing, and the kid pointed it out to me, the teacher. I'm a little hurt by things like that in the beginning, but I know I'll learn from it.

Lucrecia, former third-grade teacher now a principal, from Anchorage, says she wasn't aware of "the emotional level" that this work would evoke in her: "It was a whole different philosophy for me. The way I looked at the world. Children taking responsibility for themselves; that was very different for me." She spoke about the positive reactions she had when she moved to Anchorage from Mississippi:

I was coming from an environment where everybody had been basically black or white but nobody talked about racial issues. The school I entered was a very multicultural setting. For the first time in my life, I was hearing people say, in a school setting, "It's okay to be different. You are all good people. You all have something to contribute." And I was exposed to a rain-bow coalition of children who were learning how to get along. It was just wonderful.

The Issue of Instructional Time

As we argue that educators must find time to teach conflict resolution and bias awareness, we face a skeptical audience. There isn't a teacher in the profession who will say that there is ever enough time to teach everything in all the curricula he or she is supposed to cover. The frustration level is high.

Every new school year there is something else that teachers are told they need to add to their repertoire. In fact, in no other profession do people continuously take as many classes, workshops, and "in-services" in order to learn new skills and subjects. Television, computers, CD ROM, the Internet—more and more technological developments are continuously exposing young people to a greater and greater amount of knowledge. So teachers have to employ a variety of techniques, from computer training to second language strategies, to help young people gain access to all of this information and to ensure equality.

How can the new lessons of emotional and social learning fit into this schedule? Teachers in peaceable classrooms teach RCCP despite the time crunches. They find ways to make it happen. Basma explains, "It doesn't have to be a 9:00 A.M. thing every day. You can just say, 'Okay, let's do this.' I used to make an RCCP time in the beginning, but now that the kids are aware of it I use it throughout the day."

As teachers, we all have our areas of strengths and weaknesses, our likes and dislikes, all of which affect how we teach and what we emphasize in the curriculum. Teachers trained in the skills of the peaceable classroom learn to weave them into the fabric of everything else they do.

There are essentially four ways to teach these skills, which we call direct teaching, teachable moments, infusion, and modeling.

In *direct teaching*, teachers use the prescribed lessons and units to teach skills in conflict resolution and intergroup relations. Students learn how to think and talk about conflict and diversity issues in new and constructive ways. Students are given a chance to practice new skills based on the themes of the peaceable classroom. Direct teaching is often used in the beginning of the year, to establish a common vocabulary. Kids learn that put-downs are not okay, that they are striving to reach win-win solutions, that paraphrasing is important for active listening, and that negotiation and mediation are the way conflicts are best resolved. Direct lessons are presented in blocks of time called workshops, usually about twenty minutes to an hour in length, depending on the age group.[5] They are interactive, provide plenty of time for practice of skills and discussion, and allow students to evaluate their own learning experience as well as the content of the lesson. Workshops may happen once or twice a week over a period of several weeks throughout the year.

The second method often used in our program is that of *teachable moments*: teachers pointing out incidents in life that reflect concepts being taught in the classroom. Events that occur in the larger community, neighborhood, or other public arenas can provide for powerful teachable moments, and when a conflict arises in the daily life of the classroom or the school, this is a prime opportunity for involving kids in thinking of creative solutions.

Diane Levin, in her book *Teaching Young Children in Violent Times*, tells about young Ken, who during class freely brought up his visit to his mother in the hospital after she had been shot.[6] Since the other children all lived near Ken, they'd all known about the shooting, so the teacher decided to let the outside come in and began to help them continue the discussion. They learned that Ken's mother was out of danger, which was reassuring to his classmates. The teacher ended the discussion by asking the children if there was anything they could do for Ken and his mom. Much to Ken's delight, they decided to make get-well cards for her. In spite of their fears, having a safe place to talk enabled them to feel that their actions could make a small difference in the world outside the classroom. There are countless opportunities such as this one to incorporate such learnings into kids' everyday lives.

The third way we often integrate our program into the classroom is by infusing the concepts learned in RCCP into other curricula, from social studies and reading and language arts to math, science, and health. *Infusion* saves teachers time because both conflict resolution and required content are taught at the same time. It also gives young people the opportunity to apply their skills and ideas to real-life situations. Most teachers find it natural to infuse the skills learned in RCCP directly into their instruction. Some do this in their classroom management as well, by reinforcing students when they spontaneously use conflict resolution skills. One could also start with RCCP activities and add in the academic content. For example, I might want to focus on having kids learn to listen better to each other, so I might have them work in cooperative groups to create group stories. My lesson objective would be twofold: to have the young people create a story about a topic we had been studying and to have them evaluate their own listening and collaboration skills.

After directly teaching the themes of the peaceable classroom model, most teachers teach their regular curriculum and infuse these themes into the lessons. In literature and language arts classes, for example, students read the required literature and then discuss and write about the areas of conflict in the books. A teacher named Joel told us about reading *The Diary of Anne Frank* with his sixth-graders. He found that they were very interested in the relationship between Anne and her mother, a typical teenager-parent relationship. The students had personalized the book, but they had a rather narrow view of it, so Joel asked, "How many of you have had a problem like this with your parents?" He encouraged his students to share their own experiences and then to examine other points of view. "I asked them to put themselves in the father's shoes, the mother's shoes. I got them to take another perspective."

In science, a student studying the properties of water might be asked, for example, "How is water like conflict?" He or she might answer, "Conflict is like water because it isn't always clear. It's sometimes murky . . ." Many teachers choose units of the week or month that are related to the themes of our program. These could include: peacemaking, violence, diversity, working together, building community. With these units as the link for integrating the entire curriculum, academic subjects and peaceable classroom themes flow together naturally.

Modeling, an essential approach to teaching this work, is perhaps the most important of all. Unless teachers can truly model these ways of being throughout the day, students will neither believe in them nor want to learn them. We've talked a lot about modeling in Chapter 2, and throughout this chapter, as we've shared teachers' experiences and talked about the kinds of changes that they face in their efforts to create peaceable classrooms.

Resistance to Change

The challenges we've just described—teacher as facilitator, the shift in power in the classroom, personal transformation, and instructional time—aren't the only ones we face. Often, schools are hesitant to try programs like ours because they resist change itself. This may happen for many reasons.

Teachers are often so overwhelmed by the demands already placed upon them that they feel they can't possibly take on one more new thing. The stresses that accompany teaching as a profession are exhausting, as we've noted. In fact, it is reported that nationally 40 to 50 percent of teachers leave the profession in the first years of teaching.[7]

Some teachers are resistant to this new vision of education because they don't sense the emotional pain and difficulties that young people are experiencing. If you don't experience a lot of serious problems in your own classroom you may think, "It's happening somewhere else. It's not my concern." Teachers have enough to do to juggle all of the academic content they are expected to teach, so if their students are well-behaved they may see no need for addressing these skill areas.

Other teachers do see the need to address social and emotional concerns but are resistant to teaching them. They feel that no matter how hard they try, they just can't "fix" all the children in all the ways they need to be fixed—emotionally, intellectually, socially. They may attempt to ignore these concerns. They avoid opportunities for kids to talk about issues like the ones we raise. They say to themselves, "I've got to teach. I can't look at all of the pain of these young people. I don't want to make exceptions for these children, change my expectations of them. I want them to learn." Additionally, many teachers don't know how to approach emotionally charged issues. They aren't comfortable because they don't feel they have the skills to help young people share and disclose in appropriate ways.

Still others say openly, "Nothing I can do is going to change kids' lives. I have to prepare them for junior high, high school, or college. I have too much to teach now. Let somebody else deal with the rest of it." And often they are supported by members of the public who feel that the responsibility to teach young people social and emotional skills belongs in the home alone.

The resistances teachers struggle with are very real. We need to listen to their concerns and support them wherever and whenever possible. If we want teachers to be there for kids, we have to be there for teachers too. The key is providing teachers an opportunity to grow professionally and personally. And when teachers are appreciated and nourished they are willing to give even more. Teachers leave our training feeling invigorated and supported by the fact that others among them experience similar struggles and needs. They feel a sense of emotional security, a sense of connectedness to the group. As Basma (whom we've quoted before) says, "Our training was great because we were all trained together, we all cried together. We realized a lot of things about ourselves that we may not have wanted to admit or that we may not have realized—good and bad. The training brought us closer together." And when training is over, support can't stop there. We provide teachers with additional assistance to ensure that they are comfortable and able to add these new skills into their repertoire.

Staff Development: A Crucial Support for Teachers

Although teachers report that our four-day introductory training is very helpful, development of any skill in a training context doesn't necessarily

NEW ROLES AND NEW TASKS

ensure that this skill can be transferred into a teacher's active repertoire. A unique part of our model is the extensive follow-up support we give to teachers who have attended this training in RCCP. When a coaching component is added, where opportunities to experience demonstration lessons and practice with feedback are offered, teachers get a clear sense of what it takes to really apply these new strategies competently. Bruce Joyce and Beverly Showers, who have looked at the coaching of teaching extensively, tell us that "the attainment of competence requires numerous practice sessions—from 10 to 15 times before a high level of skill becomes evident."[8]

Educators for Social Responsibility Metro, in conjunction with the New York City Board of Education, were actively involved in fine-tuning the staff development part of our model. Every teacher in New York City who has attended an RCCP introductory training receives five to ten visits to their classroom from a staff developer, an educator who has deeply integrated the principles of our work into his or her personal and professional life. Beyond their expertise in teaching RCCP concepts, staff developers receive extensive training in coaching strategies and conferencing techniques, so that they can ascertain what will be helpful to the classroom teacher and provide the needed one-on-one support. During these regularly scheduled visits, teachers have opportunities to see lessons modeled, to teach lessons and receive feedback, to discuss strategies for effective classroom management, and to set goals for incorporating the themes of the peaceable classroom into all that they already do.

In the 1990 study of the New York City program referred to earlier, 51 percent of the teachers reported devoting approximately four to five classroom periods per month to teaching the RCCP curriculum. Twenty-one percent of the teachers reported teaching as many as six to eight lessons per month. The study also reported that in addition to the training, teachers found the staff development phase to be the single most useful part of the entire program.[9]

We have found that follow-up support is essential in making this work a regular part of the curriculum. Too often, teachers are handed a manual and are expected to incorporate new and innovative curriculum into their classroom with little or no assistance. However useful, such guides often end up on a shelf, even in cases where the training was exciting and beneficial. Extensive follow-up support helps teachers take ownership of the material. When we tell teachers that we will visit their classrooms several times, they are surprised—this rarely happens with new programs.

In school districts across the nation, we are implementing variations of this staff development component, realizing the successes we have had with it in New York City. School districts are finding ways to create partnership models in which this process can use experienced RCCP teachers to provide support to their colleagues.

What Teachers Say

One very practical but very real benefit of the peaceable classroom model is a reduction in unproductive conflict within schools, especially conflict that leads to violence. Students themselves become more aware of when a conflict is escalating and learn that they have the ability to intervene early on. In the 1990 evaluation of RCCP, teachers reported moderate to a great deal of attitudinal change in students with respect to conflict. Of the teachers who responded,

> 70.9 percent indicated there was less physical violence in their classroom;
>
> 66.7 percent indicated that there was less name-calling and fewer verbal put-downs;
>
> 63.0 percent indicated there was an increased use of supportive comments by students;
>
> 69.1 percent indicated there was a willingness to cooperate on the part of their students;
>
> 77.8 percent said students exhibited more caring behavior;
>
> 71.5 percent said that students exhibited increased skill in understanding other points of view.[10]

But statistics can't capture the experience. Faydra said, "Kids are communicating more. Even though a lot of them don't have the words to express everything they feel, and even though they sometimes yell when they say it; they are saying how they feel versus just shouting or throwing something or hitting someone." Sheila continued, "I heard a student tell another student she would not talk to her friend until she cooled off. She said, 'I'm too angry to talk right now.' And this came from a girl who frequently shoots her mouth off in an instant."

Mariana remembered the day she realized that her efforts to teach these skills in a New York City classroom were worth the pain:

I had this boy Luis, who was constantly putting down kids and constantly being put down. This kid made a peace pledge: "I'm not going to fight." One day there was a meeting after lunch. Luis was fighting with these other kids and we were exploring the issues when all of a sudden a girl said to Luis, "But you signed the peace pledge." They all picked up on it. Everything I had been doing suddenly pulled together. Luis's face dropped and he said, "Oh my God, you're right." Young people begin to hold each other accountable for their behavior.

Basma, from New Orleans, shared what was for her a powerful reminder of the strength of her own work:

One of my students had a confrontation with another kid yesterday. And this morning I was speaking to the child and I said, "You know I think I'm going to have to slack up on allowing you to do errands until you exercise your behavior in a positive way." And another little girl nearby said, "Yeah, you've got to use your RCCP." She said, "See, this is RCCP. And look over here, girl," and she pointed to my board which has slogans that say, "You have choices." "You are valuable." "Respect others." I was amazed!

When conflict is reduced and diversity is valued, teachers can do what they are best at—teach. If we can develop the various skills of the peaceable classroom early on, conflicts that arise don't disrupt the regular routine of the classroom. Classes are more productive and kids learn more. Kathy, a seventh-grade teacher from Vista, California, says that she likes to begin her year with a solid two weeks or so of RCCP: "It sets the tone, helps the kids get to know each other." We talk a lot about what's acceptable behavior and what is not."

Joan, a middle school bilingual teacher, described what teaching these lessons has been like for her: "It creates another dimension with kids. They say things they might not have said to anyone. The climate in the room changes. They become more mature." And when we can teach better, we enjoy teaching more. When the level of conflict in the classroom is reduced, teachers can enjoy their interactions with their students.

Patty, a third-grade teacher, told us,

When I first heard Linda speak seven years ago she said, "The gangs are on their way to Anchorage. It's only a matter of time." Not here, I thought. Since then, numerous gang-related murders have occurred. . . . My task as a teacher has changed. I can no longer just teach basic subjects. I must teach . . . peace lessons. My classroom management is based [on these] concepts. I feel fortunate to have a classroom of young people who are open, honest, and respect each other's diversity and opinions.

The peaceable classroom teacher is an educator with a wide sense of mission. As Mildred, a New Orleans teacher, put it,

Bottom line, yes—academics are fine. We know you've got to keep the test scores up. But as far as I can see, the bottom line is, can we prepare them for "out there"? You can look out the front door of their school and you can see

the prostitutes walking up and down the street; you can see the pimps sitting on the benches; you can see the motorcycle gang, the teenagers with gang colors on. It's about preparing my students to deal with that too.

The Call to Service

Linda and I have talked extensively about the incredible teachers we have met since we've been involved in this work, teachers whose commitment to young people extends far beyond the classroom. They know that school is where many children will receive much of the nurturing they need, along with the chance to develop the skills they will need to grow into strong, emotionally and socially responsible adults.

We need to realize how so much of what we do can change a young person's life; even when we don't know it. Ram Dass and Paul Gorman wrote extensively and beautifully about service and the importance of helping one another in their book *How Can I Help?*[11] They say, "And finally, what of those moments when we question whether we've anything useful for others? What do we really have to offer, what do we really have to give? Everything, it turns out. Everything."

[**6**]

MEDIATION IN THE SCHOOLS

MYRTLE BANKS ELEMENTARY SCHOOL, New Orleans, Louisiana, November 1993.

The two sixth-grade mediators in blue T-shirts attentively watched over the playground. They saw the push from a distance. Quickly the onlookers dispersed, leaving just four students to resolve the conflict, with a parent coach nearby.

One small girl, about eight years old, was pretty mad; her lips scrunched up to meet her nose in an angry frown. Arms folded on top of one another, her body angular, she tapped her foot and shook her head back and forth. "So why did you say that then?" she yelled, almost as if not really wanting an answer, but wanting to be heard. The other girl seemed more scared than angry. She tried to reply, "I never did say that," but her words were falling on ears that weren't ready to listen.

The mediators, a boy and a girl, reviewed the rules with the two girls. "No interrupting, no name-calling, agree to solve the problem—can you agree to that?" one asked. He waited patiently until the first girl responded, somewhat pompously, "Yeah, 'cause I have a lot to say to her." The other mediator posed the same question to the other child. With eyes downcast, she nodded her head, indicating yes. Then the mediators began their line of questioning.

The boy mediator asked the first child, the angry one, "So tell me what happened." On cue, the little girl explained, "Well, she called my sister a name yesterday when she was over by the tree with April. I know she did, because April told me, and I won't have anybody talking about my sister. I won't take it." The mediator listened intently, eyes focused on the speaker. When the child was finished, he repeated what he had heard. "So yesterday Jody called your sister a name, when she was by the tree with April. You know this is true because April told you. And you don't like anybody calling your sister a name—is that right, Carrie? "Yeah," Carrie said, still a little angry. "That's right."

The tension eased as she unfolded her arms and turned to listen to her opponent's explanation. The girl mediator asked the second girl the same question. Jody began, "I didn't call her no name. April just said I did because she doesn't want me to be friends with her. She always gets me in trouble. I wasn't even over by the tree yesterday when she said I said this about her sister. And why would I say something about her sister?—she's always been nice to me. Next thing I know, she came over and pushed me."

The four kids talked for about ten minutes before the girl who was mediating asked, "So what can you do here and now to solve this problem?"

"Well, I guess I could talk to her next time before jumping to conclusions," Carrie offered.

"And I guess I need to be careful how I say things so they aren't misunderstood," Jody replied.

By now the tension had left the air. Carrie was swaying her hips, anxious to rejoin her friends in lunchtime play. Jody seemed relieved. With a glance towards each other, the mediators congratulated them. The two girls smiled and hurried off to their playmates.[1]

As an observer that day, I [Janet] felt as if I had been privy to a special event—what could have easily resulted in a bloody nose was now a conflict resolved and a friendship restored.

Peer mediation became an integral component of RCCP's work nine years ago. One of our first schools was P.S. 15, now the Patrick Daly Elementary School in Red Hook, Brooklyn. Before we began there, Tom Roderick of

ESR Metro visited the school playground with Linda at lunchtime one day to watch young people's interactions. To their amazement, they clocked eleven physical fights in a period of only five minutes. Today, a visitor to this school would have an entirely different experience. While the sources of conflict among the children remain much the same, the ways in which they handle them have drastically changed. Now, all students learn mediation techniques in their classrooms, and children look to mediation as a way to get their needs met and understood. It would be rare to see a physical fight erupt.

Although peer mediation can become an integral part of any conflict resolution effort at a school, it is not a panacea for ridding a school of all violence. In fact, schools without a solid curriculum component in conflict resolution often lack a firm foundation to support peer mediation. We believe that peer mediation should exist not as a solitary entity, but as an integral and critical part of a total school conflict resolution program that affords *everyone*, not just a select few mediators, the opportunity to develop conflict resolution skills. The reason we initiate mediation programs only in schools that have been regularly teaching the RCCP curriculum in their classrooms is to ensure greater success and to create a more widespread acceptance of the skills and culture of nonviolence. We began the peer mediation component of our work nine years ago; all of our peer mediation programs are still in operation.

While formal research is still being compiled about the effectiveness of peer mediation programs, teachers, administrators, and students repeatedly say they experience a definite positive difference since peer mediation started at their schools, particularly in decreased suspensions for physical or verbal violence. Basma said, "Before, when there was a fight, everybody was running to see it. Now they call a mediator." Mildred, a teacher in the same school, reported, "I have seen fights drop fifty percent. It gives the kids a different way of handling their problems. The mediators here now are helping the kids to work out their problems." In New York, Roberta, a principal, said, "I find much less of a call for discipline this year. There's no discipline crisis anymore." The 1990 evaluation of RCCP's mediation component, which surveyed teachers and student mediators in five RCCP schools in New York City, supports these statements.[2]

What is it about peer mediation programs that keeps them in demand in schools throughout our country? In this chapter we explore how school communities benefit from such programs. In the next chapter we let kids describe their own experiences.

Creating a Culture of Nonviolence

Mediation benefits schools by magnifying and extending the efforts of teachers teaching the curriculum in their classrooms and by helping to establish a schoolwide culture of nonviolence. Conflict resolution lessons in the classroom and mediation programs are mutually reinforcing. Peer mediation provides a practical model of conflict resolution skills at work in the world. Children learning about conflict resolution in class look up to mediators and aspire to the role themselves. Even older students respect them and appreciate that the work they do makes the school better. It becomes *cool* for kids to be helping each other. Peer mediation, then, can be a process that "pulls it all together," supporting and validating critical lessons from the classroom.

When a program first begins, the school mediation coordinator, often a teacher, counselor, or administrator, publicizes the process and encourages students to use it. In the elementary school this usually happens on the playground at lunchtime. At the secondary level, kids fill out mediation request slips through their counselors' or an assistant principal's office. Teachers begin to encourage students to resolve their conflicts through peer mediation by talking about the process in their classrooms and teaching the basic skills to their students. When they see problems escalating, they suggest mediation. This helps build the schoolwide support needed for the program. Kids watch carefully how teachers model that which they believe in. When teachers talk about mediation and use these skills themselves, students know this is important. Then they begin requesting mediations of their own accord.

An effective peer mediation program becomes a vehicle for establishing norms about how conflict is to be resolved. It enhances the culture of nonviolence and creates a more peaceful school climate. First of all, and most importantly, there are fewer fights and suspensions for fighting, because mediation provides a mechanism for de-escalating aggressive behavior.

At a Manhattan high school, Yvette broke up with Johnny. Sandra started going out with Johnny, and a friend told Yvette that Johnny and Sandra were saying bad things about her. Soon there were looks, whispers, and rumors. When Yvette showed up at Sandra's apartment building one Saturday with a knife and several friends to back her up, it was clear that the situation had gotten out of control. On Monday, when the girls came to school, stories of the incident spread quickly, reaching some of the school's trained peer mediators. Yvette and Sandra agreed to mediation. In a two-hour session, the girls worked through their problem, which they discovered had much of its source in misunderstandings deliberately sown by a mutual "friend."

When two angry students come to a mediation, the neutral third party, a peer who is not part of the school's adult power structure, sets the rules. Mediators ask the disputants to agree to solve the problem, not to interrupt, not to call each other names or use put-downs, and to keep things confidential. This discourages aggressive behavior and creates a safe context for negotiation.

The mediator helps by paraphrasing what each party says so that statements are clearly understood and not changed at a later time. The mediator guides the discussion, clarifies points, and creates a positive atmosphere. Because the mediator is neutral, the disputants trust in his or her power to help them resolve their conflict. Both parties have a mutual stake in the outcome of the mediation, and so solutions that are reached have a greater chance of sticking; there isn't a winner or a loser and neither party feels the need to retaliate or strike back.

Mediation not only allows for parties to reach a *resolution*, which is about coming to an agreement, but it also allows for the possibility of *reconciliation*—salvaging and often strengthening relationships. In the face of the explanation "You called me a name and hurt my feelings," we can agree not to call each other names again, but true reconciliation, as Richard Cohen, co-founder of School Mediation Associates, writes, "is ultimately about forgiveness."[3] We see reconciliation happen often in children's lives and mediators have the ability to be part of this process. Duvall, a mediator in New Orleans says, "It makes me feel good when I stop fights from happening. I see the same kids who were really mad at each other earlier playing basketball and walking home together."

Mediation can do more than short-circuit fights. It can become a public norm that underlies school life, changing the way the student body and school staff act when conflicts arise. Establishing a peer mediation program at a school takes time, resources, and dedication. But we can't expect to see kids change overnight. In fact, the first kids who become mediators are pioneers (it isn't yet *cool* to be a mediator).

The selection process is integral to supporting a shift in school culture. While schools vary slightly in the methods they employ for selecting mediators, they all involve young people to some extent in the process. When kids have input they select peers they feel will truly represent them. The kids selected tend to be kids who are looked up to in some way by their peers.

Interestingly, sometimes mediators are recognized for their troublesome behaviors and misdirected leadership; sometimes they are students known for high achievement and strong, positive leadership. Mediators are selected from all upper-grade classrooms and represent all groups of students, as well as all the languages spoken. In Anchorage, Alaska, some of the most remarkable mediations take place at Russian Jack Elementary School. The school has a considerable population of deaf students, some of whom of course participate as mediators. Kids inform their parent mediation coach, Vernita, who has also learned to sign, when they feel their special skills are needed.

As mediation begins to change the culture of a school, it's helpful for students to know they can ask for a mediation at any time. At elementary schools, where mediators are "on duty" on the playground, students become so accustomed to having this option of dealing with their conflicts that it almost becomes second nature. In a second-grade classroom at P.S. 321 in Brooklyn, one of the first schools to implement RCCP, a teacher was asking her students about things they could do when they get angry. As the class brainstormed ideas, one girl said, "You could always go find a mediator." The teacher guessed that the girl might have thought that mediators roamed everywhere and were always available, so she added, "Yes, if you were here at this school, you could always find a mediator." How wonderful it would be if mediators were in fact available in every facet of young people's lives—at school, at home, and in their communities!

Kids seek out mediation because they learn that fighting will often get them suspended from school, while mediation will bring them a resolution; fighting is hurtful and potentially dangerous, while mediation provides a chance to look at things differently. Leslie, an eighth-grader, put it plainly: "You have a choice. They can come to mediation and really try to work it out, or they can go to the office and let somebody else decide their fate." Jozelle from New Orleans said, "If they don't want to solve their problem, they'll get brought to the office and they'll get suspended. They'll go see the principal, and he doesn't play around."

One aim of mediation is to have an ongoing way to solve problems that doesn't entail going to the principal's office or getting suspended, but the goal, of course, is not to replace clear sanctions against unruliness or fighting. In fact, a school must have a consistent policy that enforces a prompt response when school rules are broken. While mediation is used to resolve a wide range of conflicts, even in cases where students are suspended it cannot replace a clear discipline code. At the middle school where I once worked, kids who were suspended for fighting always went to mediation, either with an administrator or with student mediators, before they were suspended or after they returned.

Mediators respected for their skills are often asked to intervene informally by their friends when conflict situations arise. The need for formal mediations in a school sometimes decreases as a result. Manuel, a fifth-grader from New York gives us some insight into this process: "I use peer pressure with my friends, too. Like if we're playing dodge-ball and sometimes they get mad and want to start a fight. I yell, 'Stop! Stop!' Most of the time they stop. Before I was a mediator I wouldn't have even used peer pressure, . . . I just wouldn't get involved."

At the Satellite Academy in the Bronx, many RCCP students say they've been able to use their training to help resolve disputes between friends and families. Robert, a senior at the school, says the guys he hangs out with in his Bronx neighborhood will sometimes seek him out to mediate their differences. "They refer to me as the Counselor," he says.

At an elementary school in California, a teacher told us about a time when she saw three of her kindergartners on the playground. Two of the taller boys were arguing and a little girl was between them, arms outstretched. When the teacher went over to ask if they needed any help, the girl responded, "Not really, Ms. Martin, I'm just *marinating*."

Mediation and School Life

Mediators are involved at every level of school activity. They conduct school-wide and district functions, and speak to small groups. Students recognize the mediators and know how and when they are available to help them. When teachers get to the lessons on mediation in their curriculum, mediators come to their classes to demonstrate and answer questions. They perform scenarios in the classroom so that students can observe the process.

At P.S. 75 in New York, all third-, fourth- and fifth-graders attend the customary mediators' graduation, a special event held to honor the completion of their training. Parents attend too. Guest speakers are invited. It's not uncommon to have the district superintendent come to congratulate the mediators. In RCCP schools, mediators' photographs often greet their peers as they enter school. Kids see the position as a powerful one, one to be respected and admired.

And because this work needs to permeate the entire school, individual schools within the district may choose to create schoolwide functions to promote and honor the contributions of young people. In Anchorage, Alaska, a mediation peace rally was held a few years ago. Over four hundred mediators from eleven elementary schools gathered together to recommit themselves to promoting peace in their schools and in the world. They began to see themselves that day as a movement, part of a national effort on the part of young people who are making a difference.

The ultimate goal of any conflict resolution program is to get young people to talk to each other in order to resolve their own conflicts fairly. A formal mediation program creates an atmosphere in which kids can choose to "talk it out" themselves informally as well.

Soon after peer mediation had been instituted at the middle school where I worked as assistant principal, I found that more and more young people began working things out themselves. Knowing that our school promoted the use of conflict resolution skills, students would come to me and ask, "Can I have a private place to talk this out with so and so?" I would arrange for the other student to come in, asking if they were willing to talk about the problem. I'd set up the ground rules and, depending on the severity of the issues and the students involved, they would sit in my office while I went about my business or I would leave the two parties and adjourn to the office next door, leaving the door ajar.

Sometimes these negotiations were simple—rumors, broken friendships, name-calling. Other times they were more involved and could have resulted in serious violence. Amazingly enough, even students who had affiliations with local gangs eventually came forward to choose the problem-solving approach. They would say to me, "So-and-so is starting up again. I'm going to lose it and I don't want to have to kick his butt." They knew that if something were to start up in school it would wind up in the neighborhood; they'd be suspended or expelled and there was a chance that somebody could get really hurt. So one student would ask for another to be called in. In serious cases like this, I would direct the mediation myself, but almost always with the assistance of mediators who shared the cultural backgrounds of the rival parties. As an administrator, at times I found that a somewhat more formal process was necessary, an official meeting in my office. In the safety of the privacy of that place, many kids expressed their anger and came to terms with how to avoid out-and-out fights or gang violence. As the culture of the school changed to support negotiation and mediation as the norm, so did more and more students.

Another important way in which peer mediation changes school norms is by establishing acceptable behavior for the students who are not involved in the actual fight or argument except as witnesses. These "non-party bystanders" can help to either escalate or de-escalate a conflict.[4] We've all seen the classic scene in which two students are "having words" with each other and a crowd forms around them, encouraging them to fight. Jeers ring out. "Hit him! What are you—chicken? Are you gonna just stand there?" In many cases the disputant doesn't want to fight, even tries to back away, but the crowd encourages him forward, sometimes even physically pushing him into a fight. I have heard countless numbers of students tell me, "I never intended to fight so-and-so, but all of a sudden, there I was, and my friends were there watching. I couldn't back away."

At Linda's alma mater, Thomas Jefferson High School in New York City, one student shot and killed another and critically wounded a teacher just a few years ago. Linda visited the school after the incident and had an intense discussion with fourteen young people, several of whom had actually watched their schoolmate dying. She learned a lot from them about their feelings about the futility of the violence that surrounds them and the hopelessness it generates. They saw no alternatives to the violence that was destroying their friends. Linda asked them about the sequence of events that led up to the horrible tragedy that day, if there was anything that anyone could have done differently that might have altered the outcome. The students ended up identifying eight or nine things—mainly things done by *bystanders*—that had escalated the conflict in the hallway.

At the time of this tragedy there was no peer mediation program at this school, due to a lack of financial resources. Perhaps Giselle, an eighth-grade mediator from a nearby middle school, best expresses the urgency we should all feel about these programs becoming part of our schools: "Believe it or not, we have had the toughest kids break down and cry in mediation. We've got to get through to kids, one way or another. I have a feeling that if they would have had a peer mediation program at Jefferson High School those two people would have never been shot."

At first Linda thought Giselle was putting too much faith in the mediation process, but then she realized Giselle was probably right. The two boys who had gotten into the altercation had had a long-standing feud that involved both their families. Disputes like this often fester until they explode because our society is not equipped to resolve them.

One reason motivating non-party bystanders to get involved is the hope of earning the esteem of the party they see as in the right. Kids want to win the approval of their peers. Rumors, for instance, often originate or get spread in the hope of gaining friendship, impressing peers, or discrediting others. And rumors lead to fights.

Perhaps one of the greatest benefits of creating schoolwide norms which support the nonviolent resolution of conflict is that the potentially negative power of the crowd begins to dissipate. Not only do kids stop taking sides when a fight or argument ensues in a lunch area, they begin to help de-escalate the situation. Often it is they who call mediators (on or off duty) to intervene.

There are times, however, when feuding parties aren't likely to seek a nonviolent approach. Mediators who are aware that a conflict could erupt in violence often advise school leaders of the ensuing problem: "Hey, this is what's brewing out there. They won't listen to us, and this might end up in a big fight after school. One of you guys needs to get involved." There were times when I received anonymous notes letting me know that something was going to happen, or that "so-and-so" might be carrying a weapon. The greater the number of students supporting the change to a norm of nonviolence at a school, the greater the chance we can prevent the violence adults wouldn't normally find out about until it's too late.

Many mediators use their skills outside of school as well, defying situations that would be classic cases of bystander complicity. One day Linda received a phone call from a woman who had seen the following interaction at a local playground in New York City after school hours.

A group of students, probably in about third or fourth grade, who were playing basketball, were being harassed by another group of slightly older kids who evidently wanted to play too. The older kids were clearly about to start a fight. The woman wanted to intervene but wasn't sure if or how she should. All of a sudden another group of young people who had been standing nearby surrounded the arguing kids in a circle and started to sing. "Peacemakers talk about it, they don't fight about it, they want to make up and be friends."[5] The kids who were starting the fight were so surprised by this behavior they quickly dispersed and the clash never took place. The woman, stunned and moved to tears by the actions of these kids, asked them who they were and where they were from. It turns out that they were mediators from the school nearby and had learned the song during mediation training.

Putting Mediation into Practice

Mediation programs are complicated structures. There are decisions to be made as to the selection process for mediators, the frequency of mediations done by them, the resources that are made available for the mediation program, the strength of the trainers, and the training curriculum offered. But there are two things that we have found especially enhance a mediation program: expanding student involvement and the use of peer mediation coaches.

When a peer mediation program takes off in a school, lots of kids want to become mediators. Members of the school community struggle with mediator selection. Inevitably, many young people are turned down. One way of minimizing this problem is for teachers to select additional *classroom* mediators. Young people can be classroom mediators "of the week" or "of the month." Teachers find that these in-class mediators help resolve the daily issues that come up in the life of the classroom and provide incentives for students to behave well and accomplish their best.

In some of our schools, Junior Ambassador and Young Ambassador programs have been established in order to involve more students in leadership positions. These ambassadors are trained in advanced concepts of conflict resolution and intergroup relations.

At Roosevelt Middle School in Vista, California, the school where I worked as assistant principal, the Young Ambassador program began when we were looking for a way to bring rival gang members together. The RCCP curriculum component had begun, but the gangs seemed to be changing the climate of the school faster than the new curriculum was. The program began with a small group of about thirty student volunteers from different backgrounds of race, language, gender, academic standing, and behavior in school. Together, we taught this group key concepts about understanding differences and how to create unity. They attended intensive workshops in conflict resolution skills and intergroup relations. These students became leaders at the school, involving themselves in schoolwide activities that promoted acceptance and appreciation of diversity. Their mission statement was "Increase the peace, decrease the violence, and appreciate people of other cultures."

At Roosevelt there are now over a hundred Young Ambassadors in a population of about fifteen hundred students. (There are only thirty-five peer mediators.) Teachers and school leaders continue to find this group to be critical in establishing a culture of nonviolence and appreciation of diversity. The elementary schools in Vista California have begun Junior Ambassadors programs.

We believe there is a huge benefit in creating a "critical mass" of students—other than those trained as mediators—who support the norm of nonviolence and are respected by peers and adults. Young Ambassadors also involve themselves in community functions. In Vista, they have spoken at city council meetings and have been guest speakers at conferences and other important events. Young Ambassadors have also visited elementary schools to teach classroom lessons and have worked with developmentally disabled students. A few years ago, several kids from this program worked with two teachers to create local public service announcements called Peace Increasers—thirty-second "spots" about valuing diversity. These PSAs were submitted to a nationwide contest sponsored by the cable station VH1. Out of over a hundred submissions nationwide, Roosevelt's Young Ambassadors were awarded a one-thousand-dollar check for their efforts and were featured on a national television show, along with several other nationwide programs, as "ordinary people doing extraordinary things."

At Roosevelt Middle School, many Young Ambassadors ultimately become mediators, which requires yet another level of dedication and formal training.

We find the Young Ambassador program a useful addition to our RCCP program. We recommend it, for all grade levels, at schools that are willing to support such efforts with dedicated teacher leadership and schoolwide involvement.

The Peer Mediation Coach

The role of the peer mediation coach is crucial. At our schools, we employ parent coaches, generally people who are experienced in supervising kids during school recesses. The coach assists the mediation coordinator in arranging mediators' schedules, talking with teachers, and supporting mediators in skill development and other needs. The parent coach gets to know the mediators very well. Not only are the coaches available for supervision of mediations, either on the playground or inside a mediation room, but they also become mentors and resources for the students. Students speak highly of their mediation coaches. Kristin, a mediator at Vista, where two dedicated parents shared this role, said, "I think the mediation coaches do a great job. They jump in to help just when you need them. They support us and do their best to make us our best." Erica, an eighth-grade mediator at the same school, agreed: "Their feedback, both good and bad, is really helpful. It gives you insight on different areas that need improvement plus it boosts your self-confidence." Jana, a fifth-grader from New York, said, "I will always remember the mediation coach who supported me. . . . Even if it didn't turn out for the best she'd say, 'You did a good job and you can learn from your mistakes.'"

We find parents to be especially enthusiastic and effective coaches. Having parents work as coaches also sets the stage for other work with parents in the district, often becoming the liaison between the school and the community when RCCP's parent component begins.

A Story about the Power of the Process

One day Linda was asked by the directors of the two small alternative high schools that share the building in which the national RCCP office is also housed to mediate a situation that had already escalated into violence. Four months earlier, a fight had erupted between two rival gang members at the two high schools—leaving eleven students suspended and several hospitalized. The students' suspension time was drawing to an end and they would be returning to school the following day. The directors requested that Linda conduct a mediation with the key students involved. Linda explains,

Although I was scheduled for a speaking engagement out of town the next day, I realized the severity of the problem and arranged to leave later. I also realized I had to break all my own rules about the mediation process. I had to work alone because I couldn't find a partner on such short notice and I was mediating a group of young people who were from a different cultural background and gender from my own.

I decided to ask two safety officers to sit in with me, a Latina woman and

an African-American man. The students in both schools saw these two adults as kind and supportive individuals. Although I believed in the power of the mediation process, I had never met any of these young people before. An ounce of prevention would be better than the risk of potential physical violence.

As expected, eleven male students of Latino and African-American backgrounds arrived at my office door. They were obviously tense and angry sitting on opposite sides of the table. I explained the guidelines they would need to follow and asked for agreement. I got it, and we proceeded. Slowly, these young men began to let out their feelings and frustrations. They kept to the guidelines impeccably: they spoke one at a time, there was no name-calling, and they were working to solve the problem.

Two and a half hours later a resolution was in sight. The issues were about territory and turf. Concerns centered around who was getting to use the gym more often. As a resolution grew nearer, I repeated the agreements they were reaching (which included calling off a major fight). I decided to ask each student if there might be anything that would get in the way of their resolution. Ruben said, "It's just too bad that Georgie isn't here!" A gang member from the opposite camp agreed. My heart sank. I knew that all the work they had done could be useless if Georgie were to escalate the situation. It appeared that Georgie had a lot of clout in this arena. Ruben, who appeared to be one of the leaders, said, "I'll talk to Georgie over the weekend and let him know that it's off."

At this point, I intervened. I explained that this would be difficult to trust. So Ruben volunteered to call Georgie right then and there. He asked if Rodney, a leader from the other gang, could go along to witness this. An amazing trust was beginning to build. Rodney, Ruben, and I went into the next room.

The other students, much more relaxed now, remained in the room with the two safety officers. Ruben called Georgie and told him what had happened in the room that day. He referred to me as "the peace lady" and let Georgie know that the fight had been called off as a result of our mediation. From the sound of Ruben's reply, Georgie must have thought that he had *gone nuts. In an excited voice, Ruben said, "No, Rodney agrees with this too! He's right here." And he handed Rodney the phone.*

It was at this point that I realized the level of trust that had developed over a two-and-a-half-hour period with young people who had literally almost killed each other just four months before. Tears filled my eyes as I watched Ruben and Rodney, who had returned to the room together and were now telling the others what had transpired. Their feelings of empowerment and definite camaraderie were evident. I left town later that day, as planned, but not without establishing a line of communication with these two young men, who faithfully reported to me by phone each day for a week. The agreement held for the remainder of their senior year.

I remain in awe of the utter power and simplicity of nonviolence—how we all really yearn for another way of doing things. Another two students were added, that day, to my list of great teachers.

[**7**]

SIGNS OF HOPE

WE HAVE TALKED ABOUT the benefits schools are experiencing from participation in diversity education, conflict resolution, and mediation training. In this chapter we'll listen to the voices of the young people who are part of the solution.[1]

Angel

One day I was in the park, and there were these kids from a day care center. They were on the seesaw and they were both talking. They started out talking nice and then they were talking meaner and meaner and then they started arguing and then they came up face to face. And then I thought, "Let me mediate them. Let me give it a shot."

I told them that I was Angel and I asked, "Would you like me to help solve your problem?" And one said yes. The other kid said yes too. So we went to the shade in the corner of the park. I explained the rules. I said no name-calling, be as honest as you can, no interrupting. One of them looked madder than the other so I started with him. He talked. He said that the other boy was telling him that his mother was on drugs and all that. So I paraphrased it. And then the other kid said that no he didn't. He didn't mean to say that, he was talking about something else.

So I asked the first kid, "What could you have done differently?" And he said that he could have asked the other boy why he said what he did. He could have asked, "Why did you say that? Why did you say that my mother was on drugs?" And he could not have come up to his face. And the other kid said, "I could have not told him that his mother was on drugs which I didn't really mean to." So I said, "How could you solve the problem? What can you do now to solve the problem?"

So the other kid said, "Shake hands, and I'll be his friend again." And the other kid said, "I will not make fun of his mother no more and I'll shake his hand and be friends." And they both shook hands and I realized, I mediated this problem. I thought I couldn't do it, but I did it.

Although young people like Angel are working double time—in their schools, their homes, and their communities—to make a difference in the lives of the people around them, much of what we hear about young people today isn't about the good deeds they are doing. Instead, we hear stories about the horrible things young people do. And yet only a small percentage of today's youth are responsible for the heinous crimes we hear of; in fact, these crimes are committed by only 6 percent of young people in our society.[2]

Since the inception of RCCP's peer mediation program in New York City in 1987 (and its national dissemination, which began in 1990) some ten thousand young people have served as RCCP peer mediators nationwide. They, along with many others, are working steadfastly to combat the reality behind the negative images we have of youth. As they wage peace with their peers and younger children, they are proving that there is another way of resolving conflict. They believe that they can help turn the societal trend toward violence around. It is their dedication to this work and their strong convictions that are the reasons why we, as adults, continue to be so hopeful that we can reclaim our schools, homes, and communities as violence-free growing zones.

Listening

One point is clear. In the schools we travel to all across the country, kids we speak with say they want to become mediators. The role has become a prestigious position to have in a school, but when we listen to these young people talk about *why* they want to become mediators, it seems that most young people really care about others and really have a desire to make a difference.

I always wanted to figure out ways to help people solve fights and also teach them different ways of doing things, instead of using fists and hurtful words. [Nishala, fifth grade, New York City]

I decided to become a mediator so I could stop the crime on the street. I might be able to help stop people from using drugs, bringing guns to the middle schools and high schools. All that's not necessary. I've seen people shoot each other when I was smaller. They would have never started an argument if they would have known some of the skills I'm learning. One of them would probably have walked away and forgot about it. [Carl, fourth grade, New Orleans]

By listening, we've learned how being part of programs like ours makes young people feel they have the ability and the skills to do something about the violence they and their peers are confronting, whether they see it in their neighborhoods or only in "the news."

These young people *believe* in what they do. They take their position in the schools very seriously. As Jozelle, a sixth-grade mediator from New Orleans, said, "If the kids don't listen to us and we don't stop the violence on the street, I don't know what's going to happen."

Adults confirm the commitment of these young people. Cindy, a middle school teacher, shared,

One of the math teachers held an auction at lunchtime. One of the mediators was supposed to go to a mediation and [so] he missed the auction. His name got called to win a prize and because he wasn't there, he missed it. All I heard him say was, "Gosh, you know, I missed out. I'm bummed." It takes a lot for a kid this age to have that kind of dedication.

When mediators are called upon to do a mediation they don't ask questions, they don't complain. Being a mediator is their job. More than their peers, they tend to report on time, make up missed work after school, and keep up their grades, and they are diligent about sharpening their skills and supporting each other so that the work gets done efficiently. Often mediators sacrifice their lunch periods and free time with their friends in order to volunteer their time. Fifth-grader Manuel explained what this is like for him: "My friends peer-pressure me to play. But I tell them no, I can't do it. Sometimes I don't want to leave because I have gym or an important game to play, but I go anyway."

Free time is important to kids, but sometimes this job takes precedence.

As we talk with young people, they elaborate two central themes: how they have changed—in radical or subtle ways—and how they've seen their schools change.

Mediators realize that positive changes come with time and practice, that learning these skills and making them a part of their lives requires a long-term commitment. What's so rewarding for us to see is how young people can expand their own intrapersonal awareness. They can talk about their own behavior in light of past and present experiences, think about how to manage and regulate their own behavior and emotions (a process that many adults don't address until later in life.)

Not all mediators have walked the straight and narrow all of their lives. Often we've heard about how being a mediator helped stop someone from using violence to get what they needed or wanted in various situations. In fact, some of these young people set out to become mediators because they knew they needed some "polishing"; they wanted to strengthen their personal characters, to put an end to getting into trouble, fighting, and bullying, and to stop the violent roller-coaster they were on. Edgar still wears the clothes that represent the Latino gang he associates with, but he's really trying to separate himself from them. Sometimes he hangs with the mediators and sometimes he hangs with the gang. "I used to always kick back with my homies. But too many of my friends are in jail or dead. I wanted to have a life." Calvin, a high school freshman, shared this:

You want respect, but there's only one way that you see you can get that respect and that's by being tough, bold. That's the way I got respect, by being the most aggressive person. I've changed a lot. I try to stay friends with everybody and not by being mean. . . . It's the way I look at people now, listen to them and talk to them. People actually say to my parents "He's a nice kid," not "He's real tough." It's a different kind of high and it feels good.

Brandon learned how to be tough early on in life. Being held up at knifepoint one day when he was nine years old made him streetwise real young. After that, he chose to be the aggressor rather than the victim. He describes what that was like:

After this, I just bullied people around. Got my own way. Didn't have many friends. Kids were scared of me. One day I punched this kid right in the face. Broke his glasses. At first I felt good about it. My friends thought I was cool. Then I saw he was crying. This kid hadn't done anything to me. I started feeling bad. . . . When this program began at my school, my dad wanted me to join. I thought, Yeah, right. This wasn't for me. But soon everything started to change. I began to get my respect another way.

For some of these young people changes included forming new friendships with "positive peers," other mediators and friends who didn't get into trouble. Anthony said, "I don't hang around with the same people I used to because they always fight and stuff. I hang around with the mediators now." Being part of this positive group of leaders, Edgar, Calvin, Brandon, Anthony, and others found the strength to stop their old patterns, supported by new friends and adults who recognized that they were trying to change. They learned better ways to resolve conflict so that it didn't have to lead to violence.

In some cases, learning better ways to resolve conflicts means simply walking away, a major accomplishment for a kid who may be used to "getting into somebody's face" all the time. Other times it means using negotiation and mediation skills. Stan, an eighth-grade mediator from California, said, "I've got a bad temper. I still do, but I've learned skills that help me calm myself down rather than get angry right away."

Mediators notice other changes in themselves such as an increase in their self-esteem. They begin to feel better about themselves because of the choices they are making and the respect they earn from their peers, teachers, and parents. Eighth-grader Matt told us, "Mentally, mediators know they're doing something good for the school and that will increase anyone's self-esteem."

Mediators learn how to communicate their own feelings as well as to understand others' points of view. An eighth-grader named Katie said she never knew how to tell people how she felt before. "Now I can assert myself," she continued. "I don't have to keep it in anymore."

Sixth-grader Veronica learned what it feels like when someone teases and makes fun of another person. She never thought about this until she began to talk about feelings in her weekly mediation meetings. Like many kids her age, Veronica used to tease people. "Now," she says, "I think about being in other people's shoes, and it just isn't nice. Nobody deserves to feel badly about themselves."

Many kids have spoken about improved relationships with friends and family members, and improvement in academic grades. All in all, they are aware that they continue to learn from each other and from the struggles they see in other young people their own age. Lori, now a high school student, expressed it best: "After a while, you don't even know that you're doing things differently. It all just becomes part of who you are."

And for some, having conflict resolution and mediation skills gives them the personal courage to better their own lives and those of others. They intervene on the streets, in their homes, in their neighborhoods. Seneca and other young adults from Satellite Academy in the South Bronx were featured in a television special on violence and violence prevention. A newspaper reporter who interviewed them was still skeptical that kids could be nonviolent in the violent world of the South Bronx, so he asked them, "Do you find you use these skills outside the school as well as inside the school?" They all said yes, and Seneca told the following story:

Not too long ago I was getting pretty sick and tired of leaving my apartment every morning in the projects and seeing the drug dealers deal drugs openly on my floor, the seventeenth floor. My seven-year-old sister and eight-year-old brother have to pass this every morning as they wait for the elevator. So one day I decided to negotiate with the drug dealers. I said to them, "You know, I really can't stop you from deciding to sell drugs, but I'd like to ask you something and I'd like to tell you why. I'd like to ask you to stop dealing on the seventeenth floor. It's really upsetting to me that my little brother and sister have to go to school every morning seeing this." They didn't say much right away, but the next morning they weren't there and they haven't been there since. But you know, I still don't sleep well at night. . . . Because I'm still thinking of all the little kids on the sixteenth floor and the eighteenth floor.

Mediators also speak about the changes they observe in their schools. Above all, they see a decrease in physical aggression. Lori told us, "Kids just aren't fighting the way they used to anymore. People used to get into fights almost every day. . . . Now they come to mediation first." Discipline is administered when it is merited, but kids are using mediation even after they've gone through formal school disciplinary channels. Katie explained, "If you've done something wrong, you're still going to pay the consequences. Most kids understand that. But everybody knows about mediation and wants to go if they have a problem." Edgar said, "A few years ago, everybody was throwing gang signs at our school. Now you don't see that anymore."

When a program has been in place long enough, mediators are often at a loss for work! According to Adam, a sixth-grade mediator from Anchorage,

"This year there aren't many fights because we started the program three years ago. There was a whole bunch of arguments and stuff before mediation but not much now. Sometimes its boring on the playground because there's nothing to do. Our principal, Mrs. Johnson, used to have a lot more kids in her office."

Kids say that student mediators have become role models, as admired as local sports heroes and "sheroes." Eighth-grader Stan says, "People usually look up to me, especially little sixth-graders. They ask, 'Aren't you a mediator?'" Stan is a strong leader at his school. He knows that he influences other students. "I don't want to toot my horn or anything, but I can have a lot of influence at this school, negative or positive. And I tell new kids coming in, 'You should try out next year. I think you'd be a good mediator.' And they do."

Kids note that where it used to be taboo to talk about racial and cultural differences, now they are discussed in the open. For some mediators, talking openly for the first time about differences—racial, ethnic, gender, religious, physical—has greatly affected them. Matt described how his attitudes about people of backgrounds different from his changed:

Before I was in this program I was close-minded about certain racial differences. In my mind, I associated some people with certain behaviors. I didn't like doing this, but I did it. Now every time it happens I say to myself, "Matthew, you have to stop doing this." I'm not prejudiced, but I do stereotype some people.

What Helps Peer Mediators Do Their Job

In our efforts to strengthen our programs, we asked mediators what helped them to have successful mediations at school. Their honest feedback was extremely helpful to us in thinking about improving our program and we hope it will be useful to other individuals and programs as well. Above all, mediators feel safer and more sure of having a good mediation when they work with partners. Jozelle said, "I work best with Daisy. People are always coming to us to solve a conflict." Duvall explained why working in pairs is better: "If I take two students by myself, they'd only start fighting again. That's why I call another mediator so they take one and I take one. . . . Sometimes I forget the steps but my partner jumps in to help."

Mediators also say that when the student body knows about conflict resolution it makes their job easier; when kids learn conflict resolution in the classroom "they have a little bit of an idea of what mediators do." As Nishala said, "If they had lessons, they'd understand what I understand. It's hard for me to explain it all to them."

Kids are well aware that they have to remain neutral and keep confidentiality when helping to resolve a conflict. Ralph commented, "It's real important not to take sides in a mediation. It's also important not to solve the problem . . . , but to help them come to a solution." Nikita admitted her frustration when kids don't come up with solutions: "The hardest part for me is I want to tell them the solution. When I ask them, 'What could you have done differently?' You want to tell them but you can't. Mediation isn't about giving them suggestions. Sometimes you know that kids are still mad at the other person, even though they've said 'I'm sorry.'" Sixth-grader Veronica said, "I go into my head and I imagine myself in someone's shoes and how they must feel. . . . I tell them that they can trust me and I won't tell anybody about their conflict. Then they agree to mediation."

Having an adult coach nearby during mediations provides the mediators with safety and with expertise when needed. In our program, the parent coaches get to know the mediators very well. Not only is the coach available for supervision of mediations, either on the playground or inside a mediation room, but this person becomes a mentor and resource for the students.

The Heart of the Matter

The following stories were told by young people Linda and I know personally. All the students interviewed are or were mediators in RCCP schools.

They have important information to share with us about what they have experienced as a result of participation in peer mediation programs at their schools. Over the twenty plus years we have been in education, Linda and I have learned how important it is to listen, honor, and learn from what young people have to say. They are the dream keepers. As we listen to their voices, their opinions, their experiences with others, we adjust our own perspectives and we grow.

Marisol

I'm an eighth-grader at Roosevelt Middle School in Vista, California. I have been a mediator for one year. I am Latina, Mexican-American, born in Vista, California. I live with my mother and father and my two older brothers.

I became a mediator because I thought I would help people solve their conflicts instead of making more problems for themselves and others. I thought being a mediator would also help me solve my problems at home. I was getting into a lot of arguments with my mom.

I was proud when I was selected. My attitude and grades began to change when I became a mediator. I used to get low grades, but now I'm doing better than that.

Since I've become a mediator, I learned how to do things differently. Before I would have problems with my friends and I would get aggressive with them. Now I ignore it, or I ask them, "Why are you telling me this?" I tell them how I feel and then they understand. I've seen a lot of difference in how I get along with people, especially with my parents. I used to talk back to them a lot. And they've seen a big difference in me, too. Now, I am able to talk it out without having any problems like I used to have.

When I started school in sixth grade, RCCP was just starting. There was a lot of violence, lots of problems with the eighth-graders, gang violence. There would always be fights. The bathrooms would be written all over. Now there's a big difference. You don't hear about many fights. You don't hear about kids ditching. You don't hear about writing on the bathroom walls.

I'm proud of being a mediator. I've seen that I'm helping people. I even did a presentation for some elementary students not too long ago. They really look up to us.

I have a lot of friends. Many of them get into trouble with their families a lot. Some of them are in gangs. I try to help them. When they think about doing something that could get them into trouble, I say, "Let's do this instead." And I've seen that they're changing a lot too, with their parents and friends.

I know that when you try, you can get what you want, and I like trying. I'm sure that people who want to have a better life, not join in gangs and stuff, would be interested in this. I think that people push kids into staying in their gangs and that's why they stay. But I think if kids could really see what we're doing now, they would want to get involved too. They'd want to join us, instead of gangs. It's hard once you're in a gang to get out. I ask my friends to join my group but they feel they can't get out. It's too hard for them.

We need to get out there and tell people that violence isn't what they need. I've got to start with my own friends 'cause I really want them to leave their gangs and be in good shape. I feel bad about so many of my friends being in gangs. I feel I've got to make a difference for them, and I'm going to try.

Tiffany

I am a sophomore in high school. I am Filipina-American. My dad tells me there's Spanish and Hawaiian in my blood, maybe even some Japanese. I live with my parents, my sister, and my older brother.

When I first learned about conflict resolution and intergroup relations, I was in the sixth grade. There was this new program they were starting up called Young Ambassadors and some of my friends were interested in joining. I was in student government and I was so shy. I didn't really want to do this, but it seemed different. "Should I go?" I thought, "Should I go?" I was so scared, so nervous. I don't remember the questions they asked me in the interview, I just answered them. My assistant principal told me that they were bringing together kids from different backgrounds so that there wouldn't be any gang rivalry at our school. I thought, "This is crazy."

But I was accepted and soon lots of new doors opened to me. Everyone at our school was coming together from different groups. They were expressing how they felt about things, just coming together. Being in the group, I opened up to my peers. I was frank with them. It was weird to be friends with different kids, kids I would have probably never spoken to, even gang members. I used to just stay away from them because I was scared of them. I stereotyped a lot.

And talking wasn't easy for me. When I was growing up we didn't talk about feelings. We were dictated to and that's how it had to be. I've always had a lot of pressure from my family. They tell you get straight A's and you get straight A's. There's no question about it. At times I felt like I couldn't get those A's, but I would never tell my parents how I felt.

Through RCCP I learned that you have to express yourself. At first, it was weird for me to say how I felt. I thought, "I can't say that. Everybody would know how I feel." That must be how I got so shy, because I couldn't say how I felt. When people would ask me, "How do you feel when this happens?" I would know the feeling, but it was hard to express it. I could say something simple like "I feel sad," but there were all these emotions running through me. As time went on I began to find the words for the way I felt. Even though I was learning to express myself in the meetings, when I went home I still kept things in.

Becoming a mediator even helped me more. I learned how to listen, how to hear others' points of view. How to use creative questioning to be able to get to the root of a conflict. Little by little I was able to say to my parents, "I feel really pressured when you do this." I'd tell my parents what I think. I understand it's just that they expected a lot from me but I'm also learning that there are some things I just can't do, and I need to let them know that when I feel this way. Now that I'm getting older my parents realize that this is a different world, this isn't like when they were growing up. People here are individuals. They have their own minds.

Being in this program, I learned a lot about myself and others. It's given me a positive outlook on life. It's given me skills that will help me get far in life, that will help me in the future. We may have the smarts in English and everything, but communication, that's the way the world works. I feel good inside because I know I'm helping someone. I know I'm making progress. I'm stating my beliefs, my position, and I'm respected for the way I feel.

I think kids like this work. A lot of people do because they want to change the world, to make a difference. They see what we are doing as the first step. We used to even write down when we helped someone on a walk-the-talk sheet. Instead of writing the negatives, we wrote about the positive things we were doing. Some of the students even taught their parents these skills.

Not all mediators have an impeccable, peaceful life, because everyone is human. We make mistakes. We use what we know, but not twenty-four hours a day. But everybody learning these skills is determined to spread the word about it, to tell everyone, "Yeah, this is going to be a perfect world one day, and we all have to believe in it." If we change one person's life, it makes us feel so much better.

Lanitra

I'm African-American and I was born in South Central Los Angeles, on Grape Street in Watts. There's a lot of violence going on in Watts. Where I lived on Grape Street, guns were an everyday thing. On Grape street, every house on the block sold drugs. The police had a thing called the batter ram, kind of like a big tank car where the police would come unexpectedly and knock your house down to get all the drugs. I used to see the guys always carrying the guns from the house to their cars when they thought the police would be coming. It was normal to see the guys at night just hanging out with their guns.

Violence was a normal part of growing up. My mother and father were divorced. My mother worked hard to raise me and keep me away from the violence. But just walking down the street you'd often see someone you knew getting beat up by somebody for something. And you just kept on walking 'cause there wasn't anything you could do. You didn't have to look for violence, it was just there.

There were other kinds of violence around me, too. Things happened in my life that I didn't even know were violent until now. The way some of my friends and family members treated each other seemed normal when I was growing up. When you don't know any better, you just accept things. You keep them inside, you tell no one. That's what I did. Now, I struggle with changing the way I accept this kind of violence in my life. I know another way. But patterns are hard to break.

In my fifth-grade year we moved to Oceanside, California. By the sixth grade, I went to Roosevelt Middle School. I was an at-risk kid and I was only in the sixth grade, hanging with the wannabe gang members. This was the year that they started the Young Ambassadors program at Roosevelt. My assistant principal asked me to get involved in it instead of going to the office all the time. I used to keep meeting her in the office a lot.

This group was trying to bring together positive and negative role models and work together to make the school a safer place. It was kind of hard to believe in this group, so I wouldn't come to the meetings at first. I didn't tell anybody about nothing that had happened to me in my life, or how I felt about anything until I came to this school and they were saying, "You need to tell people how you feel." I tried to play hard at first; I didn't have to tell people "Well, I feel mad" or whatever. I thought I was real big and bad. I wasn't going to use this stuff. It was just another thing to make the teachers happy and to get out of class.

But then it was like, "Well, I do have this stuff inside of me that I want people to know about and I do feel upset. I am hurt by certain things. I want to be able to tell my mother how I feel inside." And soon—I didn't even know that I was using I-messages—I did tell people how I felt. I learned that I became a better person when I started doing that. I was becoming a better person on the outside 'cause I was telling people how I feel, not just being mad at someone and wanting to fight that person over nothing. And the stuff on the inside, I was letting my feelings come out, not just making believe that all that happened to me didn't happen to me. I had had some hard times and I was kind of upset because of this.

By seventh grade, I started doing better in school, going to school often, staying out of the office, getting good grades. My grade-point average went up very high. I became a mediator and in eighth grade I became the Commissioner of Peace, our name for the president of the Young Ambassadors. Being a mediator made me feel good helping people and I was helping myself learn about situations in my life and helping other people who had the same situations as me. It felt good knowing that I could help other persons solve their problems, that I could help myself avoiding situations that needed to be avoided.

I've changed in a lot of ways. I used to just hang around one group of people. Now, I'm culturally aware of everyone that's in my school. I hang around with so many different people, not just my black friends. I don't walk by that person just because they're white or from another group.

I still use my skills. I'm using them at home and even in my new school. The teachers and administrators call on me to help with the problems because they know I have the skills. Now it kind of comes naturally, helping people or helping myself. I'm doing better with myself now, understanding myself, expressing myself. I know I'm going places, and it feels good. One thing I wish is that everybody was learning this way of communicating. The kids growing up in Watts need these skills too.

Chris

I've been a mediator for one year. I go to Russian Jack Elementary School in Anchorage, Alaska. I'm in the sixth grade.

I'm a Cherokee Indian. I grew up in a small town in Oklahoma. It was mostly Cherokee and different Indian tribes. There was a lot of discrimination in that town and in the school that I went to. The Indians made fun of *the whites and the white kids called us all kinds of names. It was tough on both groups. Maybe if there would have been a mediation program in that school things would have been different.*

I wish people would understand more about each other. Like in the movies they show the Indians fighting all the time. They kill people and have long hair and stuff. It's not really like that. The Cherokees weren't warring people. They stayed away from war. They weren't afraid of it, it's just that they had to adapt to a whole way of life, especially after the Gold Rush, and they moved into Oklahoma. In the movies they make up all this stuff about Indians killing people. Indians are mostly just the opposite of how they show them.

When I first moved to Alaska, I used to be so self-conscious about my country accent. The kids used to call me "country boy." They'd make fun of the way I talked. Back then I had to take it. I didn't know what else to do about it. Now I help other kids that have the same problems I had. I help them reconcile their differences through mediation.

I feel that conflict resolution is important for everybody. Even adults can use this at work. Like, for example, if someone in their office were to get into an argument they could use their skills. That's if they want your help. Some people don't want help. At school, the kids are ready. They want help, so it works.

I wasn't always the most peaceful person either. One day at my old school I made fun of some kids. The next thing I knew there were four of them on me. I was alone. One punched me in the stomach and another in the face. I guess I asked for it though, I called them wimpy and little. I wouldn't be saying that stuff now. My parents are proud of my work, and so are my teachers. Teachers thank me for helping out their students.

I did this mediation one time for these two little kids. It was kind of cute because those kids were just sitting there looking at each other with their mean-looking little faces. Then when it was over they were smiling and I knew it was because I helped out.

When I'm older I hope to be an archeologist and do lots of scientific re-

search. They say you have to talk to people in different countries and stuff, get permission to excavate. I think I'll be able to use my skills in that job. They'll help me talk with people.

Leroy

I'm eleven years old. I'm in the sixth grade at Myrtle Banks Elementary School in New Orleans, Louisiana. I live with my mom and dad and my little sister. I first came to this school when I was in the fourth grade. By the time I was in the fifth grade, I became a mediator. I think Miss Johnson picked me to be a mediator because she thought that I could handle the job and help solve a lot of fights. I used to be bad, too. And I think she thought this could help me.

I was excited about being a mediator. The training was great. We did a lot of role plays and talked a lot about peace and what mediation is all about.

Being a mediator isn't easy. It's a lot of responsibility. Some kids have been suspended from mediation. Like last Tuesday, I almost got into a fight but I decided not to fight. We were playing a game and this boy thought I was cheating so he swung at me and missed. I told him that I wasn't going to fight him because I'd be suspended from mediation. He thought I was scared, but I wasn't. I felt all right although I was mad at first when he almost hit me. I was proud of myself because I didn't fight. If it had been in the past, I would have fought him. I always fought in the fourth grade.

I'm changing a lot now. I'm not even hanging around with certain people because they always fight. I'm hanging around with Carl now. He has a temper, but he stays calm with it. He's a mediator too.

I feel safe at this school. Everybody knows me and nobody messes with me. All the little kids look up to me. They want to be mediators too. If you want to gain respect in this school you should become a mediator.

I don't feel so safe where I live, though. Last night somebody got shot around there. It was around 11:00 P.M. I looked outside to see what happened and saw a man running. Then he collapsed. I was scared at first when I saw him running. There were a lot of shots before he collapsed. Everyone ran out to see who it was because lots of people have seen people they know shot before.

My little sister—she's in the second grade—thought that the man who fell was my daddy because he had a cool shirt on like the one my daddy has. But the next morning when we got up we saw him. I knew that it couldn't have been him because he had on different shoes. After it was over, I turned on the cartoons, Tom and Jerry. I watched them all night, trying to get it out of my mind. I had never seen anyone get hit. I thought I'd dream about it all night.

I try to use my skills as a mediator. They work real good at school, and sometimes they work in other places. Like last year when I went trick-or-treating with my mama, sister, and friends. Two of my friends started fussing over the candy. I took some out of my bag and gave it to them and said, "What are you-all fussing over candy for? You can always get more." I always try to solve problems. It makes me feel good inside.

Sometimes its hard to use the skills in the neighborhood 'cause some kids are just plain bad. They throw bottles at grown-ups and curse at them too. You can't do nothing with people like that. And sometimes you just have to avoid conflict. Like, I live on the third floor of the projects. At night the building hallways are always pitch black because they take the light bulbs out and use them on the porch so they can play cards. I'm too scared to go upstairs, so I either stay inside or go in before it's too dark.

If I had the power to change the violence in the world, I'd create a special place for all the violent people where they can't escape, like the one in California with the water around it. And all the good people, they'd live in a special home. They'd be in a big building. All the older people would be safe there and my teachers too, Mr. Thomas and Mrs. Johnson.

Joshua

I'm eighteen years old and I attend Satellite Academy in the Bronx. I'm a mediator now and will soon be graduating from school. But before I got myself together, I went through a lot of problems. I was always messing up in school. I fought, disrespected people, broke bottles, played hooky, hung out, used drugs. You name it, I did it.

Being a male and growing up at the same time is hard, especially in the environment I live in. And to have a mother that was my father too—it was hard to understand and respect her. I was disrespectful to my mom. I was doing what I wanted to do because I felt like I was a man already. I would do things to fit in. If you do something wrong, to some people you hang out with it makes you look good. A lot of people think that being feared is the same as being respected. A lot of respect on the street is being the Man or having all the money or the cars or killing a lot of people or being a sperm donor—getting a girl pregnant and leaving her. What I didn't know then but I know now is that when you respect yourself, that's real respect.

I've learned a lot since I started with RCCP. If a person doesn't like one thing about you, or if he doesn't like what his friends say about you or if he's jealous or has any negative thoughts about you, he would probably like to start a dispute. And let's say you fight. What's going to happen after you fight? You fight again. Try to hurt the other person, shoot him, stab him, or kill him. So instead of going through all that, if you don't act on what you feel, then it won't escalate. I'd rather be a wimp than jeopardize my life. People that are less violent may let things happen to them, but at the same time they're strong. You don't have to be physically strong, but mentally strong.

Before I got involved with conflict resolution, I'd have an argument with someone on the street and let's say they pulled out a weapon. Before, I would have been quick to react—I would have argued or even took it to another level. Now I know that I can think my way out of it. I'd ask, "Do you think that pulling out a weapon will help you?" Or, "Where will you go from here after you use the weapon on me?" I would give him ideas to help him think "Is it worth it?" So instead of reacting fast, maybe he'll think first. People do a lot of things without thinking.

Once I moved to this neighborhood and came to Satellite, I became an

A student and I completely changed. I had people here to help—I couldn't have done it myself. But you've got to let yourself be helped. Here we are all equals. The students and teachers aren't on different levels. We all listen to each others' opinions. Teachers listen to students' opinions and students listen to teachers' opinions. And here, if you can't accept mediation to settle your disputes, you have to leave. When you have people, the way we do here, to encourage you, it makes you bigger and stronger. And if my teacher makes me feel like this, imagine what I can do for someone else. That way, one person can change a whole bunch.

I got fed up with myself. I was hurting myself physically and mentally. I was hurting my family, too. I want to be somebody in life, have a job, a future. I knew that I couldn't do that if I didn't have an education. I try to stay out of problems as much as possible now. I want to go to college. I know if I get into problems either I'll be locked up or I'll be dead. And I don't need that for myself or my family.

This program can change even the worst kind of guy if they want to change. Even a bad person is human. They still have feelings. If they see bitterness, they will react to it. No matter how macho they try to be in front of their friends, when they're by themselves they still cry, you know?[3]

Jill

I grew up in Orange County, near Los Angeles. My mom and stepdad raised me. I am an only child.

I really had a fun childhood. I lived a very normal childhood. I moved to Oceanside at the end of fifth grade. For the first time I saw people from different races, kids in gangs. I thought, "What's going on?" I was really confused. It was a whole other world for me. I liked it because it wasn't the nice little preppy, snobby place that I grew up in.

During my seventh-grade year I got interviewed and accepted as a Young Ambassador at Roosevelt Middle School. I got so educated about accepting other people for who you are, not just from the outside but in the inside. I learned what gangs are all about and how to accept and respect other people, no matter what their background or group. I've always had a lot of different friends, never just one type of friend.

Then I became a mediator and that was wonderful. It gave me a sense of responsibility. I felt good about myself and confident enough to share myself with people who were having a conflict. It was a great feeling knowing that you could help people so that they didn't end up in a fight and end their friendship.

I loved being able to help people and talk to them without telling them what to do. It was kind of like a job and I loved it. I think kids listen to kids because they are their peers. There's something that clicks and they can listen better with kids instead of with an adult. There's a different connection than with adults.

I also learned how to confront situations when it was necessary and avoid them when it was better to do so. One day I was walking home from school with some friends. We passed the park, and there was this guy there with his girlfriend. All of a sudden he yelled out, "Shut up!" We were talking and laughing, so my friend Iris thought he was talking to us. I assumed he was talking to his girlfriend and I just ignored it. But Iris yelled out, "Did he just tell us to shut up?" She yelled it really loudly so he could hear it. So he answered, "Yeah, I did." Iris said, "Oh." We kept walking and then he started throwing his Cryp signs at us. So Iris jokingly said, "Yeah, I'm from the Bloods." That did it. And just those two silly words, "Shut up," had started this whole scene.

By now, he was so offended that he started coming at us like he was going to kill us. I was scared. We all were. He could have had a gun on him and blown us away. My heart was beating so fast and I had these incredible butterflies in my stomach. We just kept walking and were almost to Iris's house when he got into his car and started driving really crazily. We hid behind a bus. We heard the car stop. Yvonne was the oldest one among us. She looked more like she would have said something, so he automatically went for her. He got out of his car and started walking toward her, rolling his shirt up like he was ready to fight us, maybe kill us. Somehow I prayed that he was proba-

bly just trying to scare us. So we kept walking and he finally slowed down and yelled after us, "Remember, I know where you live." He got in his car, screeched his tires, and drove away.

We sat there thinking and calming down. I thought, "I can never walk home again. Now I'm considered a part of a gang. I'll always have to look behind my back." I knew that I'd never want to be in this situation again. I was angry at Iris because she doesn't think about anything. She put our lives in danger. If she hadn't responded in that way, this would never have happened. If Iris had been a mediator, she would have known better not to escalate that situation.

I've always had a pretty good sense of myself. I never had trouble expressing my mind and telling other people how I felt. It's just that when I talked I wouldn't listen to other people. I would blabber on about how I felt and that was it. I learned how to listen and put words into ways where people would understand. Being involved with RCCP, I became calmer and expressed my feelings without being mad or frustrated. Today I can express my feelings and I know it's okay to cry, I know when I'm sad, and when I'm happy.

Growing up as a white female American there have been times when I'm really confused. I've had people put me down because some of my best friends are African-American. I've been accused of being too white, or trying to be black, or of not understanding. I've always accepted people by their color, race, and sex. This is who I was and RCCP supported who I was. It helped me understand why some people are prejudiced, how they think and how to work through these issues.

It makes me sad that the world is this way, but I know who I am. I feel like I have a future, a direction. I know I can and will accomplish something in life.

Edgar

My name is Edgar, actually it's Edgardo. I'm Mexican-American. I'll be a ninth-grader soon and will be going to Vista High School.

When I was in the seventh grade, I got this letter saying that I was recognized as a leader and would I like to attend a Young Ambassador meeting.

It made me feel good that people thought I was a leader, that people believed in me. I decided to attend the meeting because it was about learning other ways to handle problems without fighting. I always expressed my feelings with fighting, but I wanted to change that because I didn't want to mess up my life.

When I first got to middle school, I kicked back with the gang members. I was doing what they wanted me to do, not what I wanted to do. If it weren't for this program I probably would have dropped out of school by now because I would have just been into what they wanted me to be. I'd probably have gotten suspended. I'm glad I chose this way instead of becoming a gang member.

I was raised in the gang culture. I always looked up to my sister. She's six-teen right now and she was a hard-core gang member. She used to take me to parties in Escondido. Her boyfriends used to come to our house and bring gang members. They'd take me cruising with them. I looked up to my sister, so I went. One of the reasons we moved out of Escondido was because my dad wanted us to get out of the barrio. I've got four other sisters and a brother. All of them are younger than me. They all look up to me. I don't want them to be like my older sister. I want them to have a good life.

My friends give me a hard time because I'm a mediator, but I don't listen to them. I hear them but I ignore them.

My parents are happy that I'm a mediator. When I came out in the news-paper last year they showed it to the neighbors. This made me feel real good.

I'm hoping I could go to college. My parents aren't college-educated. I'd like to go. I believe in myself. I think I can get ahead in life. I want to get a good education and be somebody. I want to depend on myself, not on anybody else. I learned this mainly from my parents, and from my peers. I know I'm going to make it and nobody is going to stop me.

I hang around with all kinds of kids. I play basketball with Brian and Kevin and some of the homeboys say, "What are you hanging around with those white boys for?" I ignore them. I like playing basketball with my friends so I just ignore them.

In this program I've been able to help people solve their problems without fighting or getting into trouble. This program is good to start at a school. It makes you become more joined together and it helps the school become a better one.

I've seen changes in some of the kids at school since we started this program. They look at things differently now. They don't act the same, they try to be more peaceful now. I think we are really changing the gangs on this campus. There used to be a lot of gangs before, writing in the bathrooms and all that, but it's sort of stopped. It's more peaceful now. I think the gang members are scared now. They know that more people are trying to stop them from doing what they want to do and that sooner or later they're going to lose control of what they are doing. They think they're the highest rank in school, that they run the school. But I think they're getting scared because they know they're not anymore.

Mohammed

I'm in the seventh grade at West Side Academy in New York City. I've been a mediator for three years. I'm Egyptian. I come from a different background than many of my friends and I know what it feels like to be different. We should all be treated equally no matter what the color of our skin.

I always wanted to be a mediator. I used to look up to the mediators when I was younger. Before I started mediating, if someone did something to me I would just do it back to them without thinking. Now I think twice. Mediation taught me to calm myself down, not to react right away. It taught me to have patience with myself. And now with my brother, I'm pretty nice with him. But don't worry, I still fight with him sometimes. Now my brother is a mediator too. He's almost three years younger than me.

I feel better about myself since I'm a mediator. I feel that I'm giving something to the community and that makes me feel happy. It gives me more self-esteem.

I was real excited about becoming a mediator but I thought it was going to be a piece of cake. I just thought, "All right, they're in trouble and we'll just help them talk it out." But now I see it's very hard. First you have to calm down the kids who are in a fight and then you can talk to them. It's hard, but I still love doing it.

A good mediator is someone who can keep things confidential, has a good personality, is honest and good with people. He doesn't have to be great in math. He has to have a good heart.

One time at recess two friends were playing football. When the quarter-back threw the ball another kid on the same team knocked him down by mistake because he wanted to catch the ball himself. And then they started to get into this big fight and asked for a mediator. Sometimes I have to ask the kids, "Do you really want mediation or are you just doing this to stay out of trouble?" I had to tell these two kids, "Look, this is not a joke. We're here to help you. If you can't help us, we can't help you."

I think mediation is having a good effect on this school. Students are start-ing to feel like we're their parents. We're little parents and we take care of them. If they have a problem, we go to them and help solve their conflict. They're understanding what mediation really is. I've been at this school for seven years. I see a difference.

If we didn't have this program in my school, there would be a lot more violence—people just beating up on kids who are more helpless. But we're helping them in this way.

I see what's outside and it's terrible. Being a mediator you can solve things in an environment where you don't have to fight. There's enough fighting outside already. And although I'm only one person, I belong to a big group. This big group can have a big effect on this school. It's a start. We have to start somewhere. This is the start of the big race. We have to start with the schools and hopefully the kids see the mediators and will try to be like that.

I'm happy to be part of this program and I hope I stay in it for a long while.

Jonathan

If I hate someone and commit a violent act and they come back and do it to me, we both end up hurt. It goes on and on and on. My children would do *it to their children and their children would do it to their children. It's best to reciprocate hate and violence with love and understanding. We should try to send that message to our children and so on. [Like] somebody once told me, "An eye for an eye makes the whole world blind."*

Tanya

It's up to us to make the change. We are all a part of the things that go wrong in our world. It's up to us to have open minds and not to judge anybody by the color of their skin, or their religion. I believe in the concept of treating others the way you want them to treat you. Put yourself in someone else's place before you do anything that you wouldn't want done to you. It's not good for us to look on the outside. Look within yourself. It's up to us to help each other.

Leadership for Tomorrow

Listening to these voices we know that we are succeeding beyond teaching young people a new paradigm and equipping them with social skills. We are instilling in them the knowledge that they are powerful, that what they are saying does matter. Their voices speak loudly, and they are listened to.

As we look at this expanding global village we live in, the importance of young people's leadership becomes ever more evident. As adults, many of us desire to make changes, but changes require much effort and time before we witness results; we know how difficult it is to erase the learning of the past, to see things from a different perspective. Today's youth are making these changes now. They are learning early on that nonviolence and appreciation of our diversity is the normal, natural way of living. They are learning these lessons in peaceable classrooms and in peaceable schools. And they are carrying their convictions out into the world around them.

Our work of the last ten years has allowed us a rare glimpse of how that world can be. Not too long ago, Archbishop Desmund Tutu of South Africa was addressing a group of young people who had been "children of war," victims of devastation and loss of extreme dimensions. These young people had since risen from the trauma of their past to heal themselves and help others. Archbishop Tutu said something to them that day that holds true for the thousands of mediators in our program. He said, "When you are walking down the street and someone looks at you and says, 'Who are you?' you tell them, 'I am a sign of hope.'"

Our own living signs of hope are walking down many streets in this country every day proving that violence is preventable, not inevitable. These young people are our greatest teachers.

[**8**]

You and I do not have to wait for a great cause to make a commitment to personal
service. It can start with those nearest to us: our family and friends.
- Mahatma Gandhi -

OUR VISION OF EDUCATION emphasizes the role of schools as places
where children practice managing their emotions, handling conflict, and
standing up to prejudice, but parents have an obvious and critical role to
play in reinforcing these lessons of the heart at home.

Parents as well as young people struggle with such influences as free-
floating anger, the glamorization of violence, and the increase in bigotry in
our society. We find that often, just as young people and teachers need to
be explicitly taught skills in emotional literacy, conflict resolution, and bias
awareness, so do parents. The parent component of our work has been essential to the progress we have made with kids. In fact, the schooling we describe is most effective when parents reinforce these lessons at home. The
issues we address apply as much to parenting as to schooling, and there are
some very practical ways in which the methods we teach at schools can be
brought into the home.

In our work with parents, we offer a series of four three-hour workshops,
called Peace in the Family. Parents come to the sessions hungry for support

and eager to learn these new skills. At the workshops they can stop and think about how they act as parents—what works and what they would like to do differently. We provide concrete skills in active listening, I-messages, win-win negotiation, and many of the other strategies that we also teach young people.

We start by having parents explore their own approaches to conflict as these relate to their parenting styles. They take a closer look at their beliefs, values, and behavior around conflict and diversity issues. We then begin to offer some practical techniques for opening up lines of communication between them and their children. They are given plenty of time to practice these new ways of interacting. Our hope is that parents leave the training with a better sense of the role they can play in creating a more peaceful and just world.

Our work with parents parallels the themes of the peaceable classroom—especially in building a caring community within the context of the workshops. "We shared a lot of things happening in our lives and made good friends" was how one parent described the bonds that parents made with one another. "I was surprised to see how many parents had the same problems with their children." Another parent said, "We had some good laughs. A lot of things are hard for parents, but it was fun to figure them out together."

These days the task of parenting is often an isolating experience. As we recreate an experience of deeper community in these workshops, parents get a chance to learn from and be supported by each other.

Kim, one of our veteran parent trainers, remembers the following story:

At the beginning of one parent workshop series, a father dropped off his wife at the workshop. We were able to coax Dad in, even though he emphatically said, "I am not going to stay—this is for mothers!" By workshop number four, there was not a dry eye in the room when Dad, who never missed a session, tearfully expressed his appreciation for what he had learned, saying, "I only want to make life better between me and my son."

As the peaceable classroom provides an opportunity for young people to experience the bonding kids need for healthy development in a school setting, "peaceable homes" can complement and support this experience. A home that is nonviolent in its structure and day-to-day life can serve as a crucial safety net for children. Where there is peace in the family, children grow up with more immunity to at-risk behaviors related to violence and discrimination. When parents and schools become partners in modeling these skills, children have an even greater chance of witnessing positive examples and learning how to handle themselves in a variety of circumstances. As Kim says, "If we demonstrate peaceful responses, our children start to learn by example. Children don't always do what you say, but often what you do. A product of my involvement is that I am trying to 'example' the behavior I expect from my children."

We find our work with parents is taking place progressively earlier in the process of implementing RCCP within a school district. When we first started, the parent component usually began well after the curriculum and mediation components were in place; in the newest districts, parent training has taken place right along with teacher training. We're finding that the sooner we can elicit the help of parents, the better RCCP starts to flow in a school environment, and the greater are the positive changes in our young people. Hearing the same message in both the home and school strengthens the framework kids need to counteract the destructive messages and norms our wider society still tolerates about conflict, violence, and diversity. Clearly, when parents and schools are in this boat together a very powerful alliance is created on behalf of our children.

Emotional Literacy in the Home

Parents can play a key role in supporting emotional literacy education by raising children to be in touch with their emotional selves. First, however, those of us who were raised in environments which taught us to ignore our emotions, or that only some emotions were okay ("Don't come out of your room until you have a smile on your face"), have to unlearn some of the messages of our own childhoods before we can teach our children to share their feelings and express them appropriately. Most often the way we were raised determines how we act as parents, unless we consciously seek another way.

We need to see how we sometimes reject children's feelings with unthinking remarks such as "Stop crying right now—there's nothing to be afraid of," "Don't be like that," "I'm ashamed of you." I (Linda) remember doing at a parent workshop a version of an activity we also do with teachers, the one that involves setting up a scenario of a day in the life of a child who is constantly bombarded by put-downs.[1] This particular day, I was co-training with my friend and colleague Emma González with a large group of parents. I was holding up the large red paper heart and we were creating a story about a day in the life of seven-year-old Carmen. I'd say, "You're pathetic. You can't do anything right," and rip off a piece of the heart. "You disgust me—just shut up." Rip. By the third rip, after "You just don't try hard enough," nearly every one of the entire group of sixty mothers was crying. I had never experienced such a dramatic emotional response to this activity. They began to talk about how they said similar things all the time to their children because they thought it built character.

We have to keep finding ways to tell our children how much we love them and how proud we are of them. When we create a safe and loving place for parents to look at themselves, they can begin to do so. One parent told us that the part of the training on put-downs and put-ups had affected her the most. "Something I can do in the future is to take put-downs out of the fights. It's natural to get into that stuff. We all grew up that way, using lots of put-downs, but if we stop using them, we can take the fire out of the conflict."

Parents can do much more to strengthen the components of emotional intelligence. They can make a habit of naming emotions as readily as they name objects, helping kids increase their vocabulary for feelings. They can also model the behavior of calming down when they are upset and before they act—or at least talk openly to kids about losing their control if they do. This helps young people strengthen the pattern of first stopping and calming down, then thinking about their response, and finally picking the best one and trying it.

John Gottman, who has conducted research on marriage and parents' interactions with their children, found that a significant factor in developing a child's emotional competence was how parents managed moments when a child was upset, distressed, emotional. Parental response in such circumstances usually falls into certain categories. Some try to diminish the feeling—telling the child to "get over it" or, "Go to your room." Others respond with anger: "How dare you talk to me that way?" Others become the child's "emotional coach," helping the child identify the feeling and understand what is at the root of it. Gottman found that kids with parents who did this were much more stable emotionally. These parents were strengthening two important components of emotional literacy—self-awareness and managing moods.[2]

Another element of emotional intelligence that parents can strengthen in kids is motivation—maintaining hope and optimism in the face of setbacks. Children often take rejection of any kind personally. Parents can help them interpret rejection differently, to think optimistically rather than pessimistically. Say a child comes home in tears; because a friend refuses to play with him, he's convinced that there is something wrong with him. A parent can intervene by asking, "What are some other reasons this could be happening?" By exploring possibilities—for instance, that the friend was just having a bad day—the child can be gently led away from negative self-judgment.

Empathy is another component of emotional intelligence, one that unfolds in children throughout their childhood and can be strengthened in the school as well as the home. Empathy begins when an infant hears another baby cry and starts to cry him- or herself. When a young toddler sees another child fall down and get hurt, s/he will usually do something to soothe the other. As a child gets older, empathy is exhibited by the ability to take other people's perspectives and to read their feelings. Parents, acting as emotional coaches, can help. When a child has done something upsetting, "How do you think I'm feeling right now?" can be a very useful question. Parents can also encourage siblings to tell each other how they feel in constructive ways, especially when conflict arises.

Using Conflict Resolution in the Home

As with conflict styles, we can get locked into a specific parenting style, and in fact there are some parallels.

A conflict avoider or soft negotiator usually has a parenting style that does not set clear limits for children. Conflict avoiders tend to respond frequently and quickly to children's needs but reserve little time for themselves in the process. When things seem overwhelming, screaming and shouting is often the result, because feelings on both sides are being ignored.

A hard negotiation style goes hand in hand with an authoritarian approach to parenting, strongly directing and often locking into power struggles with children. Children fear getting reprimanded, intimidated, or even physically punished. Communication closes down because fear prevents children from admitting problems or giving information. Resentment builds. Authoritarian parents often show their anger through spanking. Child psychiatrists James Comer and Alvin Poussaint remind us that spanking can easily become a way to stop whatever is happening, with or without just cause; children become the focus of the parent's attention for "being bad," and they get spanked whether or not they deserve it, receiving a double message about hitting others.[3] When it's okay to spank, it's harder to convince children to talk out their problems. Children growing up with this style rely on others for advice and support, looking outside themselves instead of within for direction; adolescents who have been disciplined harshly will tend to follow their peers rather than solve problems for themselves.

A principled negotiator who is able to confront conflict nonviolently usually has a parenting style that lends itself to collaboration and problem-solving. A parent with this conflict style is able to keep communication open, exploring disagreement and generating alternative solutions together with the child. Power struggles usually decrease and needs are addressed on both sides with both the parent and the child feeling empowered and listened to. Kids who've been raised this way stand more of a chance of making wise choices for themselves than children who have had less direction than they needed or those who've experienced too strict an approach, because developing strong decision-making skills is key in functioning in a society with so many options and dangers.

Like teachers, parents often bring negative connotations to the word "conflict." Depending on their parenting style, conflict is a source of frustration, avoidance, or opportunity. Participants in our RCCP parent workshops often realize that they can learn helpful skills to deal better with conflict. Kim explains.

Many children have commented, after a fight, that fighting was the one way they knew to respond to a problem. This is because many adults don't know alternatives to teach or suggest—we either accept our lack of alternatives as being okay or we don't seek any other options. As a result of my involvement with RCCP, I have learned that there are many nonviolent ways to respond to conflict. When we are not comfortable with a situation, we must first know what our alternatives are and then choose the appropriate response.

Using conflict resolution skills with our children does not mean we as parents have to give up our authority. Young people still need limits set. In fact, a parent can always say, "This is not negotiable." But many things *are* negotiable, especially when parents expand their range of peacemaking skills.

It is important for parents to know their "anger triggers." Knowing what triggers our anger can help us manage our feelings during a conflict, and young people need to see that the adults closest to them can be angry without being abusive or out of control. Our children are usually not trying to make us mad. It just happens.

Active listening is especially crucial to open communication between parent and child. "I have a habit of finishing sentences for my older daughter," observed Heather, a participant in one of our parent trainings.

While she talks, I sit there nodding impatiently, "Uh-huh, uh-huh, uh-huh," and then I finish her thought for her. After the workshop last weekend I decided to try to stop doing that. It wasn't long before she put me to the test. But this time I was patient. I gave her my attention. I didn't interrupt her. And when she was done I actually paraphrased what I heard her saying. She was shocked. She just stood there with tears in her eyes. "Mommy," she said, "you really listened to me."

Another idea we bring to parents to help them resolve conflicts creatively is seeing the difference between demands and real needs. When a thirteen-year-old says to her mom, "But I *have* to go to this party," there probably is a real need underneath that demand: "I want to feel part of the group." It is important for parents to think about what their own real needs are as well as help their children identify theirs. There are often many ways to find a solution that meets both sets of needs, especially if we give each other clear reasons.

We help parents look at conflict as a problem to be solved instead of a contest to be won, and to understand that it is important to involve young people in the solution. A parent can say, "Here's the problem as I see it. How do you see it? What can we do about it?" Vernita Young, a parent trainer from Anchorage, puts it this way: "As a parent, I have become aware of the importance of having my children learn to be problem-solvers. I now want my children to be successful negotiators. Therefore I have to learn not to be an arbitrator in their conflicts."

And indeed we are often better off telling ourselves that our bickering children are having a valuable experience in conflict resolution and allowing them to learn to be independent problem-solvers by resolving their own disputes. We don't always have to listen in on our children's conversations and add our opinion.

Of course, sometimes we need to help. Researchers Adele Faber and Elaine Mazlish, in their book *Siblings Without Rivalry*, describe four levels of constructive intervention.[4] A parent of two siblings might say, "I can hear that the two of you are having a problem. Would you like to tell me what's happening? Who'd like to go first?" It is often important to paraphrase what each child is saying and reflect their feelings. At the second level of intervention, a parent can simply summarize the problem and say, "This is a tough one, but I'm sure you two can work out a solution that's fair to both of you. Let me know if you need my help," and then leave the children alone. It may be good to talk to them once the conflict is over, to see how they feel about the solution and help them see what they can learn from the conflict.

When the children involved feel they can exercise little or no control over the situation, real mediation is necessary. After you help the youngsters summarize what happened and what they are feeling, it may be useful to ask each child what could have been done differently, and then finally, "What can you do now to solve this problem?" At this third level, the parent stays present as a third party, right up to congratulating the kids on their solution. It is important, of course, for the parent to maintain neutrality and make suggestions only when the kids seem stuck. A fourth level of intervention is sometimes called for when the conflict is getting out of hand with great intensity of feeling. Sometimes we have to describe what we see and separate the parties from each other: "I see two very angry children who are about to hurt each other. It is not safe for you to stay together. We need a cooling-off period. You go to your room, and you go in the living room." When emotions are high, children cannot focus on the problem-solving process. One way to avoid situations like these is to intervene before an argument escalates, if possible. When children are already getting out of hand, physical intervention and direct, firm statements are critical. After the cooling-off period, a more gentle intervention might be very useful.

Raising Our Children to Honor Their Roots and Value Diversity

Just as children get their first lessons about how to deal with conflict in the home, it is there that they start to learn about diversity. As Carol Brunson Phillips, an expert in diversity education, points out,

It has been said that actions speak louder than words. And if this is so in the case of childrearing, then we must be especially vigilant in our actions to shape the values children will attach as they learn about the people in their world. If we don't, they will learn by default the messages that are already prevalent out there and both we and they will contribute to perpetuating past ideas which we do not want to replicate in our children's future.[5]

Children need to know that they can ask for help in making sense of the many messages—positive and negative—they get from society at large, by coming to us as parents and openly talking about these things. They begin to notice differences very early and they will start to hear words in conversations that will make them question where they fit in. "What am I?" they might ask when they hear words like "black" or "white." They'll be exposed—before we even realize it—to prejudice and bias.

All children suffer when issues of prejudice are not dealt with openly. For children of color, families need to help make sense of a society that is racist and sexist by labeling it as such. Otherwise, a child's self-esteem and development will be undermined. Even when surrounded by a loving, accepting family, children of color are still taking in the subtle and not so subtle negative messages of the wider world. Children who happen to be male and white and able-bodied also need help. Racism and sexism can distort their reality as well; they need to reject the myth that they are superior.

There are some practical things to remember that will help our children grow up bias-free. The following are some strategies and ideas to keep in mind:

> We can help our children by openly acknowledging not only that each person is a unique individual, but also that he or she is a member of a group, and that there is good and bad in every group.

> We can teach by example, being the first to admit our own prejudices and avoiding jokes and other expressions that stereotype people.

> We can foster respect for differences and make it okay to agree to disagree.

> We can take action when either children or adults show prejudice, instead of ignoring it or indicating approval in any way, and we can let our kids see us act on our unbiased beliefs.

Although schools can help play a critical role in countering the effects of prejudice and discrimination, parents are key in reinforcing these positive messages at home.

And of course we also have a larger responsibility. Not only do we need to give our children an anti-bias education at home and in school, we must also continue to work to create a wider society that is just and free of bigotry.

Peace Corners and Family Meeting Time

We've seen how the peace corner is a part of many classrooms. The idea of having a place where youngsters can be alone or talk something out can be useful in our homes as well. The peace corner is designed to help youngsters collect their thoughts and come to their center—not quite a replacement for the typical "go to your room and cool off" place. Youngsters might keep diaries there, favorite books, drawing supplies, anything to help them express their feelings rather than be carried away by them.

We also suggest that families set up a way to deal collectively with conflicts that affect them all. Family meetings can be helpful—time set aside to discuss problems and come up with mutually agreed upon solutions. Some families write down conflicts or family problems and place them in a "conflict jar," to be discussed during the next family meeting. Children need to be told about what's going on within the family. They need to feel included and know that problems and even arguments are a natural part of being a family. Children need to also learn that sometimes we can discuss problems when we don't even know the solutions.

Family meetings can also be a time to reinforce our values in relation to conflict. We may say, "In this family we don't hit when we're angry," or, "We talk things out instead of fighting." When the family is together, we have an opportunity to reiterate that feelings are okay and that talking things out works. Family meetings can also be a time for practicing skills in communication and conflict resolution—from active listening to I-messages—or for reading a favorite book or story. Martha, a parent of three, shared what family meetings have meant to her: "From the moment we posted the agenda and wrote down complaints to bring up at the meeting, the burden was lifted from me, the parent who's usually at home to hear about all the fights. I no longer feel responsible for solving every problem on the spot. Instead we've been working on problem-solving when we're all together and cooled off. What a relief."[6]

The Influence of Media, Video Games, and Toys: A Parent's Role

Some of us who are adults today grew up in homes that did not even have a television set. Today children can watch one violent incident on TV every six minutes. The average child is likely to watch eight thousand screen murders by the end of elementary school. A New York City fifth-grader named Jessica complained, "They say we're the future. We're going to run the world in the next few years but they treat us like we're nothing. You can't watch TV anymore because cartoons, transformers, GI Joes, practically everything has something to do with guns or something to do with destroying something else."

The link between violence on the screen and violence in our communities has been the subject of more than three thousand studies conducted in the past forty years. The majority of these studies have established a strong causal link between violence on the screen and violence in our communities. Young people in the United States watch an average of twenty-eight hours of TV weekly. During this time, if children watch only prime-time programming, they see about a hundred acts of violence. If Saturday morning cartoons are included in their weekly viewing, the violence rate increases dramatically since there are twenty-five violent acts per hour on Saturday morning cartoons—six times the rate of episodic TV dramas.[7] Toy companies have partnered with the television industry. They are in this business together, sharing their wealth and marketing strategies. Children can buy toys that interact electronically with the television set directly, or they can go to their local pizza parlors and play video games most parents have not even seen.

Recently I watched an eleven-year-old boy play a video game in a pizza place in my own New York City neighborhood. It turned out to be Mortal Kombat, a game I had heard of for years but hadn't come close to observing in all its intricacies. I watched in amazement and disgust as two figures started to fight each other to the finish, with limbs flying everywhere. The young boy's excitement grew stronger as one opponent was clearly defeating the other. The boy began jumping up and down as the words "Finish him! Finish him!" flashed on the screen. The game came to a halt. Mission completed—someone had been "finished."

How could this industry, having such influence on our children, have gone so far without being stopped? Part of the answer came to me when I realized that although I had spent the last twenty years working for the cause of nonviolence, I was exposing myself to Mortal Kombat for the first time.

The producers of violence in the media and the creators of the next video game are counting on the adults of this society not to tune in. They are counting on our ignorance or our denial of the harm such exposure brings to our children.

Some time ago, I was boarding a plane from New York to Cincinnati and noticed I would be traveling with about forty Muslim refugees from Afghanistan, mostly traveling in family units, each with a name tag and a number. They were dressed in long, flowing attire, and all the women were veiled. Half an hour into the flight, the flight attendants made their way down the aisle asking us if we would like to view the movie, the title of which did not sound familiar to me. I decided to pass. I didn't pay attention to the movie until I saw several Muslim mothers and fathers chatting back and forth and pointing at the monitor. Although I couldn't hear it, I looked up to see the all too familiar visuals—guns, shooting, people and buildings being blown up. Then I saw the adults in the families with kids begin to create makeshift blindfolds out of any materials they could find; the children remained blindfolded throughout the remainder of the movie, at least another hour.

I had many reactions at once. How could they *do* this to kids? And then came the harder questions. How can *we* do this to kids? Are we in such a state of denial that a major airline can show any level of violence on the screen while we pay our full fares and convince ourselves that as long as we don't order the headsets our children are protected? I thought of all the young children I know and love and imagined them sitting next to me. If I allowed myself to take in the meaning of what I was seeing on the screen, I too would want to shield them from the sight.

I was incensed. As I started to compose my first letter to an airline about showing violent movies in a situation where adults have absolutely no opportunity to shield children from their effect, I realized how numbed I too had been to the insidiousness of the glamorization of violence in our culture. I wondered if my letter was going to be the first that this airline received or the tenth or the one hundredth, and whether our collected protests would eventually alter what would be shown to a captive audience. As I sat and wrote, those kids in blindfolds no longer seemed such a strange sight.

The media and the music and toy industries have such an impact on our kids' lives that many of the thoughts, ideas, and behaviors they are exhibiting are no longer coming from their own minds and hearts. When we adults weren't looking, these industries claimed a prominent place in our children's lives. Most of us are still quite numb to its effects. In our workshops I've heard parents say things like, "I can't go to that movie my kid went to, I can't take the violence." Or, when questioned about the music their kids are listening to, they say, "I can't stand the beat, so no, I haven't really listened to the words." Television, music, video games, and toys are giving our children clear direction in terms of values to adhere to, behavior to follow, and ways to think.

So what *can* parents do? Clearly, whether we enjoy it or not, we must monitor what our children are listening to, viewing, and experiencing. We must advocate for regulations that will help us control our children's viewing and we must turn objectionable programs off in the meantime, explaining to our children why. We must be more aware of the music our children listen to, exposing them to music we enjoy and expanding their repertoire. We must come out of our denial of the harm caused by such exposure. Social science researchers Daniel Linz, Barbara Wilson, and Barbara Randall point to six ways media violence affects our children's behavior:

[1] *Reward for Violence.* When violent acts are rewarded or left unpunished on television, this functions as a sanction for violent behavior.

[2] *Reality of Violence.* The more realistically a violent act is portrayed, the more likely it is to be imitated.

[3] *Violent Role Models.* Children look up to characters whose use of violence is portrayed as necessary or attractive, and are more likely to become aggressive themselves.

[4] *Justified Violence.* The more violence is presented as okay, the more likely it will be copied.

[5] *Violent Connections.* If children find similarity between themselves and a character, they are more likely to emulate that violence in real life.

[6]   *Amount of Violence.* Excessive exposure to violence can produce a "psychological blunting" that can cause lack of responsiveness to real-life aggression.[8]

There is another risk, as Judith Myer-Walls points out: "Critics worry that children will imitate violent acts they have seen. A more realistic concern for me is that my children may be traumatized by televised violence. When the unthinkable is presented, not only does it become thinkable, but it may also become haunting."[9]

Violent programming, games, and music are teaching our children that their world is dangerous. These influences are also teaching them that the Rambos of this world are making the hero's choice. One of the most important things we can do is not leave a vacuum in our children's lives by neglecting to state what our beliefs are about these issues. We have to help our kids recognize what is fantasy and what is reality. Our kids need media literacy skills—explanations and discussions about how special effects are used to manipulate what we see. Our kids cannot avoid all violent toys or TV shows, but we can engage them in critical debate about the issues they raise. One father let his child watch "Teenage Mutant Ninja Turtles," but only if the child would imagine a fifth turtle named Gandhi. The father engaged his son in a deep discussion afterward on how "Ninja Gandhi" might get the turtles out of trouble without resorting to violence.[10]

Besides monitoring and engaging our children in discussions about what they are seeing and hearing, we must register our concerns publicly. I sent my first letter of protest to an airline only two years ago. We've got to let producers, advertisers, TV stations know that we won't continue to be associated with them or buy their sponsors' products if they continue to participate in making violence glamorous to our children's senses. Our responsibility is not only to try to change the direct impact these industries have on our children, but also to play a critical role in shaping their messages in a wider context. Schools and homes can work together in this arena.

A few years ago in Anchorage, Alaska, a group of kids that included some RCCP mediators were at a slumber party when one child decided to show everyone his family's gun; another child urged him to show them how it was used. In moments one child was dead, another had killed a friend, and the others will probably be traumatized for the rest of their lives. Although we had taught our kids skills to resolve conflict, we hadn't discussed a more hidden threat—the availability of guns in our society. These kids misjudged because they hadn't been taught what to do in this kind of dangerous situation.

Since half of all households in America keep a firearm for either hunting or protection, it is a startling but true fact that gun safety must be included in the discussion of safety habits in the home. According to pollster Larry Hugick of Princeton Survey Research Associates, three out of ten boys between the ages of fourteen and seventeen have handled a gun and more than half of them knew where to get one.[11] In fact, youths in small towns and rural areas are even more likely to know where to get a gun—usually in their own homes. Extensive advertising by gun manufacturers and the gun lobby has convinced many Americans that owning a gun increases their chances of protecting themselves and their children. Unfortunately, this is far from true. The Children's Defense Fund reports that a gun in the home is forty-three times more likely to be used to commit homicide, suicide, or accidental killing than it is to kill a wrongdoer in self-defense.[12] In fact, when a couple fights and a gun is available in the home, the risk of death to one of them increases twelve times as compared to the risk involving any other weapon.[13]

The risks of firearms, especially to children, are clear. Since one out of two homes does own a firearm, we need at the very least to childproof our homes for guns just as we do for dangerous chemicals, prescription drugs, and sharp objects. If we have a gun in the home, we must explain to children the dangers of touching it. Children need to know that guns can kill people or cause lifelong disabilities. They need to be taught the difference between media violence and real-life violence. And, finally, we as adults can decrease the potential of an accident by keeping firearms unloaded and locked away from children's reach, with bullets stored and locked in a separate place.

Guns in the home is an issue that families across America will have to continue to grapple with. Young Jason in Anchorage would be alive today had his playmate's family not had a gun in their home. As we as a nation debate the issue of gun control, it seems that none of us would disagree that kids should not have access to guns and that we as adults need to make firearms inaccessible to kids under all circumstances.

Parents and Schools as Partners

Researcher Anne Wescott Dodd has found that parents may oppose even innovations they have positive attitudes toward if they are not included in their implementation.[14] Parents in RCCP are involved right from the start; in fact, it is not uncommon for PTA presidents to attend an introductory training for teachers. Before we implement RCCP in a district, we have extensive contact with a number of constituencies—the local school board *and* parent advisory committees in particular.

Dodd also found that parents need to see that a given innovation has a clear link to teaching children "the basics." This is a challenge in the kind of education we advocate—especially since most parents' education did not include the social and emotional domain—but educators can help parents understand those linkages. Children are better able to learn reading, writing, and arithmetic when conflict is minimized in their lives and they feel more secure. We talk about Gardner's seven intelligences with parents. Most importantly, we invite parents to visit classrooms where RCCP lessons are being taught. Firsthand experience lets them see how their children are being helped in all aspects of their work and lives.

We consider parents and community full partners in the changes we are trying to make in schools. In working together, we underscore the fact that all of us—children, parents, and educators—need to consider ourselves life-long learners.

RCCP parents have played and continue to play an advocacy role in the development and implementation of our work. When a large group of parents in any district goes through the parent component of our work, they become strong allies in ensuring its continued expansion and implementation in the district.

Since we began in the South Orange-Maplewood School District in 1992, district support has been steady and strong. However, a few years ago, the state education budget was cut so drastically that the local school board faced difficult decisions about which programs to cut. Unbeknownst to any of the RCCP staff, a group of about twelve parent trainers wrote a letter and circulated it throughout the district, following up with phone calls to other parents, encouraging them to support the full implementation of RCCP in their district. On the evening that the school board came together to vote on budget cuts, a large, organized contingent of RCCP parents spoke up eloquently and passionately about the positive changes they had experienced in themselves and their children as a result of our work. Although the school district suffered the largest budget cut that year ever, RCCP's budget for the next school year was kept intact.

Trials, Rewards, and Hopes

Two seven-year-olds were trying to figure something out. "Let's go ask my mom—she knows everything," one said. Years passed and the two children were now thirteen and had a different dilemma: "We can't ask my mom, she doesn't know anything." And two decades later, the same two guys declare, "As my mother used to say . . ." The circle of parenthood often goes from being all knowing, to knowing nothing, to being quotable.

Parents do hold a central place in kids' lives, after all. The 1993 *Newsweek* CDF poll showed that even though the American family has undergone huge changes, young people still look primarily to their parents for support. When youths from ten to seventeen years of age were asked who were "very important" influences in their lives, 86 percent answered their parents. Other very important influences were grandparents (56 percent), places of worship (55 percent), and teachers (50 percent). Only 22 percent ranked television, movies, and popular music as very important influences.[15]

It seems our children are telling us that they would welcome parents and other caregivers playing a greater role in their nurturance, direction, and in simply making sense out of a complicated, often frightening world. Marian Wright Edelman, in her book *The Measure of Our Success: A Letter to My Children and Yours*, captures the heart and soul of most parents' hopes in a letter to her son, who was then twenty-one:

I seek your forgiveness for all the times I talked when I should have listened; got angry when I should have been patient; acted when I should have waited; scolded when I should have encouraged; criticized when I should have complimented. Most of all, I am sorry for all the times I did not affirm all the wonderful things you are and got lost in parental admonitions about things left undone. I hope so much that the balance of your childhood memories will be positive and loving.

Parents are sometimes frail and troubled, but also strong and resilient human beings—just like you—if we get the nurturing and support all human beings need. What we owe you, our children, is our best effort to be a person worth emulating. I hope I can grow big enough one day to feel I have done that.[16]

Schools need to support parents and caregivers to "grow up big enough" to help our children get all they need to feel safe, both emotionally and physically.

< IV >

BUILDING

ON

THE

PAST

FOR

THE

FUTURE

[**9**]

RCCP'S BEGINNINGS

Meaningful coincidences are unthinkable as pure chance—the more they multiply
and the greater and more exact the correspondence is [the more] they can no
longer be regarded as pure chance, but, for the lack of causal explanation, have to
be thought of as meaningful arrangements.

- Carl Jung -

THE RESOLVING CONFLICT CREATIVELY Program traces its grassroots beginnings to a crisp November evening in 1985, when a "meaningful
arrangement" occurred between Tom Roderick, myself (Linda), and Community School District 15 in Brooklyn, New York.[1] Several hundred
people—teachers, principals, students, and members of the community
were attending the district's monthly school board meeting. The focus of the
meeting was to adopt several resolutions. Top on the list was setting up a
"peace education" program in the district, and Tom and I were invited to
help. Then, as now, Tom Roderick was executive director of Educators for
Social Responsibility in New York City (ESR Metro). I was working as curriculum specialist for New York City's Central Board of Education.

Many little events and experiences finally led to having Tom and I meet
at the right time in our careers for the idea of RCCP to take shape and mate-
rialize. It seems that both of us had been preparing our whole lives for this

work, each in our own way. We shared a commitment to educating children in the ways of peace. Gandhi's words—"If we are to reach real peace in this world and if we are to carry on a real war against war, we shall have to begin with the children"—were very real to us. Now we had come across a small group of people in a corner of Brooklyn who were eager to join us in that vision.

And a grand vision it was—that in schools throughout the city, adults and youngsters would learn nonviolent approaches to conflict and respect for cultural diversity. Perhaps the New York City schools would not only embrace this goal, but also lead the way for the rest of the country.

This vision seemed in contradiction to what was going on in the world at the time. In 1985 the Cold War dominated national consciousness, fear of nuclear war was palpable, and the Reagan administration was pumping billions of dollars into an unprecedented military buildup.

Yet our work took shape and meaning from the events of the time and the collective concern of many committed people. The early 1980s had brought a surge of public concern about the nuclear arms race, and educators had become aware that children were ill prepared to cope with the intensity of the emotions evoked by the nuclear age.

In fact, a group of educators in Cambridge, Massachusetts, began to act on the notion that students needed adults in their lives who would explore and challenge the beliefs and fears they had, so that young people's lives could become less despairing. They felt that children needed adults who could encourage them to go beyond the fear and grow and develop into informed, active citizens of the future.

ESR and RCCP

It was from these concerns that Educators for Social Responsibility (ESR) grew and was founded in 1981, four years before the birth of RCCP. Sheldon Berman, past president and founding member of the parent organization, explains, "In our own thinking, we realized we needed to address some of the root causes of the arms race—and not only the arms race, but violence in general." As ESR members and staff focused on the root causes of violence, the organization, as Berman puts it, "grew into its name."

Mainly, ESR's interest was to help students engage in some critical thinking about important contemporary issues. The goal was to help students and teachers examine their biases and assumptions as well as the political and social context they were living in. ESR's work blended the intellect with the emotions and led people to examine their values. The emphasis was on encouraging students to participate actively in the issues of the day instead of giving in to the despair and apathy many were feeling.

It was in this context that the collaboration of Educators for Social Responsibility and the New York City Board of Education, in the persons of Tom and myself, moved forward with the pilot effort, first called the Model Peace Education Program, in Community School District 15. Jerold Glassman, then superintendent of District 15, and Arthur Foresta, then coordinator of special projects, spearheaded the efforts. Glassman presented the idea of creating a study group around issues of peace education to his principals. He got three volunteers: William Casey, principal of P.S. 321, who went on to become the next superintendent of District 15; Sylvia Oberferst, then principal of P.S. 230; and Patrick Daly, principal of P.S. 15, whose tragic death five years later underscored the need to expand our work. All three agreed to choose three or four teacher volunteers from their teaching staffs to accompany them to a five-session after-school workshop Tom and I were to conduct. At that time ESR Metro was only three years old. Tom remembers:

The beginning involvement with District 15 was a real stretching experience for us in ESR. We had been working with individual teachers in schools around the city, developing curriculum materials. Suddenly, we had this meeting and then here was a whole district that wanted a district-wide pro-

gram in peace education. It took some real hard work to see what these ideas—conflict resolution, peace education—would look like on a district level.

Tom and I led the sessions. Each week we focused on a different way of looking at the issues—in one session we took a global perspective, in another we studied the conflict resolution approach, and so on. At the end of the five sessions, the participants came to the question, So what direction should *we* go in? It was a unanimous decision: although the national and global perspectives were important, they wanted to start close to home at the interpersonal level, emphasizing conflict resolution. William Casey, reflecting on why, said:

I think I could probably give you a simple reason. When this program was beginning, I had spent six to seven hours a day with a thousand children for the past ten years. You become keenly aware of the part violence plays in their lives both in school—schoolyards, classrooms and hallways—and out of school, in terms of television, toys, and reading material. While I think parents and teachers were very concerned about the impact this had on kids' lives, we were all doing something individually. This was an opportunity to collectively do something about a great source of danger for kids.

Pioneers and Partners

Thinking back to our initial move toward conflict resolution, I realize that 1985 was well before the epidemic of violence had reached such serious proportions in our society. We were thinking preventively and asking what we might put in place now so that kids could be helped sooner rather than later.

As we proceeded with this focus, we began to connect to others who had also been thinking about and experimenting with teaching conflict resolution to kids. Priscilla Prutzman's groundbreaking work with Children's Creative Response to Conflict (CCRC) helped shape the themes in our curriculum. William Kreidler of Boston ESR shared with us many wonderful ideas for working with children and teachers. In 1984, his book *Creative Conflict Resolution: More than 200 Activities in the Classroom K-6* was published. Kreidler had gathered the best work of others to date, including CCRC, and went a step further. Drawing on his own classroom experience, he created many usable classroom activities. He also began to document a clear rationale for the concepts and activities we were starting to expose kids to, citing the latest research in the field. We used this popular publication extensively and relied on it in planning our own curriculum.

Early on, we also had the support of officials at the New York City Board of Education's central headquarters. Charlotte Frank, then director of curriculum and instruction, and Sylvia Schechter, then director of the health and physical education unit, encouraged and supported us and opened many doors.

There were also a handful of individual donors who were the first of many private funders to support the program over the years. These individuals as well as foundation and corporate contributors enabled the program to be developed and launched. During those early stages, we also looked to the national center of ESR for guidance as well. Many ESR members, both nationally and locally, were thinking about the connection between conflict resolution and the awareness of nuclear issues. They became excited about our direction in District 15, shifting their energies to help support the work. Our funders continue to help us maintain the quality of our work and the development of new components.

In the beginning, things were happening so quickly we barely had a chance to reflect on what we were doing. We were stretching and growing rapidly, and becoming aware that what we were attempting to do—institutionalize the teaching of this work in a large urban school system—had not been done before. We were breaking new ground. We started to be very concerned about the level of responsibility we had toward the wider educational community to make sure these pioneering efforts were in fact helping kids and making schools better.

As of 1987, RCCP had not yet expanded outside of District 15, even though there were many requests to do so from the central board and other New York City school districts. An independent educational evaluation firm, Metis Associates, had an ongoing contract with District 15, and the superintendent, William Casey, who had been one of the first RCCP principals, offered to let us use some of their time to evaluate RCCP independently. It was just what we wanted—objective feedback and information so that we could go to other districts with a sense that our work and how we were doing it seemed like a "promising practice."

It was the 1987–1988 school year. Metis Associates conducted a search for possible instruments to use for teachers, principals, and students to measure some of the effects of teaching conflict resolution in schools. At the time, the only instruments that had been used to evaluate the field of conflict resolution were self-esteem measures. We knew that the changes we were seeing in kids and teachers went beyond this, so we challenged Metis to use an experimental research design which incorporated both cognitive and attitudinal measures. They created and field-tested knowledge and attitudinal surveys. The Metis evaluations released in 1988 and 1990 pointed to the fact that we were definitely on the right track.

Most teachers agreed that student behavior had changed because of RCCP. Fully 71 percent reported moderate or great decreases in physical violence in the classroom, while 66 percent observed less name-calling and fewer verbal put-downs. Teachers reported, as we mentioned earlier, that they had changed, too. Fully 84 percent said that their own listening skills had improved. Many also noted that they had applied their increased knowledge of conflict resolution techniques in their personal lives.[2]

We knew that a more in-depth evaluation would eventually be needed, but this was a good start. After those first three years of experimenting, fine-tuning, and evaluating, we were cautiously ready to bring RCCP to more districts within the city. Our growth at this stage was deliberate and managed, since no other course would enable us to maintain the high standards we were committed to.

And so in 1988 we finally started to expand to other school districts in New York City. It got more and more difficult to convince the central board that we needed to expand slowly enough that we could maintain the quality of what we were doing. The New York City schools were beginning to experience an increase in violent incidents, and RCCP seemed like an important step to take.

The program's popularity was also fueled by a nationwide surge in violence among young people. After several highly publicized homicides in Howard Beach, Bensonhurst, and Crown Heights in New York, violence prevention became a hot political issue. The result: educational and political leaders in New York City and other parts of the country began to pay serious attention to RCCP. This led to several breakthroughs, including a NYC Central Board of Education budget for the program.

Former New York City chancellors Joseph Fernández and Ramón Cortines and other chancellors before them have supported RCCP. Despite severe budget cuts in recent years, the NYC Board of Education office of the RCCP has maintained its staff and budget. From time to time, we've had to resist the pressure—sometimes from a chancellor, sometimes self-imposed —to expand too quickly and without adequate resources.

Our way of working with schools is labor-intensive. It has to be, for violence is deeply rooted in our society, and old ways of thinking don't change overnight. Our pedagogy is experiential and learner-centered. Many teachers need support in integrating these approaches into their teaching. Without a thorough introductory course and generous amounts of classroom-based support, the program cannot take hold. Still, one of our favorite chancellors went so far as to characterize RCCP as a "Cadillac program at a time when we need economy cars." We argued with him, of course. Working day in and day out in schools, we know that RCCP is a Volkswagen beetle. We designed it in collaboration with school staff who wanted a program that would cost as little as possible but still get us where we needed to go. To strip it down any further would mean removing one of its wheels. The shell would be there, and the name, but we wouldn't be going anywhere.

As we expanded to several more districts within New York City, we began to work with the high schools, developing our secondary school curriculum and using it in the alternative high schools first. We developed our work in middle schools next, by working collaboratively with two other conflict resolution programs—Effective Alternatives in Reconciliation Services (EARS) and Victim Services' School Mediators' Alternative Resolution Team (SMART)—to create Project STOP, Schools Teaching Options for Peace. The New York City Central Board of Education received both public and private funding to bring STOP into forty middle schools. The Fund for NYC Public Education coordinated these efforts. As we began our work in the middle schools, the curriculum, staff development, and parent components were delivered by ESR Metro, using the model and materials we had developed in RCCP. The mediation component was delivered by the other two organizations. This was the first opportunity to put our full model into a school simultaneously and to work collaboratively with two other committed organizations.

Beyond New York City

In December of 1987, Tom Roderick was asked to write an article on the topic of children and violence for the contemporary issues section of *Educational Leadership*. Tom wrote a wonderful article tracing the history of conflict resolution in schools and highlighting our work in New York City. He titled his article "Johnny Can Learn to Negotiate." Since *Educational Leadership* is a journal that almost every principal in America subscribes to, we became national news.

ESR National began to receive many inquiries. One of them was from the Anchorage School District in Alaska, saying that they were ready to sponsor a course in "peace education" in three weeks! They wanted to know if someone could go to Anchorage in January to do this, during what turned out to be one of the city's coldest winters in history. Larry Dieringer of ESR National called my office to see if I was interested, and my assistant interrupted a staff meeting to call me to the phone. My immediate response to Larry was, "Are you kidding?" Several things went through my mind. There was too much happening in New York—I couldn't possibly leave. How could anything developed in urban New York be of any use to a school system in Anchorage, Alaska? And finally, could I really handle a fourteen-hour plane ride and sub-zero temperatures? I said, "Don't think I'll be able to," but when I told my staff about the phone call, they encouraged me to go. They all had a sense that what we were doing was going to catch on around the country and that we needed to humbly share what we had been learning. By the end of the day I called Larry back to say yes.

Flying into the Anchorage airport, the earth blanketed in white, the imposing mountains at a distance, the sun setting over Prince William Sound and the Cook Inlet, I wondered whether this was a crazy idea—a big mistake—or whether our grassroots origins in New York City, teaching kids "another way of fighting," had a certain universality regardless of the distance and differences that separated these two places.

In retrospect we understand how important it was to go to a place like Anchorage. Once again, a coincidental event had much to teach us. Had we not expanded to the Anchorage School District next, I suspect it would have taken us a long time to realize that our work could take hold in any school environment that was concerned about these issues—urban, suburban, or rural. Working there also confirmed to us that our model and approach were based on such sound pedagogy that they *did* have value and relevance to other school systems. The New Orleans Public Schools followed next, then the Vista Unified School District in Southern California, the South Orange-Maplewood School District in New Jersey, and, most recently, the Atlanta Public Schools.

In each place where we went, a person or a small group of people responded with enthusiasm to our work and held the vision for it to happen at their site. Seeing the need in their school districts, they convinced us that we needed to be there.

Thus, by the end of 1992, with several sites replicating our work, I was still coordinating RCCP for the NYC public schools under an agreement from the school system to be on a part-time line. It was becoming clearer that although many efforts in conflict resolution were starting in individual schools across the country, we were pioneers in working at the school district level. After over two decades in our school system, I was feeling a strong tug to leave my position there in order to concentrate on the national expansion of RCCP.

In March of 1993, Marian Wright Edelman, president of the Children's Defense Fund, received funding to bring together a hundred violence prevention experts from around the country in Washington, D.C. I was invited and spent three days with some of the most compassionate, committed people in the country, struggling to shape a national agenda for this work. In her opening greeting, as she launched CDF's new violence prevention focus, Marian said, "I hope I have the right people in the room because I need you for the next twenty years." As I went through the room meeting folks, it became evident that very few of them were educators working in schools. By the end of the third day, I was mentally composing my letter of resignation to the New York City school system. I was feeling the need to commit to this work more fully at the national level. RCCP's New York office had grown strong in leadership and ESR Metro was ever present as co-founder and co-implementer. Confident that my leaving would not hurt the city's program, I handed in my letter of resignation in May of 1993. One of our first RCCP teachers, who was then on the RCCP Board of Education staff, assumed my position; I was grateful Sheila Alson answered "the call" to move RCCP-NY forward and become its coordinator. Today, Mariana Gastón, who has been with us since the beginning of the program, serves as coordinator of RCCP for the New York City Public Schools.

Under ESR's auspices, the RCCP National Center opened its doors in New York City in the fall of 1993, with not even enough money to pay me a full salary. I was reminded of the early days, when Tom gave his services for free and I helped on borrowed time. It was all quite familiar. But we have always been believers in "do the work and the money will follow," and sure enough, we connected to a handful of foundations that helped us get off the ground. We'll always be thankful to those early donors who had the faith to join us in taking the next step.

At the RCCP National Center, we see our role as that of a catalyst in preparing educators to provide high quality instruction and effective school programs in conflict resolution and intercultural understanding in a variety of educational settings across the country. Our goal is to help transform the culture of participating schools so that they model the values and principles of creative nonviolent conflict resolution and respect for diversity. Our task at the RCCP National Center is also one of advocacy, informing school systems, policy makers, and the general public about the efficacy of such work in schools and what it takes for successful implementation. As we seek to create more peaceful, just, and democratic learning communities based on a comprehensive and sustained approach, we are always learning and adjusting. Those of us who are implementing RCCP through the country are a rather self-critical and reflective group. We consider ourselves a "work in progress." We try to learn from both what has worked and what hasn't so that we can continue to make a significant contribution to the fields of conflict resolution, social and emotional learning, and intercultural understanding.

Future directions for RCCP are already emerging. In classrooms we're seeing increasing numbers of wounded children. Many have seen traumatic violent incidents or have been abused. As we were completing this book, I made time to visit some RCCP elementary classrooms and meet some Junior Ambassadors. In a matter of thirty minutes, five children disclosed that they had witnessed or experienced serious violence—from seeing a friend shot to witnessing a stabbing in the park. Surrounded by violence, so many of our children are suffering now and are at risk for future violent behavior. We are in the process of developing a new component of

RCCP to serve these particular children, and we can't be doing this quickly enough.

Our vision has always been informed by the idea that if you want peace, you have to work for justice. But political leaders in Congress are leading the nation in the opposite direction. While global economic developments lead to huge job losses for U.S. workers, our government is abandoning its long-standing commitment to provide at least a minimal safety net for the poorest Americans. This is one reason we are also exploring ways to encourage young people to play an active role in the wider world.

Some of our political leaders have become infatuated with punishment, putting it forth as the cure for all social ills. There are 1.5 million people in prison in the United States. For the first time in the nation's history we are spending more on prisons than on education. Building jails has become our only low-income housing program. Whatever happened to the idea that an ounce of prevention is worth a pound of cure? Our ambitious three-year RCCP Research Program will be completed in 1996. It has been funded by the Centers for Disease Control and Prevention and private foundations. We hope that it will provide evidence that preventive programs can work to reduce violence. In fact, as we go to print, the researchers tell us that although the data has not yet been fully analyzed, some early hopeful signs are emerging. We want to help bring about a change of heart that will move our society away from throwing punishment at problems and toward violence prevention and addressing the root causes of violence.

Clearly we have our work cut out for us. But ten years ago none of us envisioned how far RCCP would go and how great its impact would be. "When we dream alone, it is only a dream," wrote Dom Helder Camara of Brazil. "But when we dream together, it is the beginning of reality."

The rest of our history remains to be written by the individuals who are now choosing to become part of the movement of waging peace in our schools. With us, they stand on the shoulders of the committed principals, teachers, parents, and kids who have had the courage to move forward with this work, and whose efforts and inspiration have helped us grow.

Back to Basics: Good Pedagogy

Over the years, we have learned what good pedagogy is. In developing our model, we were striving to determine what would help kids begin to think differently about conflict and diversity and what model would best assure that young people developed social and emotional skills along with their academic skills. Finally, what would it take to prepare the adults in kids' lives—parents, caregivers, teachers, and administrators—to do this?

Our decades of experience in schools tells us that learning should be experience-based, not drawn exclusively from textbooks and other standardized materials. As educators, we know that children are not empty vessels to be filled with information but active learners, each with an innate drive to be competent and to understand. Given what we know about how children learn, we recognize that the role of the teacher needs to be that of a facilitator of the learning process. Teachers can't be the authoritative deliverers of information designed to be mastered in a narrowly defined classroom context, not with the material we are attempting to bring into the educational arena nationwide.

We also know that good education is about the development of good habits—habits of mind, habits of heart, and habits of work. The cultivation of good habits of the mind goes hand in hand with the nurturing of social and emotional competencies. Good pedagogy reflects children's individuality and is fashioned to honor it.

As the incidence of violence in our society and in our schools increases, so too does the urgency of our work.

As we move forward to offer our curricula and programs to communities nationwide, we establish the goals of RCCP as the following:

> to promote more caring and cooperative behavior among young people and adults, in and out of school;

> to reduce violence and violence-related behavior among young people and adults, in and out of school;

> to bring about lasting changes in the attitudes and behavior of young people and adults in how they manage their emotions, resolve conflict, and honor diversity;

> to institutionalize RCCP in schools and school districts.

The RCCP Model

Much has been learned in the past decade about what makes for effective innovations in school systems. In 1985, we were directed mainly by our many years of experience as educators and a trial-and-error process that informed us each step of the way.

We started with work in the classroom first because we felt that all children needed to learn these skills. We were experimenting with training teachers and developing curriculum simultaneously. RCCP's curricula provide effective teaching strategies on the elementary, middle school, and high school levels. Our curriculum materials are skill-oriented; they give young people concrete strategies to become empowered to make a difference in their own lives and in those around them.

Learning these skills requires weekly practice, so teachers are encouraged to do at least one lesson a week. Lessons have been organized in a logical sequence, but teachers teach them according to the needs of their students and their academic curricular focus. We encourage teachers to set aside a thirty- to forty-five-minute period each week for a specific lesson or workshop. Teachers are also encouraged to use "teachable moments" that arise out of what's happening in the classroom or in the world at large. Participating teachers also infuse RCCP concepts and skills into other parts of their curriculum.

The lessons are built around a variety of activities, including role-playing, interviewing, group dialogue, brainstorming, and other experiential learning strategies, all of which require a high degree of student participation and interaction.

Early on, we realized that teachers, once trained, needed support to assure that what they were learning would become part of their active repertoire. As Tom Roderick and I visited the teachers in the three District 15 schools where we began the program, we weren't sure how much support teachers would need. We soon realized that teachers needed a lot of coaching to incorporate these new ideas into the daily life of their classrooms. That's why we instituted an intensive program of staff development that went beyond the twenty-four-hour introductory training to include a series of eight to ten classroom visits per year, including one-on-one consultations and after-school meetings with RCCP staff. This concentration on teachers' professional development has since been highlighted as one of the program's greatest strengths.

The peer mediation component of our work developed next. When Tom returned from being trained in a school model for peer mediation (through a program of the Community Board in San Francisco), we began to implement peer mediation in the three schools that were already deeply committed to the curriculum component. Soon we had trained our first cadre of peer mediators.

There was a lot of excitement about this new component of our work. It made what was happening in the classrooms so visible. At that time, several other efforts in peer mediation were under way in isolated schools in other parts of the country, but none had the solid foundation of a curriculum component in place first.

The idea that we should work with parents took root when we celebrated one of our first mediators' graduations. The parents of the mediators were really excited about what their children were learning and doing, and they too wanted to learn these skills. When a "mock mediation" was conducted at the graduation ceremony, a group of parents exclaimed, "That's what they're doing around the dinner table! We need to learn these skills." That spark got us thinking.

The parent training component has two models. In one model, parents receive a series of four three-hour workshops, delivered by trained RCCP staff. In the second model, parents are trained to teach other parents in turn. Potential parent trainers receive a total of forty hours of training in conflict resolution and intergroup relations, which prepares them to return to their schools and provide the twelve-hour training for other parents. As mentioned in the previous chapter, we use a parent leadership training manual to assist parent trainers.

Our administrative component happened later on, as we became more cognizant of the research on leadership and school change. We understood that in order to effectively implement this program in a school, the support of school and district administrators was crucial. We began to study the change process and assist school officials in finding the best ways to implement our program in a school over a period of time. We found ourselves conducting management retreats and other workshops for administrators so as to help them meet the specific needs of their particular schools. Our primary aim with the administrator component is to encourage administrators to embrace and model creative approaches to dealing with conflict and diversity. We have also learned the importance of site leadership support to the program. (We'll return to this topic in the next chapter.)

Thus our model of implementation has emerged from our years of experience as educators experimenting and listening to colleagues who were actively implementing RCCP in their schools. We've found the following components crucial:

> Professional development for teachers, including a twenty-four-hour introductory course and ongoing support for classroom implementation of the RCCP curriculum

> Regular classroom instruction based on K-12 curricula developed by RCCP in close collaboration with participating teachers

> Peer mediation in which carefully selected groups of students are trained in mediation and then serve their schools as peer mediators

> Administrator training to introduce administrators to the concepts and skills of conflict resolution and bias awareness in order to show them how they can use their leadership to achieve effective implementation of the program

> Parent training to help parents develop better ways of dealing with conflict and prejudice at home and become more effective leaders in their children's schools

Ideally, RCCP is implemented at the district level so as to insure an eventual shift in institutionalizing this innovation over a period of time in the school district. We start by collaborating with the superintendent, talking about what the needs of the school district are and how RCCP can help meet these needs. When a school district makes a commitment to implement RCCP, it makes a long-term commitment (four to five years) to the program. When we began, this kind of commitment seemed almost impossible. Now school systems are more aware of the need to address this issue over a long period of time before lasting change will happen.

The schools that are selected to begin the program within a district do so on a voluntary basis, and individuals who participate at the school level volunteer as well. Once schools decide to become part of the RCCP family, they develop a whole-school planning process for implementation that is appropriate to their own situation. The plan provides for curriculum implementation, the development of a peer mediation program, parent workshops, and administrator leadership training.

The Ingredients for Success

In a 1995 report of the General Accounting Office of the United States that surveyed hundreds of promising programs in violence prevention, RCCP was one of four programs mentioned. The committee interviewed violence prevention program directors, federal agency officials, and recognized experts in the field. They interviewed teachers, students, principals. They also reviewed evaluation data on these programs.[3]

In summarizing the research, the following characteristics were outlined as being key:

> A comprehensive approach
> Early start and long-term commitment
> Strong leadership and disciplinary policies
> Staff development
> Parental involvement
> Interagency partnerships and community linkages
> A culturally sensitive and developmentally appropriate approach

We feel that the components we have incorporated into the Resolving Conflict Creatively Program model—and the content we teach—reflect these criteria. Perhaps this is because we proceeded carefully, step by step, to ensure that whatever we would do would stand the test of time.

We are often asked how RCCP go so far "so quickly." Maybe what people are really wondering is how we managed to break through bureaucratic walls to create a space for a unique collaboration of a nonprofit organization and a school system in co-founding and co-implementing a program, not in one or two schools but in an entire district, then institutionalizing it in the largest urban school system in the country. Reflecting on our work over the last decade, we have identified several factors that have contributed to our success.

> We ask for a long-term commitment (at least five years) from any school system that wishes to work with us. We start with a commitment at the school district level.

> We offer a unique partnership between a nonprofit organization de-

voted to furthering this type of work (ESR) and a school system that needs it. This collaboration creates a certain leverage which ensures the program's quality and sustainability.

> We conceive of this work as a basic part of children's education, not an add-on. We have given much thought to how the program can be integrated into a school system in order to change the entire school culture.

> From the beginning, our work has been as much about issues of diversity as it has been about prosocial skills and conflict resolution. These three areas are often on separate tracks in the educational community, causing efforts to become fragmented in schools.

> Our model—its components and curriculum—was developed over the course of many years with input from the people we serve.

> RCCP's co-founders were educators with long-term experience in educational reform and familiarity with the culture of public schooling as well as good pedagogy.

> Our model involves all levels of the school community, providing training and support to students, teachers, administrators, support staff, and parents.

> Rather than having a "client approach," we have always been willing to see the collaboration between the program and the school system it serves as an equal partnership. We therefore help find local and national resources to support the effort in a school district.

> We are constantly evaluating our work. We are also willing to put what we are doing to the test of outside evaluation. Currently, with a grant from the Centers for Disease Control and Prevention, NYC RCCP has

launched the largest evaluation of a school-based conflict resolution program ever done, with a sample group of over 8,000 students. (We are presently in 325 schools nationwide.)

As schools continue to seek out ways to become safer for young people, it is helpful to remember that any innovation will require steadfast attention and commitment to the process of change.

Now let's turn our attention to the "how to's" of bringing the RCCP model to an entire school.

CREATING PEACEABLE SCHOOLS

> Sometimes consensus in community is reached with miraculous rapidity.
> But at other times it is arrived at only after lengthy struggle. Just because it is a
> safe place does not mean community is a place without conflict. It is, however,
> a place where conflict can be resolved without physical or emotional
> bloodshed and with wisdom as well as grace.
>
> - M. Scott Peck -
> *The Different Drum*

Russian Jack Elementary School, Anchorage, Alaska, May 1993.

It is springtime in Anchorage. This is my first trip to Russian Jack, an elementary school that has been part of the Resolving Conflict Creatively Program for four years now. The sun is bright and warm; the flowers are blooming in contrast to the not-so-distant mountain peaks that peer over the city with a winter-wonderland splendor.

Upon entering Russian Jack, I notice a sign posted on the entrance doorway. It reads, "Our mission at Russian Jack, a school of cultural diversity, is to ensure that each student is actively involved in their learning, while developing a positive sense of self and becoming a productive citizen who will contribute to society in a meaningful way."

Already I have a sense of this school. I continue down the hallway, taking in my new surroundings. To the right there's a large glass display case. Inside are a myriad of art projects, bright colorful masks, and drums. A sign above reads, "These masks and drums are representative of the culture of the Inuit people of Alaska. They were made by our Young Ambassadors, students dedicated to promoting a deeper understanding of the rich cultural diversity of the children at Russian Jack Elementary School."

Donna, the school's principal of six years, welcomes me. I had met Donna once before, at an RCCP advanced training for administrators. Donna offers to take time out of her busy schedule to take me around the school. As we visit, she talks about her school and how they've implemented RCCP. Heading up the stairs towards the second floor, I see a huge banner with the letters P-E-A-C-E—large, multicolored letters sewn over a pastel backdrop. It is magnificent. Young people must read this several times a day as they go back and forth to the library and their classrooms; adults read it, too.

Teachers and children alike greet us as we visit classrooms and observe them at work. They are working in groups, talking and sharing ideas. Classroom walls display several indicators that the Resolving Conflict Creatively Program is in place at this school. "Put-up" charts line walls. Words such as "I-Messages" and "Active Listening" are listed as tools to be used for communication in the classroom. There is a calmness in the air, not the frenzy one can sometimes feel in schools.

Recess begins. Donna is called to the office. I head out to the playground. It is a warm and clear day. The sun is up and shining almost all day at this time of the year. The children are playful and carefree. Mediators stand by in the lunchroom and outdoors. Several times a conflict begins to erupt, but mediators intervene immediately. I am told that the library mediation room is available in case it gets too cold to mediate outside.

Throughout the day, children and teachers share their experiences with me. They talk about Russian Jack proudly and openly. They talk about the benefits they see since RCCP has been at their school. They support their mediators, who they feel are helping to create a culture of nonviolence at this school. Young people talk highly about their teachers, principal, and mediation program. They feel safe at this school. "It's a good school," says Nikita. "Not like my other school where kids used to fight all the time."[1]

These images from Anchorage offer hints of what can happen when the kind of educational vision we have been talking about is put into practice. Earlier on, we've talked about how individual classrooms and teachers can change. But whole schools too are changing as they embrace this work. They are doing this because they know that the peaceable classroom can only work well in a context where it is supported by a peaceable school.

This chapter is about how schools can build caring communities that espouse the values and beliefs we have been discussing. It touches on some of the things administrators and teams of teachers can do to transform a school's culture, drawing from our own experience and that of other school leaders. We look at the challenges faced, the knowledge gained, and the results we have seen.

Establishing the Need

I (Janet) can still remember when Vince Jewell, Larrie Hall, and I—then administrators of Roosevelt, a comprehensive California middle school of over fifteen hundred ethnically diverse students in grades six through eight—decided that RCCP was what we wanted because it addressed exactly the issues we were dealing with at our school.

Our demographics had changed drastically. We now had a rich, diverse population, including approximately 40 percent kids of color. But our staff was primarily of white, European-American background. We needed ways to educate staff about differences and our kids needed to learn to value diversity.

We were also looking for ways to help kids settle their conflicts nonviolently. The number of fights was increasing at our school, and the level of negative verbal put-downs was even worse. Additionally, gang members were on the rise at our school, flashing their colors and signs and leaving their graffiti on our walls.

While our school was essentially child-centered (teachers related well with kids and worked hard to provide them with a strong education and relevant activities), there was still a preponderance of what some refer to as "middle-school mentality." Adults expected kids to be handled in a certain way when they broke the rules. Some teachers had a distinctly adversarial way of confronting students; their actions often escalated defiance and caused resentment in kids. We wanted teachers to view discipline not as punishment but as a learning tool through which young people could change their behaviors over time.

Finally, as school reform guided us towards participatory management and shared decision making, we realized that we all lacked the necessary skills in communication to be able to have long healthy discussions about what we wanted for our school. We needed better ways to problem-solve and negotiate. This wasn't just about kids learning about conflict resolution— we needed it too.

We talked a lot about "change" in those days. All of us kept up on the latest literature. We recognized that RCCP was more than an add-on to be done only in the classroom. We knew that it was the tool that would provide us with a foundation for the way we would do things at our school. It would give us the "common language," the common beliefs that would eventually unite us as a community of learners. It would become part of the culture. And we knew it wouldn't happen overnight. It would take time, but it would change the way we did things at Roosevelt, and that it did.

As school leaders across the country come to us at RCCP today in need of this work, we first encourage them to look within and ask themselves "where they are" and "where they would like to get to" with this work. The needs vary for different schools. Judith, director of Satellite Academy, a school where not too long before a popular student had been murdered at a party, identified the teaching of conflict resolution skills as a top priority: "Suddenly, our kids realized they would have to help each other stay alive and they began to see the RCCP as something that could help them do that."

Schools embracing our work know this isn't a quick fix, but a long-term commitment to building a new school culture. Arlene, a principal in New Jersey, explains why these efforts are worth it: "This work has made a difference in my district, my school, and in my personal life. No other program has touched so many people in my professional world and become so much a part of them—I can say with confidence that what has been learned will outlast our contact with the trainers. The language of RCCP has become woven into how we talk about what we do and how we care for one another in ways that no other program I know has ever done."

When school leaders look to us to begin implementing this work, we make sure they realize that any real, long-lasting change isn't going to happen unless it becomes a part of the school culture—the ideologies, philosophies, expectations, attitudes, and practices important to the members of the school. What is the climate of this school like? How do the people act towards one another? Is there a lot of violence? Is there an atmosphere of trust? Do people here celebrate their differences and work towards collaborative problem-solving? School culture affects every decision that is made. Ideally, it is the thread that holds schools together—a very durable thread, like the kind that is used to sew on buttons and adjust hems, the kind that doesn't easily break. While many factors influence the shaping of a school's culture, we have noted that such schoolwide efforts depend on three factors in particular: trusting relationships, commitment on the part of members of the school community, and a way for this community to take *ownership* of the process.

Building Relationships

Perhaps what we hear the most about from educators who have undertaken to shift a school's culture is the importance of working to build relationships. How do people relate to each other in the school community and in what ways must this change? We have found that relationships between individual adults, between individual students, and between adults and students become mutually supportive and strengthened through a commitment to the peaceable school. Through understanding, empathy, and respect for each other, a cooperative school spirit can be established.

When Roberta became principal of P. S. 75 in Manhattan some six years ago, the people in the school had lost trust—trust in the leadership, trust in each other. The school had no backbone, nothing to tie it together. She decided to get involved with RCCP as a way to bring this school together. "People didn't trust in this place. They didn't trust children. They didn't trust parents. They didn't trust each other," she says. "There was no such thing as a staff party. I felt that this place needed a lot of support. But I also felt they needed a method in which to communicate and do things.

Kids recognize the quality of school relationships too. Matt, a student mediator from Vista, California, said to me one day, "I think what's best about this school is the respect we kids get from the adults here. They care about how we think and what we have to say." Responses to a survey administered to students at Myrtle Banks Elementary School in New Orleans across the board pointed to the importance of the bonds kids felt with their teachers.[2] When asked what students liked best about their school, nearly every fifth- and sixth-grade student said something positive about their teachers, and that they felt teachers cared about them. Interestingly enough, in talking to teachers at this same school we heard their dedication to caring for children reflected in their own statements: "I've been here for fifteen years, and although these children come here with so many problems, I could never go teach anywhere else. These children need us here. For some of them, we're the only family they have." Clearly, relationship building is a priority in this school.

Purpose, Ownership, and Long-Term Commitment

Having a common purpose and commitment is crucial to the long-term effectiveness of the peaceable school model, a fact borne out by the literature on school change.[3]

In order to develop these commonalities, people have to create an environment in which they can discover what they really care about, and then they have to get together so they can talk about their visions.[4] When schools decide to begin this work, they first of all talk a lot—and listen, too. We've learned that involving all the key stakeholders in this process—teachers, students, parents, and administrators—early on assures that the plan and direction of the work is understood and embraced by all.

But getting to core values, the deeply held beliefs that individuals collectively agree to put at the foundation of all they do in a school, is a long-term process. This vision of what a school believes and wants to be for its young people grows over time. Trying to decide in a few meetings what a school is all about leads to mistakes.[5]

When I first started working at Roosevelt Middle School, we didn't have a written mission statement. We knew we cared about kids and child-centered education, but we hadn't put into words what we were all about as a school. I remember wondering why it was important for everyone to "be on the same page" before we tried to write our vision down. Vince, then principal, served as a great mentor to me, a model of what leadership is all about. He reminded me, "Janet, we aren't ready to write a mission statement yet. We're in transition. We need time. Not everybody's with us yet." I didn't understand that at the time. Now I do, because changing beliefs and behavior is a long-term process. Now, five years later, Larrie, who shared the assistant principal's role with me, is principal of Roosevelt. Two months ago he handed me the school's mission statement, which reads, "Our mission is to provide our school community with knowledge, responsible decision-making skills, and an appreciation of diversity by creating a safe, respectful learning environment." The vision of the school evolved over time and it now reflects what kids actually learn at that school and how this learning takes place. It wouldn't have embodied the depth of the change process in a truthful way had it been rushed.

As Lee Ann, principal of Nunaka Valley in Anchorage, said, "RCCP works and it takes time. I credit the program with being the major influence on the staff and students of our school in bringing about change. The 'culture' of our school has changed over the past five years and our reality now closely matches our expectations in terms of attitudes and behaviors."

Creating ownership, getting an active "buy-in" for a program of change, even when it is largely supported in principle by teachers, requires hard work and a clear plan on the part of the school leader. Jackie, principal of Empresa Elementary School in Vista, California, talked about this process at her school.

You need to involve all staff in the decision to implement a program like RCCP. Throughout the process we sent groups of staff members to each training cycle until every person who works at Empresa had received the [training]. The structure of the training encouraged staff to bond with one another and also to bond with the concepts taught.

My part in the development process was to keep enthusiasm for the program alive and allow it to flourish. A leadership team of staff members and I met monthly to review how the program was being embraced and what strategies were needed to maintain our dream. We developed a multi-faceted approach.

A group of third-, fourth- and fifth-graders were chosen to become Junior Ambassadors. Our well-trained problem-solvers visited all classrooms and presented RCCP lessons to other children. We recognized two children from each classroom monthly with a 'Peacemakers Award.' Classmates nominated and voted on who should receive these awards. Their pictures went up on the peacemakers board and a free pizza luncheon was given to the award recipients. Recently we received a safety grant from the state of California and provided a three-day advanced peacemaking skills training for [the] fourth- and fifth-graders who became mediators at our school.

It was also important to maintain teacher enthusiasm for the program. In

order to encourage staff to teach the RCCP lessons in the classroom, our
RCCP mentor teacher, with the input from staff, identified ten lessons for
each grade level to teach. Then particular literature selections were identified
and a lesson plan developed to support and extend learning for each of the
RCCP lessons. Also, posters that highlight specific problem-solving strate-
gies are prominently displayed in every classroom for consistency across
grade levels.

Finally, it was extremely important that every person on this campus
"talked the talk" as a model for students. When Vicki, the assistant princi-
pal, and I meet with children, staff, or parents we consistently model accep-
tance and problem-solving behavior. Our hope is that when children are
faced with a problem they will be able to successfully have their needs met
without hurt feelings or anger becoming physical. On occasion, we have also
mediated staff conflict. Since we all talk the same talk, dealing with conflict
has become a strategy session on how better to accomplish a goal rather than
a confrontation. We problem-solve anger into understanding.

Jackie's explanation give us clear insight into how the program begins to
become a natural part of the school. Teachers participate in finding new
and creative ways to teach the lessons, conduct schoolwide activities, and
create their own variations of the work—variations that are strong, sustain-
able components of the program and clearly reflective of their particular
school's culture. When this kind of ownership and involvement happens, the
leader and principal change agents can step back, just a little, while never
relinquishing their support or ceasing to model the skills themselves in all
they do.

Patience is an important part of the process too—knowing that not everybody's going to come along right away, and some may always be resistant to
any change. Even when you feel that you're well along, there will be hills and
valleys. It's not uncommon for school members to want to see change happen immediately. As an assistant principal, I had countless discussions with

teachers who'd say they didn't see the kids acting any differently either in the classroom or outside. They wanted to see results and they wanted to see them right away. I kept reminding myself of everything I had learned about change. As my professor, Ardeth Cropper of Northern Arizona University, told me, "We say change takes about three to five years. But the more complex the change, the deeper the issues, the longer it takes. Seven years is not too short a time to see institutional change occur."

Schools implement our program in many different ways, depending in part on the availability of resources. Sometimes school members are all trained at once, but often implementation begins with a small group of teachers who attend an RCCP training and return to their school to talk about it and persuade others to go. They teach lessons in their classrooms and spread the word among school members. Typically, the curriculum is first taught in the classroom, peer mediation programs are then developed, and parent training starts soon afterwards or simultaneously. The program continues into year two, three, and so forth, but many factors can delay full implementation.

Arthur Foresta, principal of P. S. 261 and one of the founders of RCCP, reminds us,

To change a school culture, which is basically what we're trying to do, really requires the involvement of the entire school community. It's not enough for children to change their behavior, or what they've learned. Also the adults in the school, the teachers, school aides, and myself as the principal, have to model basically good conflict resolution skills. It's something that we've . . . introduced to our lunchroom workers . . . [and] school aides who are in the lunchroom now have skills to mediate problems between children.

In building school communities dedicated to the beliefs and values inherent in RCCP, people must be empowered at all levels, so that this innovation lasts.

Accomplishments and Challenges

So how is a peaceable school unique?

Throughout this book we've talked about a paradigm shift in how people view a terrain left unexplored by most schools. Young people and adults at all levels of the organization talk about issues of diversity, and about how to resolve conflict, manage emotions, and express feelings, with a new level of articulation and passion. And a transformation in the relationships people establish with others emerges from the self-reflection fostered by this work.

A problem-solving approach to daily school conflict is commonplace. It would be expected at a staff meeting for people to show respect for each other by calmly stating their own views and by listening carefully and actually considering the viewpoints of others. Several times I've had staff members come up to me to ask for a mediation between themselves and a student. When we first introduced the mediation process, this was not an option: teachers were authorities and kids were kids, and when kids broke the rules they were punished. Now, teachers were setting up appointments with young people on their free time to resolve misunderstandings and negotiate possible alternatives.

Peaceable schools provide many opportunities to increase open communication among all sectors of the school community. There is an unspoken code that "at this school we talk about issues, we don't shove them under the table." In a survey administered to over two hundred young people in RCCP schools across the nation, "talking about the problem" outweighed other methods of resolving conflict, including fighting and seeing an administrator or counselor.[6] Both young people and adults have discovered that communicating about the issues is a possibility available to them, and a respected one. Often at Roosevelt Middle School, young people would approach one of the administrators and say they needed to talk to "so-and-so," because things were getting out of hand. We have sat around a table with as few as two people and as many as eight, attempting to talk about hurt feelings, misunderstandings, and attempted threats. With very little help from the adults, young people use the skills they have learned in their classrooms to tell how they feel, to ask questions, to listen, and to come to solutions about many different kinds of problems.

Teachers angry with their colleagues because of misunderstandings or hurt feelings also find themselves communicating about the issues one-on-one rather than harboring bitter feelings. And when they need the help of a third party, another teacher or administrator is often sought out to serve in this capacity. At staff meetings, teachers' concerns are addressed before the "business" gets discussed.

True respect and a valuing of diversity permeate peaceable schools. Young people and adults realize that the ways in which we interpret conflict and communication styles is very much influenced by cultural background, gender, and personal style, and they think twice before they jump to conclusions or use racial slurs to discriminate. They have the skills to "separate the people from the problem" and use these skills in their interactions. So there's a widely observed decrease in negative stereotypes as everyone becomes more accepting of differences, which opens communication between students, teachers, administrators, and parents as well.

I can remember when we first got involved with RCCP at our school. We had been focusing on talking more openly about different cultures and bringing diversity into our curriculum and school activities. Because of a scheduling problem, some students had missed a certain section on Asian cultures. One usually shy seventh-grade student came to me and said, "I'd really like to see something about Chinese people in this school. I know we've been celebrating other cultures and I wonder why we haven't done mine." I can remember feeling overjoyed by this forthrightness; although we had slipped up, I knew that we had begun to create a culture where this particular young boy felt safe enough to put his needs forward and to become a contributing member of this school.

As awareness about issues of bias and prejudice increases, everything is affected, from hiring practices to the selection of curricular materials, assembly content, and other school activities. Martine, a teacher at Roosevelt Middle School, created an entire eighth-grade unit focused on issues of prejudice and discrimination in U.S. history. This included projects, oral presentations, and an evening display for parents, and it involved teachers of other disciplines as well. Every year at Roosevelt, teachers and students sponsor a Women's History Project display. Hundreds of students spend many hours researching the lives of famous women. All entries receive a ribbon for research and creativity. For a few years in a row, eighth-grade boys have received the highest recognition for their work from their peers and teachers. The stereotypes of gender are collapsing as knowledge moves forward to take their place.

Roosevelt also celebrates a Unity Month every year. A variety of activities takes place, including writing, poster, and door-decorating focused on valuing diversity and nonviolence; a multicultural carnival with food, entertainment, and speakers; assemblies representative of guests of diverse backgrounds; and a dance festival in which groups of young people choreograph and perform their favorite ethnic dances. Each year a unity chain is hung around the perimeter of the school administration building. All participating students write a saying, thought, or word about their feelings about violence and discrimination on a strip of construction paper. Each class links their strips together, and the chains are exchanged between classes, where they are read and discussed. Finally they are recollected and hung around the administration building. The sayings are powerful, profound, and honest. This action brings young people and teachers together, and makes their commitment to nonviolence and unity evident.

Peaceable schools maintain a vigilance about changing social norms that support violent behavior. Everything that happens in the school—the curriculum, the daily bulletins, the school activities, the discipline procedures—all state clearly that violence is not okay. Teachers talk with young people about the issues they are confronting. They explore together the alternatives and consequences to their actions. Together, they build a "culture of safety," a feeling of emotional and physical security. As the environment grows more cooperative and caring, and the use of peer mediation by adults and young people increases, schools implementing RCCP show long-term decreases in physical fighting and racial slurs.

In peaceable schools there are strong sanctions against violence and bias-related incidents. Weapons are grounds for expulsion. Fighting earns, at minimum, a suspension. Derogatory racial comments are viewed as precursors to possible violent actions. They are not slid under the carpet, rather they are addressed, when they arise, through mediation or constructive disciplinary action.

Administrators struggle with the issue of school suspension. They know that suspending a student does nothing to change his or her behavior. At times, it does create a safer learning environment for others, particularly when a young person's actions consistently interrupt the teaching/learning process. But young people who are suspended are sent out into the community with few resources to change their ways and work themselves back into the school environment. So teachers in peaceable schools strive to reduce the conflicts that result in suspendable actions. Because they are preventative in their approach, fewer issues blow up in the classroom. In-school suspension rooms can also be very effective, when they are used as places for teacher and student to be apart, cool off, and problem-solve. Teachers, too, need to be willing to regroup and find ways that will help to reduce or extinguish the negative behavior.

When a student absolutely has to be suspended or expelled for a serious offense, it is important to provide opportunities for that student to receive the help he or she needs. Today we are seeing an increase in alternative schools as placements for students who have been removed from the regular education system; it is our hope that these students will be given the opportunity to learn skills in how to manage their emotions and resolve conflicts nonviolently and creatively, and that these skills are seen as core components of their educational experience. The focus needs to be on moving from punishment to positive discipline, in whatever way that can happen. A suspended student's time may be better spent learning social competency skills, doing community service, or receiving home teaching.

A fifth notable feature of peaceable schools is that power is shared in a spirit of creating a democratic environment. Principals and other administrators involved in RCCP develop their skills in communication and group dynamics. They attend introductory trainings, management retreats, and advanced workshops, and so do their staff members. They all know that organizations are healthier and consequently more successful when leadership is facilitative—when power is shared among the people in the organization.

Teamwork becomes the modus operandi for getting things done, and becoming an administrator at a peaceable school requires a whole reevaluation of how decisions are made. If we encourage openness and truth and the sharing of information, we have to be willing to make decisions based on clear observational criteria. It's then harder to be discriminatory, since it's usually subjective criteria that shut certain people out of opportunities. We can claim to have certain values and principles, but until our actions actually operationalize these ways of being, we fall short. And this shift doesn't come easily. As Naomi, principal of P. S. 198, says,

We are relatively new in this process. I say process, because I do think that it is a process. It is a process that our teachers are presently being trained in. This is our third year. We are finally beginning to see and understand that children can negotiate, children can teach us. We can learn from them. . . . We have a consensus kind of attitude in our school that's beginning to permeate the school in a way that says, "Let us talk first and begin to negotiate to solve all kinds of problems."

In our move to school reform, shared decision making, and school-based management, it's easy to make the mistake of thinking we can simply bring various people to the table for discussion around key school issues, be they parents, administrators, teachers, custodians, or support personnel. We forget that where there has been a history of unequal power between these constituencies and where people haven't dealt openly with issues of diversity, this task is not so simple. And it's especially difficult if the staff of the school doesn't reflect the wider cultural diversity of the community and student body it serves. Avoiding issues of power and pretending that all people have an equal say in our society alienates people who may never have had an equal say before. It can foster feelings of separateness and be counterproductive. When people lack skills in communication and the ability to hear each others' perspectives and points of view, we may bring everybody around the table but some may not feel like they really have a seat. It's only when the issues of power and diversity are openly explored and confronted, using all our skill in conflict resolution and a sensitivity to issues of intergroup relations and diversity, that the members of the school community can truly share in the decision-making process.

If everyone has had a chance to develop such skills, they will bring to that shared decision process a common frame, a common vocabulary, and a common way of doing things. Parents and community members, teachers and principals in a peaceable school, for instance, sometimes start a business meeting with a "gathering"—an activity also done in classrooms—to bring the group together, involve everyone immediately, and affirm individuals and the group; when tension is raised over different points of view, they consciously use active listening. When everybody has these process skills, educational reform of all kinds can be put into practice much more easily. Max Depree, chairman of the board of directors of Herman Miller, Inc., one of the top twenty-five firms on *Fortune*'s list of most admired U.S. companies, says, "Participative management without a belief in [people's] potential and without convictions about the gifts people bring to organizations, is a contradiction in terms." He continues, "Everyone has the right and the duty to influence decision making and to understand the results."[7]

The idea of any restructuring or curriculum reform is to create schools that are designed to best serve the students. In peaceable schools, administrators and staff work together to transform their schools, not simply manage them. As Larrie, Roosevelt's principal, said, "I see my role as a facilitator, . . . keeping the fire burning; making sure that the needs of teachers are being met and the people that are doing the work have what they need to continue the dream."

Finally, the development of social and civic responsibility is encouraged in peaceable schools. We are living in a time when young people and adults must be encouraged to actively take part in making a difference in their schools and communities. This will be the focus of our final chapter.

[**11**]

BEYOND THE SCHOOLYARD:
SCHOOLS AND COMMUNITIES
WORKING TOGETHER

> They were nothing more than people, by themselves. Even paired, any pairing,
> they would have been nothing more than people by themselves. But all together,
> they have become the heart and muscles and mind of something perilous and
> new, something strange and growing and great. Together, all together,
> they are instruments of change.
>
> - Keri Hulme -
> *The Bone People*

ALL THE CHANGES THAT we have been discussing and that we advocate can effect wonderful, transformative changes in schools, teachers, and kids' sense of themselves and the world. We know that because we've seen it happen.

But at P.S. 15 we created a peaceable school, a safe haven—and Patrick Daly was killed just blocks from the school.

We see our effort as part of a larger movement of social change and activism. For our work to do its utmost, there has to be a background of stability, community, love, and safety in kids' lives. We not only have to rebuild a sense of community in our schools, we have to do the same in our neighborhoods. We can't have another generation growing up without the wider supports in place from the communities they live in. James Comer, professor of child psychiatry at Yale University, puts it this way: "Children are receiving insufficient help with their development. The supportive and protective functions of neighborhoods—two subtle but essential functions—have been all but lost for many of America's youth."[1]

When I (Linda) was a child and walked the six blocks to my elementary school by myself each day, I was hardly alone. I was greeted by neighbors who knew me by my first name and watched out for me until I reached the next adult sitting on another porch.

Today some children open the doors of their homes and witness drug deals in the hallway on the way to the elevator. Going to school they pass people on the street who frighten them. One of our mediators in New York City describes it this way: "It's real bad. Sometimes when I come outside, I'm scared because there are crack people in my building, on the same floor where I live. They sell their drugs right in front of me. And sometimes I'm scared that they'll hurt me."

One of my fondest memories is the way my family celebrated birthdays when I was a child. In the morning, we chose exactly what we wanted for dinner and put on a special outfit to wear to school that day. I would come home to the love and warmth of my family, a stack of gifts, and my favorite meal on the table.

Today we live in a world that robs some children of even these happy and safe moments. Interviewed for the video documentary *The Last Hit*, Micah, who lives in a Detroit housing project, spoke about *his* ninth birthday:

On the night of my birthday, December 31, New Year's Eve, we were coming up from the basement to eat some ice cream and cake. So what happened was my mother was about to put out the ice cream and I was behind her talking to my friends, and I heard about five shots—pow, pow, pow. As soon as I got shot I saw our cabinet door open, and the other last thing I saw was the clock, and I looked dead at it and I looked everywhere, but I didn't see anybody. I saw my mother in the dining room and she said, "What's the matter? What's the matter?" I went into the bathroom—there was light there. So

I said, "I'm shot, I'm shot. Help me." My auntie came and wiped my hand and said, "You'll be all right." My father didn't know I said I was shot. He said, "You're not shot, you're not shot." But about the time we got to the hospital, that's when he finally figured out that I was shot.[2]

Every child in this country has a right to safety, especially in their own home. Not one single child growing up in America should be robbed of his or her childhood because we as adults cannot protect them.

Clearly we have made the case for the important role of schools in addressing the issues of our wider society. And yet schools working alone cannot make a big enough dent in the crisis we face. Even if we could put into place a comprehensive, multi-year commitment to the teaching of emotional and social competency and conflict resolution skills in every school in America—rural, suburban, or inner-city—we would still be unable to turn the tide. As we wage peace in our schools, children are getting strong, frequent, and extreme messages from the society at large and from their own communities. They have ready access to real and simulated violence. Some live in homes and neighborhoods where violence is often the accepted norm. An eight-year old boy from Hartford, Connecticut, said, "I like school, but I have to worry about getting home alive."

There is no single, simple remedy to this problem. Our response to these complicated issues has to be a wide-ranging and public one. When we think about solutions, our focus needs to be not on any one program or project, but beyond that—to joining a local and national movement that involves the private sector, national and local governments, neighborhood organizations, religious communities, law enforcement, researchers, businesses. We must all mobilize.

We are finally realizing that something must drastically change. As our collective psychic numbness fades away we start to feel the effects of our indifference and not one of us is left untouched. Several years ago I had the opportunity to work in Mother Teresa's Home for the Dying, in Calcutta. I learned an important lesson that gives me hope. A visitor can't miss the purpose of this place: "Home for the Dying" is written in large letters above the building in both Hindi and English. Yet a strange phenomenon consistently occurs—fifty percent of the people who are brought to this place get well and are able to leave. I'm convinced that when the severity of a problem is acknowledged, we have the best chance of healing to occur. It seems that this is where many of us are now in our society—beginning to acknowledge that the home for the dying is right here on the streets of our country and that our concerted effort *can* heal the situation. As Monica, a mediator in a South Bronx high school, put it, "I'm not going to be a statistic. I'm going to walk out of here alive!"

Several years ago, I experienced a remarkable example of community in Southern India, where I was helping in a health clinic. One day, after a long and difficult delivery, a very young mother gave birth to a child without arms. Just moments after the birth, several village women arrived. Helping the mother come to terms with what she was seeing, the women eased into picking the little girl up, figuring out how best to hold her. During the first week of this child's life, a different woman from the village would visit the family each day with yet another beautiful piece of clothing she had sewn in a way that adapted to the child's disability. By the end of the week, young Satinder had an entire wardrobe of clothing that demonstrated the collective, loving acceptance of her as the newest member of the village.

The way most of us live today seems to create more and more distance between ourselves and our neighbors, and so many of us yearn for that sense of community. We need the kind of heart-to-heart resuscitation that will transform neighborhoods into functional villages again.

Social Change

There is a two-way street here that gives us hope: while the education of the heart requires changes in society in order for its most revolutionary ideals to be realized, emotionally literate people are exactly the kind of people most likely to bring about that change.

Although the curriculum we advocate is skill-based, the development and promotion of social responsibility is an expected outcome. In our work, we are hoping to inspire everyone to play an activist role in shaping our society's future. We want both young people and adults to feel as though they can change the world by their individual actions. The peaceable classrooms and schools we work to create are more than refuges from harm, they are interdependent and interconnected models for the larger community.

Since young people from peaceable schools and classrooms have experienced the power of constructive action, they are usually more hopeful about tackling problems and effecting social change. Instead of feeling they can do very little to change the world, they are armed with the experience of having done so. The skills that we teach and the values and attitudes we nurture help young people see themselves as active citizens participating in a democratic process.

In peaceable schools, young people experience a community where empathy, equality, and respect are the norm. They have a taste of what their larger world could be like. To give young people a greater opportunity to integrate these skills and attitudes, we encourage an active engagement with the wider community while they are still in school.

A few years ago, a tragedy involving the brother of one of the children in our program resulted in a concerted response from his school, home, and community working together. Nicholas Heyward, thirteen years old, was playing with his friends with their plastic toy guns in the hallway of the housing project where he lived. Nicholas heard a noise and, thinking it was one of his friends, turned with his toy gun pointed in the direction of the sound. The noise had been made by a police officer, who fired when he saw the pointed gun. Nicholas died the next morning.

At P.S. 261, the RCCP school where Nicholas's brother was in the second grade, a crisis intervention team was brought in to deal with the shock and grief of the kids and teachers. Then came their social action. One teacher organized a letter-writing campaign with his class to Toys R Us and Kay-Bee Toys to protest their selling of look-alike toy guns; in response to their letters, and those from other young people in the community, Toys R Us agreed not to restock the toy guns and Kay-Bee agreed to pull them off the shelves immediately. In addition, with the cooperation of the students, teachers, and a local community organization called Kids Press, P.S. 261 conducted a Books for Toy Guns Campaign. For each toy gun brought in, a child received two books; a local artist took the guns and fused them into a memorial which now stands in the lobby of the school. The following letter was part of the campaign.

Dear Toys R Us,

A young boy was shot by a New York City police officer. He died in the hospital on September 27 very early in the morning. Unfortunately, more children are dying than adults these days and all for the same stupid reason: guns. In this case, the child was playing with a toy gun. A woman had complained to a police officer about it. The officer spotted the boy and his friend and shot one of them thinking the toy was real. The sad part is the young boy is dead now and he cannot be brought back. His thirteen-year-old life was cut short by a small piece of steel. I understand that the police officer had to make a snap decision and if he had waited a moment longer, he may have been the one in the morgue wearing a toe tag. But he is not the one in the morgue and unfortunately, he made the wrong decision.

Why do children play with guns? Is it because we see our "heroes" do it on T.V.? Don't people know by now that it is all fake? The reason children play with guns I think is that they see their "heroes" do it so they do it too. The way I see it is "heroes" should not be on the screen but in a classroom or a library. A five-year-old child is not going to know the difference between seeing Jean Claude Van Damme shoot someone on the screen and his doing the same thing in the real world. I think one of the country's biggest problems is that people do not know the difference between the box in the living room and the real world.

Alex O'Keefe-Bazzoni, 6th grade
P.S. 261, Brooklyn, New York

Clearly, we can all—adults and children alike—be a part of the solution. In this case, adults played a key role in helping the young people at P.S. 261 respond positively to a tragic and frightening event in the world beyond their school. Research confirms that one of the best ways to help young people develop a greater sense of empowerment is to actively engage in the real world.[3]

The Young Ambassador Program developed at the RCCP Vista, California, site provides an excellent example of young people practicing social responsibility. As we mentioned earlier, Young Ambassadors are trained as peer leaders. They meet regularly and develop a deep sense of community. In these intensive group experiences, each Young Ambassador gets a sense of how his or her interactions and behaviors affect the group as a whole, and has a firsthand opportunity to improve their ability to live and work together. As they begin to acknowledge their interconnection, they reach out to the wider community as well. Some visit elementary schools that are just starting RCCP, to encourage the kids to get involved, and others do community service in their neighborhoods. Young Ambassadors from Roosevelt Middle School participated in a graffiti cleanup in conjunction with the local sheriff's office. While the kids were painting, many community residents spontaneously came out to thank them and offer encouragement and refreshments. The same group got other kids in their school to participate in designing posters with nonviolent messages; they then framed the posters and approached local shopkeepers to display them.

Community service efforts such as these give young people a wonderful opportunity to experience themselves as part of a larger network of people helping to create a better world. Some of our community outreach in RCCP is organized and built around projects like the Young Ambassadors or the Peace Chorus in Anchorage, which performs not only at other schools, but also at local nursing homes. At other times, particular events prompt a response, and students and teachers reach out to do whatever is in their power to do, hoping others will join them. At Vista High School in California, the Peacemakers Club provided leadership in a schoolwide Hands Across the City Peace Walk in honor of Dr. Martin Luther King, Jr.'s birthday.

I first heard this story told in a speech by Deborah Prothrow-Stith:

A preacher was visiting one of his elderly parishioners in her home when the phone rang and the woman moved to the other room to answer it. The preacher found himself gazing at the many bookshelves in the room, which went almost clear up to the ceiling. He noticed that the bottom shelves were very neatly organized, and as he glanced up he saw that the clutter and chaos seemed to increase. When the woman came back into the room, she caught the preacher looking upward. "Bet you're wondering about those shelves on the top," she said. "I can clean up just as far as I can reach."

That's really what we are teaching—how to figure out what actions we each can take in our own sphere of influence to change the world around us. Gandhi's advice can help: "We must become the change we seek in the world."

Breaking Boundaries and Forging Collaborations

For schools and communities to reach out to one another, a porous boundary needs to be created between the two. Teachers, administrators, and kids need to become part of community life and schools need to let communities in.

I was walking down a street in my New York City neighborhood one day and came upon three girls, all about ten or eleven years old. One of the girls had her arm around another's shoulder, comforting her as she cried uncontrollably. The third girl seemed quite troubled, possibly guilty for having caused the situation. I decided to intervene. "I'm wondering if you need any help. I'm a teacher," I said, hoping that telling them I was a teacher would elicit their trust in a stranger's help. They began to share. The one girl had in fact said something derogatory to the girl who was upset, something unthinking about her parents not caring because she was adopted. It turns out this girl was adopted and the comments hit a sensitive nerve. I engaged them in a discussion that ended with tears of forgiveness and hugs among all three girls. As I started to say good-bye and compliment them for working it out so beautifully, one of the girls looked back at me and said, "I just have to say one thing to you. I don't think you're really a teacher because a teacher wouldn't have taken all this time with us when we're not even in school." I didn't quite know what to say. I was reminded that this is how some kids view adults in their lives—in separate corners, with clear and low expectations about who we will help and when.

Although we don't all have to advocate for the same solutions to the complicated issues communities face, we have to be more willing to find a common ground. In RCCP, we have participated in some exciting collaborations that have helped us expand our reach greatly.

In 1994, RCCP and ESR joined with Ben & Jerry's Ice Cream to develop the Kids' Conscious Acts of Peace Project. Together we created an activity guide based on our curriculum and distributed it to eight thousand schools and two hundred thousand teachers nationwide. In an accompanying essay form, students were encouraged to write about a time they performed or witnessed a "conscious act of peace" and bring that essay form, signed by their teacher, to a Ben & Jerry's shop in their neighborhood to exchange it for a free ice cream cone.

A few months later, the Corporation for Public Broadcasting (CPB) joined the project, making Kids' Conscious Acts of Peace a part of its national Act Against Violence campaign. We have extended the scope of the project through CPB's over 240 local affiliates, who distributed the revised activity guide to the schools in *their* communities and helped promote and publicize the essays.

In the summer of 1995, RCCP joined the Children's Defense Fund in their third summer of sponsoring Freedom Schools in underserved communities across the country. The Freedom Schools provide a positive summer opportunity of academic learning and social development for youth in grades K–12. They are staffed by public school teachers and college students and co-sponsored by local community-based organizations. We adapted the curriculum and parent components of RCCP, making them part of the Freedom

Schools' daily instruction. We have learned that many other places besides traditional schools can be appropriate educational settings for prevention efforts. The thirty-three Freedom Schools are serving as an important safety net for more than two thousand children each summer.

The RCCP National Center is helping to support a public school based on RCCP principles. The school, which will eventually have a maximum of six hundred students, will serve as a national model for developing a core curriculum on emotional and social learning, conflict resolution, and diversity education integrated into every aspect of the school's functioning. We at the RCCP National Center feel the need to continue serving our community, thus this new school will be located in our home city—New York.

In collaboration with Lesley College in Cambridge, Massachusetts, we are starting a new first-of-its-kind Master's Degree in Education with a specialty in Conflict Resolution and Peaceable Schools. The aim of this collaboration is to create a model teacher education program that will prepare graduates as leaders in conflict resolution and creating peaceable schools. Internships will be served in school districts in local communities in which RCCP has been completely institutionalized into the school district's mission and direction. Through this collaboration, we hope to help build a strong cadre of educators who can lead school systems and communities across the country in embracing the vision of education that we at RCCP espouse.

Practical Ways Schools and Communities Can Work Together

There are numerous ways schools and communities create these "porous boundaries" we speak of. Here are a few ideas for what schools can do:

> Get students and teachers actively involved in neighborhood efforts, from cleanup campaigns to adults volunteering for community patrol.

> Lobby for students to serve on community planning committees, so the voices of youth can help shape the community's future.

> Support local mediation centers as a way of dealing with neighborhood disputes, with peer mediators and school mediation coaches volunteering their expertise.

> Cooperate with local TV, radio, and print media by helping them to report on positive events happening in schools and co-producing public service announcements with nonviolent messages.

> Support community efforts in the martial arts and other self-defense skills by introducing young people to them during school hours.

> Invite local policy makers, police, and judges to participate in school celebrations as well as in conflict resolution trainings.

> Consider using the school's facilities as a community center, collaborating with nonprofit organizations to provide safe and stimulating opportunities for youth after school.

> Support the idea of school-based health clinics, which can help reinforce violence prevention programming.

> Work along with community artists to create murals and billboards in the community with positive pro-social peace messages.

> Co-sponsor forums where all sectors of the community—staff, parents, students, law enforcement officials, etc.—can share ideas, expertise and points of view.

> Support mentoring efforts linking up adults in the community with youth who would benefit from ongoing one-to-one contact with a caring person.

> Sponsor discussion groups that invite neighbors in the community, using such materials as the Study Circles Resource Center's guide *Confronting Violence in Our Communities: A Guide for Involving Citizens in Public Dialogue and Problem Solving.*[4] Youth can be included in the study circle as well.

Measuring Our Work

When we reflect on our decade of work of RCCP, the words inscribed on Gandhi's tomb come to mind: "Think of the poorest person you have ever seen and ask if your next act will be of any use to him or her." As RCCP completes (in 1996) the first stage of the most comprehensive evaluation of a school-based conflict resolution program ever done, with a sample of over eight thousand kids, and as new successful RCCP sites grow around the country, perhaps we should also step back and ask if what we are doing in our school hallways, yards, and classrooms will be of any use to a child in need who has touched our heart.

In the new vision of education we espouse, we believe all kids, not just a privileged few, should have the following rights:

> To go to schools, play in playgrounds, and grow up in homes surrounded by adults who protect them and listen to them, instead of having to live in constant fear for their emotional and physical safety

> To go to bed each night dreaming hopeful thoughts for their future instead of reliving the nightmares of their day

> To be able to go to the corner store and have enough money to buy a treat or simply satisfy their hunger instead of witnessing the selling of drugs

> To be raised in families where adults are ever present with their love, nurturance, clear limits, and strong values instead of coming home to empty houses

> To attend schools where valuing nonviolence and diversity is the norm instead of being overwhelmed by feelings of isolation, rejection, and failure

> To inherit a world free of violence and hatred, that children may truly know what peace and justice are

Our challenge in this next decade, in a country that now spends more on prisons than on education, is to let our next act today bring this reality closer for a child we know and love so that his or her tomorrow will be better. We believe many of us across the country are already living our lives this way. Each day people perform isolated, unseen, loving conscious acts of peace in our homes, schools, and neighborhoods. In the words of Robert Kennedy,

Each time one stands up for an ideal, or acts to improve the lot of the rest, or strikes out against injustice, one sends forth a ripple of hope, and crossing each other from a million different centers of energy and daring, those ripples build a current that can sweep down the mightiest walls of oppression and resistance. Moral courage is a rarer commodity than bravery in battle or great intelligence. Yet it is one essential, vital quality for those who seek to change a world that yields most painfully to change.

We envision the younger generation, the ones who will build the future, telling *their* kids how they learned to de-escalate violence and turn conflict into opportunity, how they learned to value each unique individual, and how they were part of building a future full of hope and gentleness. This vision continues to unfold in thousands of schools across the country, and we are grateful to be playing our part.

[N O T E S]

CHAPTER 1: A NEW VISION OF EDUCATION

1   Thomas Toch, Ted Guest, and Monica Guttman, "Violence in Schools," *U.S. News and World Report*, 8 November 1993.

2   Ibid.

3   Ibid.

4   Ibid.

5   Daniel Goleman, "Pioneering Schools Teach Lessons of Emotional Life," *New York Times*, 3 March 1992.

6   Daniel Goleman, *Emotional Intelligence* (New York: Bantam Books, 1995).

7   Thomas Achenbach's study is described by Daniel Goleman in "The Educated Heart." *Common Boundary*, November / December 1995.

8   Howard Gardner, *Frames of Mind* (New York: Basic Books, 1993).

9   Daniel Goleman, "The Educated Heart."

10   Goleman, *Emotional Intelligence*, 105.

11   Maurice Elias and John F. Clabby, *Building Social Problem Skills: Guidelines from a School-Based Program* (San Francisco: Jossey-Bass, 1992), 11.

12   Ibid., 16–17.

13   D. Elliott, "Serious Violent Offenders: Onset, Development, Course, and Termination—The American Society of Criminology 1993 Presidential Address," *Criminology* 32, no. 1 (1994).

14   William Foege, Mark L. Rosenberg, and James A. Mercy, "Public Health and Violence Prevention," *Current Issues in Public Health*, 1995, no. 1:2–9.

15 Jean Johnson and John Immerwahr, "First Things First: What Americans Expect from the Public Schools," a report from Public Agenda (New York, 1993).

16 Deborah Prothrow-Stith, *Deadly Consequences* (New York: HarperCollins, 1991).

17 Ronald Slaby, "What Violent Kids Think," *Safe and Drug Free Schools*, Fall 1994.

18 J. David Hawkins and Richard F. Catalano, *Communities That Care* (San Francisco: Jossey-Bass, 1992).

19 William DeJong, "Preventing Interpersonal Violence Among Youth: An Introduction to School, Community, and Mass Media Strategies," in *Issues and Practices in Criminal Justice* (a publication series of the National Institute of Justice), November 1994.

20 See L. D. Eron and L. R. Heusman, "Stability of Aggressive Behavior: Even into the Third Generation," in M. L. Lewis and S. M. Miller, eds., *Handbook of Developmental Psychopathology* (New York: Plenum Press, 1990).

21 R. Hammond and B. Yung, "Preventing Violence in At-Risk African-American Youth," *Journal of Health Care for the Poor and Underserved*, 1990, no. 2:359–73.

22 Bierman's study cited by Daniel Goleman in "Early Violence Leaves Its Mark on the Brain," *New York Times*, 3 October 1995.

23 G. D. Gottfredson, "An Evaluation of an Organizational Development Approach to Reducing School Disorder," *Evaluation Review* 1988, no. 11:739–63.

24 American Psychological Association, *Violence and Youth*, vol. 1 of *Summary Report of the Commission on Violence and Youth, 1993*.

25 Research by the W. T. Grant Consortium is described in Hawkins and Catalano, *Communities That Care*, 129–48.

26 Ibid., 133–34.

27 Ibid., 135.

28 See Gordon Allport, *Special Report: The Ku Klux Klan—A History of Racism and Violence* (Montgomery, Ala.: Klanwatch, 1982) in *A World of Difference: A Prejudice Reduction Program of the Anti-Defamation League of B'nai B'rith—A Teacher-Student Resource Guide* (1986).

29 Louise Derman-Sparks and the ABC Task Force, *Anti-Bias Curriculum: Tools for Empowering Young Children* (Washington, D.C.: National Association for the Education of Young Children, 1992).

30 Blanchard quoted by Daniel Goleman, "New Way to Battle Bias: Fight Acts, Not Feelings," *New York Times*, 16 July 1991.

31 Green quoted by ibid.

32 Slavin quoted by Daniel Goleman, *New York Times*, 5 September 1989, C1.

33 Robert E. Slavin, "Cooperative Learning and Student Achievement," *Educational Leadership*, October 1988, 31–33.

34 David W. Johnson and Roger T. Johnson, "Cooperative Learning and Conflict Resolution," *The Fourth R* 42 (December 1992/January 1993):1.

35 Tom Roderick, "Johnny Can Learn to Negotiate," *Educational Leadership*, December 1987/January 1988.

36 Roger Fisher and William Ury, *Getting to Yes: Negotiating Agreement Without Giving In* (New York: Penguin Books, 1991).

37 John Gottman, *Why Marriages Succeed or Fail* (New York: Simon & Schuster, 1994).

CHAPTER 2: THE PEACEABLE CLASSROOM

1 William Kreidler, interview with Janet Patti in the spring of 1995.

2 The I-message, win-win negotiation, and other conflict resolution skills are discussed at length in the next two chapters.

3 *Resolving Conflict Creatively: A Teaching Guide for Grades Kindergarten through Six*, published by Educators for Social Responsibility Metropolitan Area and the Board of Education of the City of New York (1993), 96.

4 Based on activity created by Sid Simon, in *IALAC : I Am Lovable and Capable* (Chesterfield, Mass.: Values Press, 1992).

5 Daniel Goleman, *Emotional Intelligence* (New York: Bantam Books, 1995).

6 William J. Kreidler, *Creative Conflict Resolution: More Than 200 Activities for Keeping Peace in the Classroom K–6* (Glenview, Ill.: Scott Foresman & Co., 1984).

7 Ibid.

8 Ibid.

9 Louise Derman-Sparks and the ABC Task Force, *Anti-Bias Curriculum: Tools for Empowering Young Children* (Washington, D.C.: National Association for the Education of Young Children, 1992).

10 Kreidler, *Creative Conflict Resolution*.

11 Ibid.

12 William Kreidler, *Conflict Resolution in the Middle School* (Cambridge, Mass.: Educators for Social Responsibility, 1994).

13 Carol Miller Lieber, *Making Choices about Conflict, Security, and Peacemaking, Part I: Personal Perspectives* (Cambridge, Mass.: Educators for Social Responsibility, 1994).

14 William Glasser, *The Quality School Teacher* (New York: Harper Perennial, 1993).

CHAPTER 3: HOW TO WAGE PEACE

1 Roger Fisher and William Ury, *Getting to Yes: Negotiating Agreement Without Giving In* (New York: Penguin Books, 1991).

2 "Even Weeds Have Needs," from Lindamichellebaron, *The Sun Is On* (Hempstead, N.Y.: Harlin Jacque Publications, 1990).

3 This story appears in Kesharan Nair, *A Higher Standard of Leadership* (San Francisco: Berrett-Koehler Publications, 1995).

4 Danene M. Bender, ed., *Alternatives to Violence Workbook*, compiled by John Looney (Akron, Ohio: Peace Grows, Inc., 1986).

5 Thomas Gordon's list appears in Robert Bolton, *People Skills* (New York: Simon & Schuster, 1970).

6 William Kreidler, *Conflict Resolution in the Middle School* (Cambridge, Mass.: Educators for Social Responsibility, 1994), 25.

7 Ibid., 91.

8 We first came across this now popular example in Fisher and Ury's *Getting to Yes*.

9 These and other conflict resolution techniques discussed in this and the following chapter, except where otherwise noted, are adapted, with permission, from the 1993 *ESR Workshop and Implementation Manual* (Cambridge, Mass.: Educators for Social Responsibility, 1993).

10 Virginia Satir, *Peoplemaking* (Palo Alto, Calif.: Science and Behavior Books, 1972), 78–79.

11 Bill Moyers, *Healing and the Mind* (New York: Doubleday, 1993), 8.

12 Robert Bolton, *People Skills* (New York: Simon & Schuster, 1979).

13 Thich Nhat Hanh, *Being Peace* (Berkeley, Calif.: Parallax Press, 1987), 74–79.

14 Manu Aluli Meyer, "Ho'oponopono: To Set Right," a paper to fulfill course requirement for H310C, Harvard Graduate School of Education (17 January 1994).

15 Thanks to Tom Roderick, executive director of Educators for Social Responsibility Metro for these tips.

CHAPTER 4: VALUING DIVERSITY

1 Global village portrait from World Development Forum, 15 April 1990, cited in Marion O'Malley and Tiffany Davis, *Dealing With Differences* (1994, compiled by and available from the Center for Peace Education in Chapel Hill, N.C.), 7.

2 Hudson Institute, "Workforce 2,000," also cited in O'Malley and Davis, *Dealing With Differences*, 15.

3 *Time*, 9 April 1990, cited in O'Malley and Davis, *Dealing With Differences*, 15–16.

4 U.S. Department of Education (May 1989), quoted in O'Malley and Davis, *Dealing With Differences*, 16.

5 Joan S. Lester, *The Future of White Men and Other Diversity Dilemmas* (Berkeley, Calif.: Conari Press, 1994), 1–2.

6 Ibid., 17.

7 Tools for Diversity, 1903 S.E. Ankeny, Portland, Oregon.

8 Nichole Young, letter to the editor, *Anchorage Daily News*, 27 May 1994.

9 Excerpted from Peggy McIntosh, "White Privilege: Unpacking the Invisible Knapsack," *Peace and Freedom* July / August 1989.

10 Kesharan Nair, *A Higher Standard of Leadership* (San Francisco: Berrett-Koehler Publications, 1995).

11 This and other inspirational quotes used throughout this chapter appear in "Peace Moments," a Pax Christi USA calendar compiled by Marlene Bertke (1994).

12 Lenore Gordon, "What Do We Say When We Hear 'Faggot'?" in *Rethinking Our Classrooms: Teaching for Equity and Justice*, Bigelow, Christensen, Karp, Miner, and Peterson, eds. (Milwaukee, Wisc.: Rethinking Schools, Ltd., 1994), 87.

13 These guidelines are based on those written by Patti DeRosa, of Cross-Cultural Consultation (28 S. Main Street #177, Randolph, Massachusetts 02368).

CHAPTER 5: THE ROLE OF THE TEACHER IN THE PEACEABLE CLASSROOM

1 "A Fine Line: Losing American Youth to Violence," a special section reprinted from the *1994 Annual Report of the Charles Stewart Mott Foundation* (Flint, Mich.: 1994), 29.

2 Ibid.

3 *Educators for Social Responsibility Workshop and Implementation Manual 1995*, section 8, p. 7.

4 Metis Associates, Inc., "The Resolving Conflict Creatively Program, 1988–1989: A Summary of Significant Findings" (May 1990), hereafter referred to as "Metis 1990."

5 The workshop approach that we use was created by Priscilla Prutzman of Children's Creative Response to Conflict. See Priscilla Prutzman, Lee Stern, M. Leonard Burger, and

Gretchen Bodenhamer, *Friendly Classroom for a Small Planet: Children's Creative Response to Conflict* (Philadelphia: New Society Publishers, 1988).

6   Diane Levin, *Teaching Young Children in Violent Times* (Cambridge, Mass.: Educators for Social Responsibility, 1994).

7   *Embracing Diversity: Teachers Voices from California's Classrooms*, California Tomorrow Immigrant Students Project Research Report (1990), 12.

8   Bruce Joyce and Beverly Showers, "The Coaching of Teaching," *Educational Leadership*, October 1982, 3.

9   "Metis 1990," 10.

10   "Metis 1990," 7.

11   Ram Dass and Paul Gorman, *How Can I Help?* (New York: Alfred A. Knopf, 1991), 50.

CHAPTER 6: MEDIATION IN THE SCHOOLS

1   This narrative was adapted from Janet Patti, "Perceptions of the Peer Mediation Component of a Schoolwide Conflict Resolution Program: Resolving Conflict Creatively" (Ed.D. diss., Northern Arizona University, May 1996).

2   Metis Associates, Inc., "The Resolving Conflict Creatively Program, 1988–1989: A Summary of Significant Findings" (May 1990), 12. The Metis evaluation found that:

> 85 percent of the teacher respondents agreed that students in their classes had been helped through their contact with mediators;
> 85 percent agreed that mediators' participation in the mediation component had contributed to increasing the mediators' self esteem;
> 99 percent agreed that the mediation component had given children an important tool for dealing with the everyday conflicts;
> 88 percent said that mediation helped students take more responsibility for solving their problems;

Of 143 mediators who were interviewed in the same schools,

> 84 percent said that being a mediator had helped them to understand people with different views;
> 84 percent agreed that being a mediator had given them skills they can use for their whole life.

3   Richard Cohen, *Students Resolving Conflict* (Glenview, Ill.: Good Year Books, 1995), 32.

4   Ibid., 20.

5 From *Songs for Peace*, audiocassette produced and arranged by Max Nass, words and music by Max and Marcia Nass, performed by The Playground Kids, New York, N.Y. (1989).

CHAPTER 7: SIGNS OF HOPE

1 Many of the statements by young people quoted in this chapter are from Janet Patti, "Perceptions of the Peer Mediation Component of a Schoolwide Conflict Resolution Program: Resolving Conflict Creatively" (Ed.D. diss., Northern Arizona University, 1996).

2 U.S. Department of Justice, Office of Juvenile Justice and Delinquency Prevention, "Comprehensive Strategy for Serious, Violent, and Chronic Juvenile Offenders" (December 1993), 5–6.

3 Joshua's story appeared in *Parade Magazine*, 8 January 1995, 5.

CHAPTER 8: PEACE IN THE FAMILY

1 This activity is a variation of the "heart exercise" created by Sid Simon that we mentioned in Chapter 2.

2 Gottman cited by Daniel Goleman, talk at the Learning Annex, New York City, 2 November 1995.

3 James P. Comer and Alvin F. Poussaint, *Raising Black Children* (New York: Plume, 1992).

4 Adele Faber and Elaine Mazlish, *Siblings Without Rivalry* (New York: Avon Books, 1987).

5 Phillips quoted in Louise Derman-Sparks and the ABC Task Force, *Anti-Bias Curriculum: Tools for Empowering Young Children* (Washington, D.C.: National Association for the Education of Young Children, 1992), ix.

6 Susan Beekman and Jeanne Holmes, *Battles, Hassles, Tantrums, and Tears* (New York: Hearst Books, 1993), 146–47.

7 David S. Barry, "Growing Up Violent," *Media and Values*, no. 62 (Summer 1993):8.

8 Cited ibid., 11.

9 Judith Myer-Walls, "Suggestions for Parents: Children Can Unlearn Violence," *Media and Values*, no. 62 (Summer 1993):19.

10 Elizabeth Thorman, "Beyond Blame: Media as Violence Prevention," *Media and Values*, no. 62 (Summer 1993):24.

11 "Living in Fear," *Children's Defense Fund Reports*, January 1994, 2.

12 Marian Wright Edelman, "Gun War Against Children: Enough is Enough," *Children's Defense Fund Reports*, November 1994, 3.

13 L. E. Saltman, J. A. Mercy, P. W. O'Carroll, M. L. Rosenberg, and P. H. Rhodes, "Weapon Involvement and Injury Outcomes in Family and Intimate Assaults," *Journal of the American Medical Association*, 1992, no. 267:3043–47.

14 A. W. Dodd, "Parents Have to Be Prepared to Accept the New Ideas," *Education Week*, 3 May 1995, 40.

15 "Living in Fear," 2.

16 Marian Wright Edelman, *The Measure of Our Success: A Letter to My Children and Yours* (Boston, Mass.: Beacon Press, 1993).

CHAPTER 9: RCCP'S BEGINNINGS

1 Portions of this chapter were adapted, with permission, from "We Made Our Dream Real," an article by Tom Roderick that appeared in Educators for Social Responsibility Metro's newsletter, *Action News*, October 1995.

2 Metis Associates, Inc., "The Resolving Conflict Creatively Program, 1988–1989: Summary of Significant Findings" (May 1990).

3 U.S. General Accounting Office, *School Safety: Promising Initiatives for Addressing School Violence*, report to the Ranking Minority Member, Subcommittee on Children and Families, Committee on Labor and Human Resources, U.S. Senate (Washington, D.C.: U.S. General Accounting Office, April 1995).

CHAPTER 10: CREATING PEACEABLE SCHOOLS

1 Adapted from Janet Patti, "Perceptions of the Peer Mediation Component of a School-wide Conflict Resolution Program: Resolving Conflict Creatively" (Ed.D. diss., Northern Arizona University, 1996).

2 Ibid.

3 Thomas J. Sergiovanni, *Building Community in Schools* (San Francisco: Jossey-Bass, 1994), 100.

4 Peter Senge, "On Schools as Learning Organizations: A Conversation with Peter Senge," *Educational Leadership*, April 1995.

5 *Journal of Staff Development* 14, no. 1 (Winter, 1993):10.

6   Janet Patti, "Perceptions."

7   Max Depree, *Leadership Is an Art* (New York: Dell, 1989), 24.

CHAPTER 11: BEYOND THE SCHOOLYARD

1   Comer quoted in "A Matter of Time: Risk and Opportunity in the Nonschool Hours," a report of the Task Force on Youth Development and Community Programs, Carnegie Corporation of New York (December 1992), 19.

2   Micah's story is transcribed from the video *The Last Hit: Children and Violence*, available from Film Ideas, 3710 Commercial Avenue, Suite 13, Northbrook, Illinois 60062. Tel: (800) 475-3456.

3   Sheldon Berman, "Educating for Social Responsibility," *Educational Leadership* 48, no. 3 (November 1993), 76.

4   *Confronting Violence in Our Communities: A Guide for Involving Citizens in Public Dialogue and Problem Solving* is available from the Study Guides Resource Center, Pomfret, Connecticut.

EDUCATORS FOR SOCIAL RESPONSIBILITY

ESR is a national nonprofit organization promoting children's ethical and social development through its leadership in conflict resolution, violence prevention, intergroup relations, and character education. It supports schools, teachers, and parents with professional development programs and instructional materials and is the organization which sponsors the RCCP National Center.

Educators for Social Responsibility (National)
23 Garden Street
Cambridge, MA 02138
1-800-370-2515
(617) 492-1764 phone
(617) 864-5164 fax

Educators for Social Responsibility Metropolitan Area (N.Y. chapter)
475 Riverside Drive, Room 450
New York, NY 10115
(212) 870-3318

For readers looking for activities to implement the ideas in our book in the classroom, ESR offers curricula and other practical guides, including the following.

Teaching Young Children in Violent Times: Building a Peaceable Classroom by Diane E. Levin, Ph.D. A practical guide designed for teachers from preschool to grade three.

Elementary Perspectives: Teaching Concepts of Peace and Conflict by William J. Kreidler. Activities for teachers and students, K–6, for exploring peace, justice, and the value of conflict and its resolution.

Conflict Resolution in the Middle School: A Curriculum and Teaching Guide by William J. Kreidler. More than 150 activities to help middle school students effectively handle conflict at this developmental stage.

Making Choices about Conflict, Security, and Peacemaking by Carol Miller Lieber. A two-volume high-school curriculum that explores the roots of everyday interpersonal conflicts and their relationship to local and international conflicts.

RESOLVING CONFLICT CREATIVELY NATIONAL CENTER

RCCP, an initiative of Educators for Social Responsibility, is a pioneering school-based conflict resolution and intergroup relations program that provides a model for preventing violence and creating caring learning communities.

RCCP National Center
163 Third Avenue #103
New York, NY 10003
(212) 387-0225 phone
(212) 387-0510 fax

United States General Accounting Office (GAO) report *School Safety: Promising Initiatives for Addressing School Violence*, April 1995. (The report highlights RCCP as one of four promising violence prevention programs.)

U.S. General Accounting Office
P.O. Box 6015
Gaithersburg, MD 20884-6015
(202) 512-6000 phone
(301) 258-4066 fax

National Institute of Justice "program focus" report *Building the Peace: The Resolving Conflict Creatively Program* (1994).

National Criminal Justice Reference Service
Clearing House
(800) 851-3420. Document #149549

Metis Associates, Inc., program evaluation *The Resolving Conflict Creatively Program, 1988–1989: Summary of Significant Findings* (May 1990).

Metis Associates, Inc.
80 Broad Street Suite 1600
New York, NY 10004
(212) 425-8833 phone
(212) 480-2176 fax

The RCCP Research Program is an intensive evaluation of RCCP in New York City currently underway under the guidance of Educators for Social Responsibility Metro. The evaluation is made possible by a major three-year grant from the federal Centers for Disease Control and Prevention as well as grants from private foundations. It involves a wide range of methods to gather information on RCCP's effectiveness, including student and teacher surveys; interviews with teachers, students, parents, and administrators; and observation. The research itself is being carried out independently by scientists from the National Center for Children in Poverty of Columbia University's School of Public Health and the Education Development Center. Some preliminary information about first year results is available as of the fall of 1996 and second year results will be available in the winter of 1997.

National Center for Children in Poverty
Columbia University School of Public Health
154 Haven Avenue
New York, NY 10032
(212) 927-8793